Symbolism

Symbolism

A Comprehensive Dictionary

Compiled by
Steven Olderr

McFarland & Company, Inc., Publishers
Jefferson, North Carolina, and London

For
Patricia Pingatore Olderr
a rose by another name

Library of Congress Cataloguing-in-Publication Data

Olderr, Steven.
Symbolism : a comprehensive dictionary.

1. Symbolism — Dictionaries.   I. Title.
CB475.O38   1986   001.51   85-42833

ISBN 0-89950-187-7 (acid-free natural paper)

Printed in the United States of America

McFarland   Box 611   Jefferson NC 28640

Foreword

Use this book as you would a conventional dictionary. When you look up a word that stands for a symbol, it should be with a specific use in mind; symbols commonly have contradictory meanings, and it is only the context in which a symbol is used that will tell you which definition is appropriate for your purposes.

Contents

Symbolism is in the realm of the arts, not the sciences. Even the technical terms of symbolism are inexact. Attribute fades off into emblem, emblem into association, and so forth. You will find terms that are clearly attributes, and terms that are clearly emblems, and others that are both or neither. Some are primarily literary, some primarily artistic. If you try to read this dictionary as a textbook you will probably be disappointed, but if you are looking up a symbol from a particular work of art or literature, then everything will make a great deal of sense. The purpose of this dictionary is to make the artist's or author's meaning come clear.

Terms

The definitions that follow are as accurate as one can hope for. They are not universally used exactly as described here, and undoubtedly you can think of examples where the distinctions are blurred. Perhaps if they were more necessary to understanding what an artist or an author was trying to say a greater effort would be made to standardize their use.

Allusion — a reference to an historical, literary, or artistic person or event. "To have an albatross around one's neck" is an allusion to Coleridge's poem, "Rime of the Ancient Mariner."

Association — something linked in memory or imagination with an object, idea, person, or event. The letter "A" is associated with beginning.

Attribute — an object closely associated with or belonging to a specific person, office or event. Scales are an attribute of Justice personified.

Emblem — an object or representation of an object suggesting another object or a person. Three feathers are an emblem of the Prince of Wales and of Wales itself.

Symbol — something which is itself, yet stands for, suggests, or means something else by reason of relationship, association, convention, or accidental relationship. A dove is a symbol of peace.

Allusions, associations, attributes, and emblems are all symbols, but not all symbols are one of the foregoing.

A

A primal cause; the Trinity; initiative and leadership; beginning; associated with happiness, creativity, the new year, spring, Aries, the sun, the number one, Minstrel in tarot deck

A.M. stands for Ave Maria; an attribute of the Virgin Mary; associated with Annunciation • **on a shield** attribute of archangel Gabriel

abacus an attribute of Arithmetic personified; the mysterious way of the Orient; sometimes an emblem of the Orient

Abbadon evil wars

abandonment death; guilt; loss of contact with God or nature; prelude to resurrection

abatina in flower language: fickleness

abecedary in flower language: volubility

ablution purification, especially of subjective and inner evils

abnormality an indication of magical powers

abortion indicates a defect in the soul or spirit; denial of nature

absinthe (both the plant and the liquor) grief

abstinence the soul refraining from temptation

abyss depth; inferiority; the Underworld; associated with the Great Mother, and earth-god cults

acacia fecundity; reproduction; prosperity; the soul; immortality; friendship; associated with the Ark of the Covenant • **Jewish** sexual abstinence; the month of Purification • **enveloped in flame** the "burning bush" of Moses and, hence, the giving of the Law • **flower language** chaste love; friendship; *rose acacia*: friendship, platonic love, elegance; *pink acacia*: elegance; *white acacia*: elegance, platonic love; *yellow acacia*: secret love

acacia gum menstrual blood

acacia thorn the divine power to repel evil

acalia in flower language: temperance

acanthus heavenly gardens; heaven; immortality; felicity; art; the fine arts; love of art; artifice; solicitude about lowly things; stunting and regression; the awareness and pain of sin; associated with Cancer • **flower language** the fine arts; artifice; persistance; persistent genius

ace (playing cards) the best • **ace of hearts** family ties • **ace of spades** death; the highest ranking card; blackness; a Negro

ache mental or spiritual disorder

achillea millefolia *see* **milfoil**

aconite *see* **wolfsbane**

acorn life; strength; virility; latent greatness or strength; independence; a germinal idea; protection against the plague; sacred to Thor; attribute of the Golden Age personified • *see also* **oak**

acrobat inversion; reversal

Adam wisdom; temptation; the weak, sinful side of man; the pristine equality of man; primitive agriculture; kingly power

adamant (mythical stone) hardness; tranquillity of the soul; sometimes associated with the Underworld or Hell

adder hidden evil; deadly malice • *see also* **serpent**

1

Adonis (mythology) youthful beauty; early death

adonis (plant) in flower language: sorrowful memories; painful recollections

adultery forsaking a higher life for a lower one

aegis protection; productive power; the nutritive principle of nature

aerolite *see* **meteorite**

Africa youth; primitiveness

afternoon autumn; a fatigued or languorous state

agate long life; health; acquired wisdom; calmness; courage; eloquence; sanctity; success; protection against snake bite, contagious diseases; birthstone for June

agnus castus in flower language: coldness; indifference

agriculture fertility; fecundity; cyclic existence; cultivation and concern with the soul • *see also* **farmer**

agrimony in flower language: gratitude

ailanthus virtue growing out of, but untainted by, sin

air the masculine principle; the mental plane; creation • **mountain air** purity; heroic and solitary thought • **night air** evil

airplane ambition • *see also* **flight**; **vehicle**

Ajax strength; courage; offense

Aladdin's Lamp male masturbation and its objectified emotional consequences

alabaster purity • **box, vase, or dish of alabaster** attribute of Mary Magdalen

Alastor an evil spirit that haunts a family; man's inner evil driving him to sin

alb an undertunic in Greece and Rome, later a woman's chemise, and then adopted for wear by priests of a goddess • **Christian** chastity; purity; eternal joy; the innocence and the prophetic office of Christ; when the sleeves, chest, and hem are embroidered, the five wounds of Christ are symbolized

albatros good luck; beneficent nature; distant seas; long sea voyages; guilt

Alcestes sacrifice

Alchemist (tarot) *see* **Temperance** (tarot)

alchemy salvation; illumination; foolish occultism

alcohol conjunction of opposites

alcove feminine symbol of containment; childbirth; doorway to another world

alder tree solidity; firmness • **alder bark** fire • **alder blossoms** water

alexandrite emblem of Russia; undying devotion; associated with June

algae long life

alligator *see* **caiman**; **crocodile**

allspice languishing • **in flower language** compassion

almond awakening, wakefulness; revival; spring; hope; divine approval or favor; sweetness; delicacy; virginity; fruitfulness; prophecy; haste; hope; death; attribute of the Virgin Mary, Aaron • **flowering almond** attribute of the Virgin Mary, Aaron • **flower language** stupidity; indiscretion; thoughtlessness; the impetuousness of youth; *flowering almond*: hope

alms *see* **charity**

alms box charity; benevolence

almuce dignity

aloe sorrow; embalming; purification of the dead; contempt; bitterness • **myhrr and aloes** the Passion of Christ • **flower language** affliction; grief; bitterness; religious superstition

alpha and omega (Greek letters) the beginning and the end; creation and destruction; Christ

altar the intersection of heaven and earth; worship; the presence of God; the Eucharist • **altar with flames** the sacrifice of Christ; the Jewish altar of sacrifice • **two altars** Cain and Abel • **altar shaped as a table** the Last Supper • **altar shaped as a tomb** the death of Christ; reminiscent of the early Church where the Eucharist was celebrated in the catacombs

althaea frutex in flower language: persuasion

alyssum exemplary modesty; attribute of Tranquillity personified • **flower language** worth beyond beauty

amaranth a cockscomb; foppery; affection; steadfast love; crown of saints; love of God excluding all other affections • **globe amaranth** faith; stability; cheerfulness; steadfast love; decorum; indifference • **flower language** immortality; *globe amaranth*: unchangeableness

amaryllis pride; haughtiness; beauty; splendor; timidity

amazement part of the process of spiritual awakening

Amazon (mythological woman) fearlessness; the higher emotions which oppose the desires

amazone friendship

amber (stone) sorrow; joy after sorrow; the sun; immortality; fertility; electricity; attribute of Apollo, Helios, the tribe of Benjamin; protection against evil and disease • **China** courage

ambrosia (mythological food) truth; wisdom; love; the nourishment which these foregoing qualities provide in the soul

ambrosia (plant) in flower language: love returned

amethyst sympathy; sincerity; humility; chastity; abnegation; happiness; wealth; usually deep love, but sometimes dalliance; associated with Pisces; birthstone of February • **Christian** absolution; episcopacy • **purple amethyst** penitence

amice the cloth that covered Christ's head when he was mocked by the soldiers at the Praetorium, hence, the

Helment of Salvation; divine hope; purity of heart and soul

amphibian the parting of spirit and matter; evil

Amphion beguiling charm

amphisbaena an ambivalent situation; the anguish caused by ambivalence

amphora a feminine symbol of containment; the womb • *see also* **jug; jar; urn; vase**

ampulla consecration

amputation castration; weakness or defect in the soul • **amputation of thumbs and great toes** incapacitation of a warrior • *see also* **maiming**

amulet the higher nature of the soul; the divine present in the worldly; resistance to evil

analogion the word of God

anchor hope; steadfastness; salvation; Christ; attribute of St. Clement of Rome, St. Nicholas of Myra; as a 19th Century sailor's tattoo: service in the Atlantic

androgyne *see* **hermaphrodite**

androsphinx union of intellect and physical power; the Beast of the Second Coming of Christ

anemone (flower) anticipation; frailty; early death; brief blossoming; sorrow; the Crucifixion of Christ; associated with Adonis, Cancer • **early Christian** the Trinity • **flower language** sickness; expectation; *garden anemone*: forsaken; *meadow anemone*: sickness; *pasque flower anemone*: you have no claims, you are without pretension; *wood anemone*: forlornness

angel spiritual influences acting upon the earth; messenger of God; saintliness; sweetness • **heraldry** belief; gaiety; striving for perfection; a good reputation; dignity; inspiration; a purified existence • **Note**: attributes for specific types of angels are not always used consistently • **black angel** death • **angel with book** a Cherub • **angel with candle** a

Seraph • **angel with crown** a Dominion • **angel with red roses** a Virtue • **angel with a throne** a Throne • **angel with armor** a Power or other lower order • **angel with scepter** a Dominion; divine authority • **angel's head with wings** a Cherub • **blue angel** a Seraph • **red angel** (or golden yellow) a Cherub • **black angel** death • **angel's feet emerging from cloud above mountain** Nahum's vision • **angel holding a flaming sword** judgment; expulsion from Eden • **angel holding a sword upright** justice • **angel sheathing a sword** God's wrath turned aside • **angel kneeling** intercession • **angel holding a lily** purity; the Annunciation; Gabriel; a Virtue • **angel holding a censer** heavenly adoration • **angel holding a branch with white flowers** mercy • **angel holding a trumpet** Resurrection Day • **angel holding a chalice** the agony of Christ in Gethsemane • **angel with a dragon underfoot** Michael • **angel with one hand extended** guardianship • **angel with two hands extended** invitation • **angel bearing a sacramental wafer** attribute of St. Bonaventura • **angel bearing an inkhorn** attribute of St. Matthew

angelica ecstasy; magic; inspiration • **flower language** inspiration

angrecum in flower language: royalty

ankh see **cross**

annointing (with oil) endowing the soul with divine love

ant industry; humility; foresight; modesty; wisdom; community spirit; considered an aphrodisiac; the fragility and impotence of existence; attribute of Ceres • **in swarms** anger • **heraldry** cleverness; artfulness

antelope struggle; presumption

anthurium the heart; emblem of Martin Luther

Antichrist adversary of the soul

Antigone faithfulness; nobility

anvil the brain; the intellect; the force that created the universe; primal furnace; earth; matter; the feminine principle; attribute of a warrior, of St. Adrian, St. Eloi, Vulcan • **with cross or swords** male and female; forge of the universe • **tied to the feet of a woman** Juno as Air personified

ape sin; malice; lust; cunning; fraud; vice; scoffing; the slothful soul of man; levity; Taste personified • **ape in chains** the Devil; **ape with an apple in its mouth** the Fall of Man • **early Christian** heresy; paganism; the Devil • **Middle Ages** painting; sculpture • see also **monkey**

Aphrodite related to spring, April, dawn, fish, fertility, ritual prostitution, Cyprus

Apis see **bull**

apocynum see **dogsbane**

Apollo see **sun**

apparition see **ghost**

apple earthly desires; indulgence in earthly desires; the Fall of Man; procreation; discord; immortality; rejuvenation; death; beginning; autumn, but also a herald of spring; deceit; unity; temptation; sexual enjoyment; the female sex organ; joy; attribute of the Three Graces, Venus, Venus' handmaidens • **three apples** (often also with three roses) attribute of St. Dorothea • **golden apple** discord; immortality; attribute of Vigilance personified and of the harpies that accompany Avarice personified • **apple in the hand of the Christ child** Christ as the new Adam; the fruit of salvation; alludes to Christ as the redeemer of man from Original Sin • **apple in the Virgin Mary's hand** Mary as the new Eve • **apple in Adam's hand** sin • **heraldry** love; rejuvenation; fullness of life; earthly kingdom • **apple eaten with honey** for Jews: the hope for sweetness and joy in the future •

apple tree • man's happiness; associated with Taurus • apple cider rural festivities • flower language temptation; *blossom*: preference, fame speaks one great and good; *thorn apple*: deceitful charms

apricot woman; self-fruitfulness; vulva • apricot flower timid love

April beginning; youth; inconstancy; the New Year

apron service; purity of life and conduct; Ancient Craft; attribute of masons and other craftsmen, Freemasonry, housewives; slave nature; repression or cover of sexuality

aquamarine (stone) associated with Aries, Aquarius, Neptune; birthstone for March, occasionally October

Aquarius associated with the loosening of bonds, the immanence of liberation; the dissolution or decomposition of the world of phenomena

aqueduct channel of truth from a higher to a lower nature

Ararat (Mount) the second cradle of humanity; the "navel" of the world

arbor vitae in flower language: unchanging friendship; live for me

arbutus associated with the Golden Age

arch the female principle; heaven; sanctuary; triumph; a secret place • single arch triumph; the heavens; associated with Jupiter; the sky • multiple arches hospitality • gothic arch aspiration; spirituality • romanesque arch dependability; authority • trefoil or three-lobed arch the Trinity • chancel arch passage from this world into eternal life, or from the Church Militant to the Church Triumphant • broken arch defeat

archangel primordial divine power on the highest level • *see also* angel

archer soldier of the lower classes; Sagittarius

Archpriest (tarot) *see* High Priest

Archpriestess (tarot) *see* High Priestess

Aries associated with the creative impulse, dawn, spring, the beginning of any cycle or process

Aristotle Logic personified

ark the Church; Noah; the Deluge; salvation; the covenant God made with Noah and the Church; the Ark of the Covenant; baptism; the womb • Noah's Ark resurrection, and the meanings listed above

Ark of the Covenant Old Testament worship; the presence of God; the Savior; the Virgin Mary; Jewish worship; associated with Cherubim

arm action; activity; protection; defense; strength; generally, the position shows the activity, e.g., offering, worshipping, inviting, etc. • raised arms invocation; self-defense • a maiden's arms upraised, sprouting branches Chastity personified; associated with Apollo • a maiden whose arms are sprouting myhhr branches, with nymphs standing nearby holding a baby birth of Adonis • a group of maidens, arms upraised, sprouting poplar branches the Heliads • hairy arms Jacob's deception of Isaac • *see also* triscele (triskele)

armillary the universe; astronomy; an attribute of Astronomy personified

armor self defense; security; resistance to evil; protection; chivalry; the Christian faith as protection against evil; attribute of the Archangel Michael, St. Liberalis (especially when shown leaning against a spear or holding a banner); attribute of any warrior saint • armor with red cross attribute of St. George of Cappadocia

arms (body) *see* arm

arms (military) *see* weapons

arrow a spiritual weapon; fertility; rain; lightning; war; famine; disease; the sun's rays; the hunter; the light of divine power; the plague; remorse; persecution; attribute of Apollo, Diana, Sagittarius, St. Christiana • **arrows with bow** attribute of Esau, Cupid, Venus, Apollo, Diana, Luna, America personified, putti • **three arrows** attribute of St. Edmund • **arrow held by maiden with a millstone** attribute of St. Christina • **arrow piercing the hand** attribute of St. Giles of Provence • **arrow piercing a nude man** St. Sebastian • **arrow piercing a heart** love, especially romantic love • **arrow piercing a stag protected by a man** the man is St. Giles of Provence • **two arrows piercing the breast or a heart** St. Augustine of Hippo • **arrow(s) held by a rudely dressed woman** St. Ursula • **golden arrow** kindles love • **lead arrow** drives love away • **a bundle of arrows** attribute of Concord personified

arson regression, especially male

Artemesia (wife of Mausolus) a widow's devotion to her husband's memory

artery channel of truth from a higher nature to a lower one

arum soul; ardor; hermaphrodite • **flower language** ardor; *spotted arum*: warmth

ascending an increase in intensity; a raise in value or worth; the human condition being transcended and a higher spiritual level being attained

Ascension Day victory; trancendence

asceticism voluntary abandonment of worldly activities in preparation for renewed life on a higher spiritual plane

ash leaved trumpet flower *see* **trumpet flower**

ash tree Yggdrasil, the meeting place of the gods; lamentation; grandeur; nobility; prudence; adaptibility; flexibility; modesty; emblem of Odin; associated with Libra • **her-**aldry** power; toughness; rebirth; intelligence; source of wisdom • **China** a staff made of ash indicates mourning for a father

ashes death; mourning; defeat; humility; penitence; failure; the lower mind; death of the body; an ending that is also a beginning; the shortness of life; worthlessness • **eating ashes** utter misery • **ashes and dust** mourning; penitence; deep humiliation

Asmodeus lechery; revenge

asp the sun; life; royalty; power; Cleopatra's suicide, and by extension, any suicide • **Greece** protection; benevolence • *see also* **serpent, uraeus**

aspalathus the wisdom of the Lord

asparagus once considered an aphrodisiac, hence: sexuality

aspen fear; excessive sensitivity; trembling; horror; lament; pride; emblem of Judas; in legend, the wood of the Cross • **flower language** lamentation

asperges expulsion of evil; purity; purification; holiness • **asperges with water pot** attribute of St. Martha

aspergillum exorcism of evil spirits; attribute of St. Martha, St. Benedict, St. Anthony Abbot, and other saints famed for their contests with the Devil

asphodel regret; death; humility; attribute of the Virgin Mary • **Greece** associated with the dead, Hades, the afterlife, Persephone • **flower language** my regrets follow you to the grave

aspiration the yearning of lower nature for the higher

ass (animal) humility; patience; stubbornness; ignorance; honesty; courage; wisdom; cleverness; greatness; the Gentile nations; the flight of the Holy Family; peace; salvation; lust; foolishness; sentimentality; inconstancy; pride; conceit; jealousy; a man between 80 and 90 years of age; emblem of the early Judaic Christians; associated with Silenus, Saturn, the poor, the sun, Ra, Balaam; attribute of Zechariah, the personifications of Sloth, Inconstancy, Stupidity, Temperance • **ass with a millstone** an attribute of Obedience personified • **kneeling ass** attribute of St. Anthony of Padua • **stumbling ass** an unbeliever • **jawbone of an ass** attribute of Samson • **ox with an ass** attribute of the Nativity • **ass with two burdens** refers to Issachar • **coat or cloak or an ass' skin** humility • **heraldry** stamina; patience; contentment

Assyria in the Old Testament: punishment from God

Astaroth accusation; inquisition

aster in flower language: **China aster** afterthought; variety • **double aster** I share your sentiments • **single aster** I will think of it

Athena wisdom; Wisdom personified; man's higher nature; emblem of Athens; associated with spinning, weaving, and other women's crafts

Atlas strength

attic the head; the mind; the conscious; the past; that which is repressed

aureole divinity; supreme power; normally only used for members of the Trinity, occasionally used for the Virgin Mary • **gold or white aureole** member of the Trinity, the Virgin Mary • **blue aureole** celestial joy • *see also* **glory; nimbus**

auricula in flower language: painting; *scarlet auricula*: avarice

aurora borealis omen of war, bloodshed, disaster, death of a king or leader • **Norse** associated with Valkyrie

automobile *see* **vehicle**

autumn death; deterioration; middle or old age; harvest; incipient decay; the afternoon

awl classical Rome: euphemism for penis

awl root associated with Bacchus

axe thunder; lightning; the power of light; the sun; the critical faculty; primitive warfare; war; fertility; execution; chastisement; attribute of a divinity, a carpenter, St. Matthew, St. Benedict, St. Boniface, St. Thomas of Canterbury, St. Joseph (especially when shown with carpenter's tools), John the Baptist • **axe embedded in monk's head** the monk is St. Peter Martyr • **axe with one or two oars** attribute of St. Simon • **axe and trident** fire and water, respectively • **double headed axe** the sun; attribute of royalty, St. Cyprian • **double headed axe with crown** attribute of St. Olaf • **double headed axe with a stone or open Bible** attribute of St. Matthias

axle phallus; axle of the universe; Tree of Life

axle tree axis of the universe; the sun

azalea herald of spring; fragile and ephemeral beauty; fatal gifts; temperance; woman • **China** woman • **flower language** temperance

B

B associated with the Savior, science, the moon, the High Priestess in the tarot deck, spirit, life force, emotion, cooperation, introspection, the number two • **as a brand** punishment for blasphemy

Babel (Tower of) sinful presumption; an impractical dream; pride; confusion of speech • **Christian Science** false knowledge

baboon enlightenment; stupidity; lust; associated with Capricorn • **Egypt** death; time • *see also* **monkey**

baby *see* **infant**

Babylon luxury; vice; the material world; idoltry; worldliness; corrupt and fallen existence; desertion of matter by the spirit; the Terrible Mother; the Anti-christ; associated with scarlet women

Bacchante storm spirit; involutive fragmentation of the unconscious; a woman given to debauchery and sin

Bacchus the uninhibited unleashing of desire; sin; corruption; debauchery; the antithesis of Apollo

bachelor's buttons in flower language: celibacy

backbone *see* **spine**

bacon wealth; life; money; material support; female sexual pleasure

badger vigilance; savagery; ferocity; clumsiness

bag secrecy; winds; scrotum; female symbol of containment • **pig skin bag** attribute of a tinker • *see also* **money bag; purse**

bagpipe wind; melancholy; associated with shepherds and peasants; in modern times, associated with Scotland

baking love making; pregnancy

balances judgment; death; constancy; sobriety; equality; justice; Christ; any binary function, good / evil, life / death, etc.; emblem of Libra; associated with September; attribute of Toth, Osiris, Themis, Mercury, the archangel Michael, Justice personified • **balanced on a razor's edge** attribute of Opportunity personified • **sword thrown into a balance pan** refers to Brennus • **unbalanced balances** the trial of Christ

balcony love; romance; spying; authority

Balder the life principle; love; eloquence

ball the earth; perfection; eternity; childhood play • **golden balls** associated with the harpies that accompany Avarice personified • **bouncing ball** chance; fate • **three balls**

emblem of pawnbrokers; attribute of St. Nicholas of Myra • **tennis ball** youthfulness; fate-tossed man • **classical Greece** fecklessness; chance; humility; attribute of Victory personified, Fate personified • *see also* **globe; orb; sphere**

balm annointing; cure; relief; kingship • **balm tea** cure for melancholy • **flower language** sympathy; *Balm of Gilead*: healing, cure, relief; *gentle balm*: pleasantry

balsam consolation; emblem of the Virgin Mary • **balsam with an olive** the dual nature of Christ • **flower language** impatience; ardent love; rashness; *red balsam*: touch-me-not, impatient resolves; *yellow balsam*: impatience

bamboo longevity; constancy; emblem of the Orient • **Orient** Buddha • **China** modesty; protection from defilement; openmindedness; culture; refinement; a staff of bamboo indicates mourning for a father

banana the tropics; continuing life; wisdom; associated with the monkey and ape families; simian nature

banana tree continuing life

bandages the winding sheet of the tomb; swaddling clothes • *see also* **wounds**

banner victory; triumph; protection; attribute of warrior saints • **red banner** revolution • **waving a banner** dispersal of evil spirits • **banners in superfluous numbers** agressive militarism • **banner and white horse** attribute of St. James the Greater • **white banner with red cross** attribute of St. Ansanus, St. Ursula • **banner with cross or words "Ecce Agnus Dei"** attribute of John the Baptist • **banner with cross held by lamb** Christ's victory over death; attribute of John the Baptist, the sibyl Phrygiana, St. Reparata • **Christ with a banner** refers to his rising from the grave, the descent into Hell, and appearances on earth after the Resurrection and before the Ascension • *see also* **flag**

banquet *see* **feast**

banshee death; messenger of fatality

banyan tree the close union of the spiritual and physical in man; expanding knowledge

baptism purification; rebirth; death and interment of the old, birth and resurrection of the new

bar on a female symbol (circle, oval, etc.): indicates virginity, chastity

barber gossip; primitive medicine

barberry in flower language: sourness; sharpness; ill temper; tartness

bard *see* **poet**

barkeeper *see* **tapster**

barley love (especially red barley); poverty; jealousy; prophecy; divination; resurrection; grains of barley are a spermatic image

basement *see* **cellar**

basil poverty • **flower language** hatred; poverty; linked to death and destruction, especially in the Middle East where it is planted in graveyards; *sweet basil*: good wishes

basilisk evil; poverty; death; the Devil or Antichrist; cruelty; mesmerism

basin (or basin and ewer together) cleanliness; innocence; purity; Pilate washing his hands; the humility of Christ's love; attribute of a barber

basket the maternal body; the feminine principle; fertility; vulva; scrotum; charity to the poor; attribute of St. Philip • **in bulrushes** the birth of Moses • **infant in basket** the birth of Moses • **with flowers or fruit** opportunity; reward; fruitfulness; plenty; victory; success; attribute of Hope personified • **three maidens with baskets on their heads** Mercury • **man suspended in a basket by a rope** St. Paul • **Christ with baskets of bread** Feeding of the 5,000

bat (animal) night; death; misfortune; black magic; infernal power or being; desolation; witchcraft; terror; madness; revenge; idolatry; longevity; wisdom; a woman between 80 and 90 years of age; an attribute of the Devil, Dracula, Pride personified • **Bible** idolatry • **heraldry** cunning; coolness in the time of danger • **China** happiness; longevity; good luck; *five bats*: the blessings of longevity, wealth, health, virtue and a natural death

bat (fuller's) *see* **fuller's bat**

bath purification; initiation; regeneration; luxury; immersion in a warm bath in particular suggests a return to the womb

battering ram destruction; fertilization; phallus

battle axe *see* **axe**

bay (plant) in flower language: red bay love; memory • **rose bay** (oleander) danger; beware • *see* **laurel**

bay (topographical feature) vulva • *see also* **harbor**

bayberry candles the new year; good luck; prosperity

beacon *see* **lighthouse**

beads memory; the rosary (which see); the female principle • **blue beads** protection against the evil eye • **gold beads** protection against the evil eye, malevolent spirits, and throat diseases • **string of beads** children • **stringing beads** sexual intercourse

beans false philosophy; energy; ghosts; resurrection; reincarnation; a humble food; connected with witches; attribute of Gratitude personified • **black bean** a negative vote • **white bean** a positive vote

beanstalk a generally favorable symbol; the ladder to heaven; the Universe Tree

bear bravery; strength; self-restraint; cruelty; evil influence; a problem of difficulty; obstacle; violence; clumsiness; solitary life; martyrdom; Satan; Gluttony personified; nobility; stubbornness; silliness; ugliness; triviality; melancholy; voluptuousness; the Terrible Mother; the dangerous aspect of the unconscious; crudity; emblem of Russia; attribute of St. Euphemia; pessimism or declining prices on the stock market • **Bible** (old Testament) the Kingdom of Persia • **China** strength; bravery • **heraldry** power; tenacity; ferocity • **bear and lion** emblem of the Devil

beard honor; sovereignty; age; in early art, it indicated a person still living (the dead were shown clean shaven) • **cutting a beard** infamy; shame; penance; servility • **bearded woman** a witch, however, for Egyptian queens, it indicated sovereignty • **blue beard** evil • **gold beard** the sun; attribute of a sun-hero • **gray beard** old age • **red beard** attribute of Thor, Odysseus, the Devil • **white beard** attribute of a sage, St. Rornvald, St. Paul the Hermit, St. Bernardino of Siena

bearded crepis in flower language: protection

beating see **flagellation**

beauty nobility; charity; virtue; immortality; strength

beaver industriousness; engineering; wisdom; self-mutilation; self-sacrifice; peace; now an emblem of Canada, formerly an emblem of Germany • **U.S.** female genitalia • **early Christian** the Christian who makes sacrifices for the sake of his spiritual life • **heraldry** sacrifice; peacefulness; tolerance; vigilance; industry; skill (especially in castle building)

bed repose; marriage; procreation; copulation; rest; illness; childbirth; secrecy; anguish; reflection; languishing; a phase of thought or opinion; dispensation of justice; luxury • **man carrying bed** Christ's healing of the paralytic

bee industry; creative activity; obedience; diligence; good order; bu-

reaucracy; wealth; eloquence; a soul; sweetness; prophecy; the zeal of the Christian in acquiring virtue; death; immortality; chastity; continence; fertility; creativity; wisdom; flattery; temptation; madness; punishment; Assyria; the virginity of Mary; the risen Christ • **Egypt** regal power • **Hebrew** government in good order • **heraldry** sovereignty; well governed industry; the Carolingians • see also **beehive**

beech victory; honor; connected with Jupiter, books, sexuality • **flower language** prosperity

beehive the Church; cooperation; the papacy; abundance; well-being; activity; society thriving on rapacity; attribute of St. Bernard, St. Ambrose (especially when pictured with two scourges), St. Chrysostom • see also **bee**

Beelzebub gluttony; worship of false gods

beer masculinity; the drink of the common man; in very ancient times, the drink of the gods (later replaced by wine)

beetle death; witchcraft; fairies; sundown; life reduced to smallness; a stupid person; the Self • **heraldry** modesty; a reminder of worldly sorrows • see also **ladybug, scarab**

beggar indigence; poverty; independence; attribute of St. Elizabeth of Hungary

beheading separation of the body and spirit; an opinion, idea, or institution at the end of its cycle; typical punishment of the upper classes (the poor were hanged) • see also **head**

belfry call to prayer; religiosity undone by clerical weakness; the head

Belial gambling as a vice

bell virginity; alarm; death; fertility; health; vulva and phallus together; the priest; the heavens; the exorcism of evil spirits; call to worship;

freedom; Christ's joy; the coming of Christ in the Eucharist; attribute of St. Anthony the Great, David, Music personified • **bell on a crutch** attribute of St. Anthony Abbot • **golden bells on the hem of a garment** attribute of Aaron • **hanging bell** the connection between heaven and earth

belladonna *see* **nightshade**

bellflower in flower language: • **white bellflower** gratitude • **pyramidal bellflower** constancy

bellows flattery; temptation; attribute of Cinderella • **old man with a bellows at furnace** an alchemist • **the Devil with a candle and a bellows** the Devil's attempt to extinguish spiritual life; attribute of St. Genevieve

belly physical man; the antithesis of the brain or spirit; gluttony; destruction matter; sensuality; compassion; intuition *see also* **stomach**

Belphegor sloth

belt virginity; power; strength; virtue • **twisted belt** a woman in love • *see also* **girdle**

belvedere in flower language: I declare against you

Bermuda in Elizabethan England: enchantment, tempest, brothel district, underworld district

berry fruit of marriage; close relation; immortality; knowledge; rejuvenation • **berries on a branch** friendship; ephemeral beauty

beryl love; everlasting youth; inner happiness; goodness; charm against death, seasickness, eye and throat ailments; associated with Scipio

betony in flower language: surprise

Bible the Word of God; sanctity; holiness; spiritual guidance; truth; Protestantism in particular, Christianity in general • **opened to the Gospel of St. Matthew** attribute of Saint Barnabas, Saint Bartholomew • **opened to Romans 13** attribute of St. Augustine of Hippo • **Old Testament** Jewish worship; attribute of St. Stephen • *see also* **book**

bilberry in flower language: treachery

billows overwhelming trials; loss of control

bindweed in flower language: *great bindweed*: insinuation; *small bindweed*: humility

birch meekness; gracefulness; beginning; the new year; self-propagation; charm against witches; phallus; associated with the end of the world in Norse mythology; attribute of Friga, the Norse goddess of love; associated with love and death • **birch rod or switch** school authority; corporal punishment

bird the soul; thought; imagination; spiritualization; the spirit; supernatural aid; air; wind; time; immortality; creation; the female principle; aspiration; prophecy; love; freedom; haste; betrayal; attribute of Juno personifying Air; birds that are solitary by habit usually represent the isolation of those who live on a superior mental plane • **talking and singing birds** amorous yearning • **black bird** in ancient times: inspiration • *see also* **blackbird** • **white bird** in ancient times: eroticism; in Christian times: divine messengers, purity, beneficence • **red bird** in ancient times: the supernatural • **flock of birds** usually have a negative connotation • **flock of birds taking flight** orgasm • **blue bird** the impossible; ideas • *see also* **bluebird** • **brass backed bird** fever • **metal bird** Phoenix • **birds with food** attribute of Elijah • **birds feeding on grapes** the faithful gathering sustenance from Christ, usually through the Eucharist • **birds in a vine** souls abiding with Christ • **bird freed from a cage** the soul freed from the body • **bird tapping at a window or flying into a house** death • **bird in a cage** hope of freedom or of salvation; a kept woman • **car-**

nivorous bird greed • giant bird creative deity; storm • bird of prey flying from left to right before a battle omen of defeat • heraldry eagle claw or leg: one who preys • *see also* specific birds: dove; eagle; vulture, etc.

bird cage man's contrariness; imprisonment; deceit • bird freed from a cage the soul freed from the body

biretta black: attribute of a priest • purple attribute of a bishop • red attribute of a cardinal • *see also* cardinal's hat

birth Sunday's child is full of grace • Monday's child is fair in the face (or, full in the face) • Tuesday's child is solemn and sad • Wednesday's child is merry and glad • Thursday's child is inclined to thieving • Friday's child is free and giving • Saturday's child works hard for a living *or* Born on a Monday, fair of face • Born on a Tuesday, full of (God's) grace • Born on a Wednesday, sour and sad (or, full of woe) • Born on a Thursday, merry and glad (or, has far to go) • Born on a Friday, worthily given (or, is loving and giving) • Born on a Saturday, work hard for your living • Born on a Sunday, you'll never want (or, lucky and happy and good and gay)

biscuit dryness; the consecrated Host distributed without love

bishop the spiritual principle; spiritualized mental qualities; religious authority • bearing a youth aloft St. Nicholas of Myra • struck by a Jew the Jew is Rebellion personified • foot on a fallen oak St. Boniface

bison *see* buffalo

bite seal of the spirit upon the flesh; love mark; mark of divine love; the dangerous action of the instincts upon the psyche, especially in the case of an animal bite

bitter herbs servitude; slavery; affliction; misfortune

bittern grossness; rudeness; desola-

tion • flocking together presage of a storm

bitterness suffering undergone in purification of the soul

bittersweet (plant) truth

black penitence; death; grief; mourning; ignorance; time; primordial chaos; mineral life; fertilized land; germinal stage of a process; mortality; punishment; womb; error; nothingness; depression; wisdom; instinct; evil; sin; superstition; the absolute; sleep; the Devil; humility; associated with Capricorn; constancy; anything to do with the earth • black and white together humility and purity of life (respectively); clarity; the printed word • black with dark red Satan • red and black life and death (respectively) • black clerical garments the hope of inner resurrection through service to God; humility; penitence • Christianity liturgical color for Maundy Thursday where there is no Communion, and for Good Friday • black flag death; pirates; execution of criminals; World War II submarines — success in battle • black hand or spot impending death or murder • black blanket hung on an Elizabethan theater: a tragedy being performed • China evil; *black clouds*: portent of floods; *on stage*: a man with a black face is a humble but honest person

blackberry repentance; worthlessness; associated with death, fairies, the Devil

blackbird the Devil; an underworld deity; bad luck; evil; the darkness of sin; temptation; cunning; vigilance; resignation; an attribute of St. Benedict • heraldry a clear sounding family name • *see also* subheading under bird

blacksmith related to thought; mental qualities disciplined by the spirit; Vulcan (especially when depicted forging weapons); sometimes there is an infernal aspect; associated with Creation • **blacksmith shoeing a horse, having first removed its leg** St. Eloi

blackthorn bad luck; difficulty; strife; associated with Scorpio • **flower language** difficulty

bladder grief; attribute of a fool

bladder nut the rosary • **in flower language** amusement; frivolity

blaeberry in flower language: ingenuous simplicity

blanket comfort; security; the night sky • **black blanket hung on a theater** indicated a tragedy was playing

blindfold moral or spiritual blindness; sin; ignorance; an attribute of Cupid, Idolatry personified, Avarice personified; on Justice personified, the blindfold indicates impartiality; on Nemesis and on Fortune personified, it indicates randomness

blindman's bluff trying to solve a problem without sufficient knowledge

blindness darkness; ignorance; error; prophecy; euphemism for castration; mentality immersed in the concerns of the lower life; the mind not awakened by the spirit; lack of spiritual perception; may be an indication that a person has heightened or supernatural powers

blister on the tongue: sign of a lie

blood sacrifice (especially when spilled); passion; war; life; Christ's redemption of man; the soul; guilt; covenant; fertility; martydom • **menstrual blood** connected with magic, witchcraft • **blood on doorpost** the Passover

bloodstone mourning; birthstone of March; associated with Aries; charm for courage, presence of mind; vitality

blowing female orgasm; passion; euphemism for fellatio

blot death; the abnormal; defective-

ness; sin; the transitory; associated with the passage of time

blue • the sky; sanctification; sincerity; piety; intuition; time and space; truth; eternity; sorrow; devotion; heavenly truth; occasionally a royal color; harmony; candor; glory; spirituality; innocence; courage; fairness; love; justice untempered by love; coolness; coldness; puritanism; constancy; calmness; philosophical serenity; contemplation; heavenly love; heaven; the unveiling of truth; modesty; hope; religion; faith; the subconscious; despair; loss of love; despondency; discouragement; half-mourning; non-erotic, tender love; passivity; the spirit of man; fidelity; peace; tranquillity; divine contemplation; expiation; humility; chastity; innocence; sincerity; piety; mediation; purification of the mind; associated with Sagittarius, Libra, the planets Jupiter and Mercury, the Virgin Mary, the Trinity, God the Father, Jupiter, Juno, sometimes Christ in his earthly ministry and the Holy Spirit • **Great Britain** associated with the Whig party • **China** a blue sedan chair belonged to a high government official • **blue clothes** attribute of a servant or peasant • **blue flower** spiritual happiness; magic or special powers • **blue ribbon** Order of the Garter; first prize in a contest • **blue and red** love and authority (often used for the color of God's clothes) • **heraldry** faithfulness; loyalty; steadiness; spotless reputation; humility; chastity; science • **Middle Ages** associated with worldly love, folly • **bluish green** associated with Scorpio • **violet blue** associated with Capricorn • **pale blue** associated with Venus • **light blue** associated with Uranus, the sky, daytime • **dark blue** associated with Capricorn, a stormy sea, night sky • **indigo blue** *see* **indigo** • **ice blue** associated with Cancer

bluebell sorrowful regret; constancy; kindness • **flower language** constancy; kindness

bluebird happiness

bluebottle happiness; the modesty of the Virgin Mary; celibacy; single wretchedness; hope in love; emblem of Germany • **flower language** delicacy; felicity

bluejay *see* **jay**

bo tree heavenly light; contemplation; Buddha

boar intrepidness; licentiousness; irrational urge toward suicide; courage; fertility; low animal nature; attribute of Lust personified • **boar surrounded by hunters** refers to Meleager • **boar underfoot** attribute of Chastity personified • **China** wild boar: the wealth of the forest • *see also* **sow; swine**

boat the human body; the womb or cradle rediscovered; a venture; security; resurrection; attribute of St. John the Hospitator • **Egypt** the throne of a god • **blue boat** Charon's boat on the Styx • **"little" boat** vagina • **woman pulling a boat upstream** Claudia • **woman holding a boat in her hand** Claudia personifying Confidence or Trust • *see also* **ship; ark**

boathook • **boathook with a fish** attribute of St. Simon • **with a builder's square** attribute of St. Jude • **with saltire cross** attribute of St. Andrew

boil (disease) a psychological affliction or spiritual shortcoming

boiling fury; an extreme state

Bologna (Italy) a model of the city: attribute of St. Petronius

bolt *see* **latch**

bondage immobilization through sin or evil; man tied irrevocably to the Creator and the universe • *see also* **entanglement**

bone life; resurrection; death; the indestructible part of man; not to be confused with **skeleton**, which see •

shank bone for Jews, a reminder of burnt offerings and of the ancient glory of the Temple • **jawbone of an ass** an attribute of Samson

bonfire death; resurrection; fertility; warning; victory

bonnet a green bonnet is the attribute of a bankrupt person

book wisdom; secret knowledge; divine knowledge; magic; spiritual or mystical power; the Bible; related to the Creation, knowledge; teaching; an attribute of Clio, the archangel Uriel, prophets, the Apostles, the Doctors of the Church, authors, the sibyls, the Virtues, St. Anne, St. Bernard of Clairvaux, St. Bonaventura, St. Thomas Aquinas, and other saints famous for their learning • **closed book** secrecy; chastity; attribute of St. Jude • **open book** the Bible; perfect knowledge; dissemination of the truth • **monk with an open book** often the rule of the order • **lovers sharing a book** Poalo and Francesca • **book and sword offered to sleeping warrior under a tree** the warrior is Scipio • **book pierced by a sword** attribute of St. Boniface, St. Anthony of Padua • **book with a fish on it** attribute of St. Simon • **book with 2 vials** attribute of St. Januarius • **book with flaying knife** attribute of St. Bartholomew • **book with cross laying on it** attribute of Faith personified • **book with seals on it in the lap of Christ** the Apocalypse • **St. John eating a book** the Apocalypse • **book with a chalice** attribute of St. Chrysostom • **book between two Doric columns** attribute of St. Athanasius • **book with an eagle on it** attribute of St. John • **book with spear** attribute of St. Thomas • **book with sword** attribute of St. Matthias, St. Paul (especially with legend "Spiritus Gladius") • **book with "alpha" and "omega" printed on it** Christ • **sealed book** the Virgin Mary •

closed book with seven seals and a lamb Christ; John the Baptist • book with halberd attribute of St. Matthias • book with scroll or tall cross attribute of St. Philip, St. Andrew • book with stone and whip attribute of St. Jerome • book with writing table and pen attribute of St. Ambrose • three books with pen attribute of St. Hilary of Poitiers • see also Bible

borage the flower: bluntness; talent • the whole plant roughness of character • flower language bluntness; rudeness

boring (drilling) sexual intercourse

bottle salvation; rain; refreshment; intemperance; consumption of alcoholic beverages; phallus; anything swollen • gold bottle attribute of a banker • with an alcoholic beverage sign of a tavern • with colored liquid sign of a pharmacist, later also of a confectioner or grocer • smashed bottle attribute of Jeremiah

bottomless pit or well insatiable desire

bough friendliness; hospitality; protection • bearing fruit or blooms ephemeral beauty • of gold the rays of the setting sun (needed by a sun hero to enter the underworld) • tent of boughs the Feast of the Tabernacles • see also branch

bouquet sweet thoughts; a tribute • flower language gallantry; but note that a large group of gathered flowers means, "we die together"

bow (archery) war; power; death; hunting; exhausting strain; the will; the tension between physical and spiritual forces; worldly power; weapon of the hunter, the common soldier; emblem of Saggitarius; attribute of Diana • bow with arrows penetrating inquisitiveness; fire and lightning; action as a means of effecting the will; attribute of Apollo, Cupid, Esau • golden bow attribute of Artemis • silver bow attribute of Apollo • bow with quiver attribute of Orion, sometimes Hercules

bower the feminine principle; the Virgin Mary

bowing honor; respect; humbleness

bowl limitation; family; poverty; begging; charity; gossip; attribute of the Virgin Mary, Diogenes, St. Alexis, the Cumean sibyl • overturned bowl the emptiness of worldly things • filled bowl riches; plenty; gluttony

box the feminine principle; the unconscious; treasure; secrets; the maternal body • alms box charity; benevolence • closed box secrecy • box of ointment attribute of St. Mary of Bethany, St. Mary of Egypt, St. Cosmas, St. Damian, Mary Magdalene • see also Pandora's Box

box tree prosperity; grace; tenacity; stoicism; incorruptibility • flower language stoicism

boxwood the abiding grace of the Church

boy immaturity; the future; neophyte • see also child; man

bracelet continuity; wholeness; marriage; eternity; a cycle; learning; a gift to bind; attribute of royalty

bracken see fern

braids attribute of a young girl, but also of a courtesan

brain fantasy; memory; reason; intellect

bramble lowliness; envy; remorse; sin, sometimes major sin (especially when growing); death; entanglement (q.v.); Christ's crown of thorns; attribute of the Virgin Mary • Jewish divine love; dangerous pride • see also briers; thorn

branch offspring; phallus; flagellation; scourge; martyrdom, (especially a branch with thorns); attribute of Isaiah • branch with berries friendship • branch with green leaves friendship; a tavern; protection • see also bough branding membership in or separation from a group; subjugation; humiliation; punishment • the letter "B" as a brand blasphemer • see also tattooing

brass boldness; shamelessness; baseness in comparison to gold or silver; obstinate resistance; mentality; firmness; strength; hardness; drought; eloquence; sometimes associated with the underworld, and the Devil • Bible a holy metal • Middle Ages strength; durability; Christ's divinity

brazier attribute of Constancy personified • woman snatching coals from brazier Porcia • soldier with hand in brazier Mucius Scaevola • brazier with wood and knife associated with Abraham and Isaac

bread fecundity; life; goodness; hospitality; the means of sustaining life; the Eucharist; care and nurture; food of the poor • breaking of bread hospitality; killing, in a rutual sacrifice • loaf of bread charity to the poor; attribute of St. Benedict; can have a sexual connotation due to the shape of the loaf • loaf of bread with a snake emerging from it attribute of St. Benedict • loaf of bread carried by a raven God's providence; attribute of Elijah, St. Paul the Hermit • two loaves of bread attribute of St. Philip • three loaves of bread attribute of St. Mary of Egypt • bread with chalice the Eucharist; refers to Melchizidek • bread and water prisoner's food • round loaf of bread fertility; sacred food • piece of bread something valueless • crust of bread something valueless; poverty; deprivation • Christ with baskets of bread Christ's Feeding of the Five Thousand • white bread food of the rich • brown bread food of the poor

breast(s) charity; innocence; devotion; motherhood; nourishment; protection; fertility; consolation; wisdom; prudence; happiness; hope; love • in a plate attribute of St. Agatha of Sicily • woman with one breast exposed attribute of a warrior or courtesan • bare breasts candidness; humility • woman squeezing her breasts generosity • woman with bare breasts and veiled face Prudence personified • multiple breasts fertility • breasts thrust forward courage; challenge; wantonness • woman nursing a child motherhood; love; Charity personified • woman nursing an old man Cimon and Pero • woman expressing milk from her breasts Mercy personified; Benignity personified • woman nursing more than one child Earth personified; Charity personified • breast milk from a Muse falling on a book or musical instrument inspiration

breastplate righteousness as a defense; courage; heroism; judgment; attribute of Aaron, Old Testament priesthood • mounted on a pole attribute of Minerva, and Minerva as Wisdom personified

breath soul; spirit; purification; the divine element in man

breathing assimilation of spiritual power; life; passion

breeches (trousers) superiority; adulthood

breeze the spirit energizing the mental plane; the clearning away of misconception; amorous yearning; fertility; the voice of the gods • see also wind

briars see briers

brick(s) dependability; substance; permanence; birth; emblem of the Babylonian goddess Mami • England lower class upstart • bricks and whip Israel's Old Testament captivity and forced labor • making bricks without straw punishment

bride the Church; the soul; fertility; freshness; innocence; inexperience; expectation • bride and groom together the Church and Christ (respectively)

bridegroom fertility; freshness; expectation • *see also* **bride**

bridge connection between worlds; the relation between heaven and earth; a transition from one state of being and another; change; the desire for change; peace • **heraldry** patience; stability; justice

bridle law; restraint; worldly interests and cares; attribute of the personifications of Temperance, Fortune; attribute of Nemesis • **old man bridled, on all fours, ridden by a woman** Aristotle and Campaspe

briers sins, sometimes major sins (usually when growing); death; grief; rejection; modesty; solitude; parasite • *see also* **bramble; sweet brier; thorn**

brimstone punishment for sins; distraction

briony *see* **bryony**

broccoli tranquillity

bronze mentality; firmness; endurance; purification • **Greece** a bronze gong was sounded at the death of a king, and the eclipse of the moon

brooch may indicate the wearer's trade • **as a gift** broken love or friendship • **in the shape of an animal** endows the wearer with the characteristics of the animal

brook deceit; spiritual guidance; morning; vulva

broom (for sweeping) victory; dominance; insight; wisdom; power to do away with worry and trouble; servility; witch's steed; attribute of housewives, well-meaning fairies; emblem of housework • **broom placed by a cottage door** the woman of the house is not at home

broom (plant) war; servitude; humbleness; rejected love • **flower language** neatness; humbleness • **heraldry** House of Plantagenet

brown the earth; penitence; grief;

barrenness; poverty; depression; spiritual death and degradation; renunciation of the world; modesty; autumn; melancholy; monasticism; sorrow; calmness; trustworthiness; conservatism; practical knowledge; Victoriam lack of emotion or spirituality; associated with Virgo, the planet Neptune; drabness

brussels sprouts light heartedness; gaiety

bryony associated with witchcraft • **flower language** black bryony: be my support • *see also* **mandrake**

bubble hollowness; emptiness of material existence or personality; a dream; fragile hope; joy; brevity of life; lack of substance; gaiety; mindlessness; folly

bucentaur the dual nature of man

buckbean in flower language: calm, repose

bucket attribute of St. Florian, and Fortune personified; knocking over a bucket full of water — death

buckeye emblem of the state of Ohio; alternate name for the **horse chestnut** tree, which see

buckle self defense; protection; virginity; aristocracy; fidelity in authority; the goodwill and protection of Isis • **heraldry** tenacity; steadfastness; readiness

buckler divine defense

bud(s) future promise; virginity; patent or undeveloped power; youth; immaturity • **half opened** vitality

Buddha love; contemplation

buffalo untamed nature; base forces; emblem of the American West • *see also* **water buffalo**

bugle call to action; sign of a cuckhold; the Horn of Salvation; emblem of the U.S. Cavalry • *see also* **trumpet**

bugloss attribute of Lying personified; once used as a cosmetic • **flower language** falsehood

bull the masculine; fertility; the father; power; male sexual desire;

brute strength; fecundity; Taurus; peace; self-denial; patience; a man 20 to 30 years of age; hoax; rising prices or optimism on the stock market; linked with heaven, death, sacrifice; attribute of St. Sylvester, St. Ambrose • **Egypt** temperance • **brass bull** attribute of St. Eustace • **white bull** Zeus; attribute of Dionysus • **white bull bearing a maiden to the sea** Zeus raping Europa • **black bull** death • **bull tied to a fig tree** lascivious fury appeased; a man subdued in marriage • **bull with wings and nimbus** emblem of St. Luke • **two fire-breathing bulls** refers to Jason • **woman tied between two bulls** St. Thecla • **bull with censer** Day of Atonement • **heraldry** magnanimity; valor; power; servility • *see also* **cattle; calf; cow**

bulldog perserverance; tenacity; stolidity; generosity; courage; emblem of Great Britain; attribute of St. Margaret of Cortona

bullfinch a scholar; imitation

bulrush salvation; lack of stamina; an attribute of Moses; the humble faithful who abide with Christ • **flower language** docility; indiscretion

bundle burden; problem • *see also* **fasces; sheaf**

burdock in flower language: persistence; don't touch me; rudeness; pertinacity

burglar *see* **thief**

burial honoring the dead; sorrow; consummation, in its various senses; return to the primal parent; initiation into manhood

burning passion; lust; indignation; shame; venereal disease

burning bush *see* **bush**

burr importunity; coherence; discomfort • **burr sticking to one's clothing** being in love

bush a spot for lurking, ambush, spying, illicit love; barrenness; usefulness • **burning bush** the Annunciation; the giving of the Law to Moses;

the Virgin Mary; divine love; the Church being persecuted but not perishing

buskin nobility; vulva; tragedy, especially in drama

butter divine love and wisdom; luxury; food in general • **butter being churned** creation • **buttered hay** deceit; cheating

buttercup insanity • **flower language** cheerfulness; childishness; ingratitude; desire for riches

butterfly the soul; freedom; unconscious attraction toward light (God); life; rebirth; joy; conjugal bliss; the psyche; inconstancy; love; liberty; frivolity; transitoriness; rashness; wantonness; lightness; spring; resurrection; eternal life; Easter • **red butterfly** a witch • **butterfly in a house** forthcoming   wedding • **heraldry** frailty; transitory life

butterfly weed in flower language: let me go

buzzard despicability; death; old age

C

C the crescent moon; associated with intellectual qualities, optimism, happiness, success despite obstacles, the number three; corresponds to Earth or Venus, the Empress in the tarot deck

cabbage disentanglement; peasantry; emblem of the sun, the self-willed • **flower language** gain; profit

cabin the rustic or outdoor life; adversity; hermitage

cabinet heart

cable strength

cacalia in flower language: adulation

cactus protection; the desert; a waste land; warmth; ardent love; grandeur • **flower language** warmth; *serpen-*

tine cactus: horror

caduceus moral equilibrium; good conduct; self control; health of the body and spirit; emblem of the medical profession; union of the sexes; fertility; phallus; eloquence; reason; peace; truce; commerce and industry • attribute of the archangel Raphael, Mercury, Hercules, Venus, Anubis, Serapis, Thoth, Asclepius, a sacred person, a herald, an ambassador, a messenger, a doctor, Peace personified • **caduceus in a woman's hand** felicity; peace; concord; security; fortune • **Rome** moral equilibrium; good conduct

cage imprisonment; marriage; cruelty; slavery; bondage • **caged bird** the soul longing for freedom • *see also* **prison**

caiman attribute of America (both continents) personified • *see also* **crocodile**

Cain agriculture; jealousy; rage; vengeance; the Jews killing Christ

cairngorm patriotism; homesickness

cake feast; fertility; offering to a god; food of the rich

calabash *see* **gourd**

caladrius Christ • **turning away from a sick person** death • **turning toward a sick person** recovery

caldron *see* **cauldron**

calf weakness; sacrifice; the prodigal son's return; immaturity; innocence; endearment; childishness; folly; stupidity; a boy of up to 20 years of age; the young Dionysus • **golden calf** refers to Aaron • *see also* **cattle; bull; cow**

Caliban spiritual decay

calla aethiopica in flower language: magnificent beauty

Calliope eloquence; heroic poetry

calliope emblem of the circus

calycanthus in flower language: benevolence

camel asceticism; patience; long-suffering; endurance; resistance; temperance; obedience; submission;

prudence; slyness; greed; salaciousness; pride; emblem of the Middle East; attribute of the personifications of Asia, Fury, Discretion, Obedience • **Middle East** royalty; dignity • **heraldry** stamina; contentment • **camel's hair clothes** penitence; royalty; attribute of John the Baptist

camellia japonica ephemeral, fragile beauty; exotic, seductive beauty; pure beauty; emblem of Japan • **flower language** *red*: unpretending excellence; *white*: perfected loveliness

camomile love in adversity • **flower language** energy in adversity

camphor chastity; an attribute of the Virgin Mary; an anti-aphrodisiac; a charm against evil spirits

canary grass in flower language: perserverance

Cancer the mediator between the formal and non-formal worlds; the threshold through which the soul enters upon its incarnation

cancer spiritual decay; impending doom; a debilitating situation

candelabrum life; spiritual life; the spiritual light of salvation • **two branched candelabrum** the presence of God; the dual nature of Christ • **three branched candelabrum** the Trinity • **seven branched candelabrum** the Menorah, which see • *see also* **candle; candlestick**

candle life, especially that of an individual; hope; learning; festivity; the external soul; charm against evil spirits; Christ as the light of the world; romance; attribute of St. Genevieve, Faith personified • **two candles** the dual nature of Christ • **three candles** the Trinity • **five candles** the five wounds of Christ • **five candles lit, with five candles unlit** the five wise virgins, and the five foolish virgins • **seven candles** a perfect number, hence, Jesus • **bayberry candles** the new year; good luck; prosperity • **burial with an un-**

lighted candle an excommunicated person • **blue flame on a candle** a spirit passing • **spark in a candle flame** a stranger or letter will come • **vigil candle** the presence of the Host at the altar • **crossed candles, or candles with an iron comb** attribute of St. Blaise • **heraldry** transitoriness • *see also* **flame; candelabrum; Menorah; candlestick**

candlestick the beauty of ripe age • **seven golden candlesticks** the seven early Christian churches of Asia Minor • *see also* **candelabrum; Menorah**

candytuft indifference

cane (walking cane) old age; cripple; blind • **white cane** blind • **gold headed cane** attribute of a doctor, a gentleman • *see also* **crutch**

cannon war; destruction; fecundation; attribute of St. Barbara

canopy regal dignity; protection; paradise; the celestial realm • **China** official rank • **round canopy** the sky; the sun • **square canopy** the earth

Canterbury bell in flower language: acknowledgment

cap used to hide the horns of a cuckhold • **cap with colored feathers** fancy; unaccountable actions • *see also* **hat**

capon a dull fool; a love letter; a bribe for judges; a eunuch • *see also* **rooster; hen; chick; chicken**

Capricorn prosperity; the dual tendencies of life toward both the high and the low, the physical and the spiritual

captive the spirit held latent • **captives** attribute of St. Vincent Ferrer

car *see* **vehicle**

carbuncle (stone) martyrdom; blood; suffering; Christ's Passion; constancy; self confidence; energy; strength; charity; anger (especially when related to the eyes); love • **five carbuncles** the five wounds of Christ

cardamine in flower language: paternal error

cardinal flower in flower language: distinction

cardinal's hat attribute of St. Vincent Ferrer, St. Jerome (although he was not a cardinal) • **lying on the ground or hanging in a tree** attribute of St. Bonaventura

cards playing cards: gambling; idle pastime; attribute of Vice personified

carnation endurance; love; fidelity; the Virgin Mary; first love; admiration; fascination; divine love; female love; caprice; associated with Scorpio • **red carnation** betrothal • **white carnation** (U.S.) Mother's Day • **flower language** fascination; woman's love; *deep red carnation*: alas, my poor heart; *striped carnation*: refusal; *yellow carnation*: disdain • **heraldry** caprice

carnelian distinction; in the Bible, an emblem of hope and patience

carnival an invocation of primoridal chaos; the desperate quest for a way "out" of time; the desire to concentrate all the possibilities of existence in a given period of time

carp endurance; perseverance; fortitude; voracity; war; energy; courage; longevity; a talkative person; complaint; a "masculine" fish • **eaten as food** poverty • **China** perserverance

carpenter Christ; God; the creator; Daedalus; St. Joseph • **building an ark** Noah • **visited by an angel** St. Joseph • **building a wooden cow** Daedalus working for Pasiphae

carpenter's square *see* **square (carpenter's)**

carpet luxury; sovereignty • **unrolling carpet** • the unfolding of life • **red carpet** honor; special treatment

carriage elegance; vehicle of the upper classes • **golden carriage** spiritual qualities allied with wisdom •

pumpkin carriage attribute of Cinderella • *see also* **vehicle**

carrion low life; the flesh; death; despair

cask famine; the maternal body • **bottomless cask** useless labor; the apparent futility of earthly existence • *see also* **box**

casket death • **three caskets** Epiphany • *see also* **sarcophagus; chest**

cassock devotion to Christ and the Church • **white cassock** attribute of a pope • **red cassock** attribute of a cardinal • **violet or purple cassock** attribute of a bishop • **black cassock** attribute of a priest • **black cassock with red piping** attribute of a monsignor or a dean • Cassocks of other colors may indicate that the person depicted was originally a member of a religious order, and the cassock is of the color used for habits of that particular order.

castle safety; impregnability; heavenly wealth; authority; sovereignty; defense; the transcendant soul; an embattled spiritual power ever on watch • **black castle** abode of Pluto or an evil power; evil; an alchemist's den • **castle of light** treasure; salvation; abode of a heavenly power, or a good power; spiritual attainment • **turreted castle** attribute of David, the Virgin Mary • **heraldry** grandeur; nobility; solidity; strategy • *see also* **palace**

Castor and Pollux brotherly love; power in battle; safety at sea; the dual worldly and spiritual nature of all things

cat domesticity; sensuality; ease; cruelty; spite; laziness; salacity; magical forces; guardian of marriage; love of freedom; self-indulgence; resentment; lust; cleanliness; playfulness; grace; longevity; coquettishness; languor; melancholy; cunning; treachery; an attribute of Cupid; a man between 70 and 80 years of age

• **heraldry** courage; liberty; individualism; vigilance; indefatigibility; cunning; strategy • **black cat** death; bad luck, except in Britain, where it is good luck • **white cat** good luck, except in Britain, where it is bad luck • **Angora cat** expensive luxury; a pampered and spoiled person, especially a woman • **tortoise shell cat** good luck • **Siamese cat** exoticism • **coat or cloak of cat skin** humility

catastrophe the beginning of a transformation; the end of a cycle or period

catchfly in flower language: pretended love; snare • **red catchfly** youthful love • **white catchfly** betrayed

caterpillar parasite; man in this world

cathedra episcopal dignity; authority; jurisdiction; knowledge; teaching • *see also* **throne**

Catherine wheel solar wheel, which see

Cato moral virtue

cat's eye (stone) platonic affection

cattle emotions; desires; baser mental qualities • **cattle in pasture** agriculture; peace • **fat cattle** prosperity • **lean cattle** famine • *see also* **cow; bull; calf**

Caucasian the spiritual side of man; higher nature • *see also* **complexion**

cauldron martyrdom; witchcraft; mother; womb; resurrection; transmutation and germination of the baser forces of nature; attribute of St. Boniface • **cauldron of boiling oil** punishment; attribute of St. John, St. Ansanus, St. Cecilia, St. George • **eagle rising out of cauldron** attribute of St. John • **witch with a cauldron** Medea • *see also* **kettle**

caulking the limitation of ideas

cave the secretive; security; impregnability; the unconscious; the womb; mother; Hell; resurrection;

burial; fertility; the human mind; the heart; refuge; primitive shelter • **two caves** associated with Obadiah

cavern *see* **cave**

cedar constancy; virtue; beauty; mystery; longevity; steadfast faith; the Lord's tree; incorruptibility; majesty; power; royalty; immortality; fertility; mercy; purification; vengeance; prosperity; growth; height; occasionally, God's power to weaken the strong; emblem of Christ, especially a cedar of Lebanon • **India** fertility • **China** fidelity • **Greece** emblem of Artemis • **cedar of Lebanon** emblem of Christ, Lebanon • **flower language** strength; *cedar leaf*: I live for thee; *cedar of Lebanon*: incorruptibility, strength, constancy

cedrela tree in China: the patriarch of a family

celandine in flower language: joys to come

celery-leaved crowfoot *see* **crowfoot**

cellar the unconscious; the instincts; childhood recollection; regression; the morbid terror lurking in the subconscious

censer purifying fire; spiritual nature; prayer ascending to heaven; worship; the priesthood; flattery; attribute of Aaron, Levi, St. Laurence, St. Stephen, the Lady of the Lake, Asia personified • **Old Testament** the plea that prayers would be acceptable to God • **censer and crown or scepter** associated with Melchizedek • **priests with censers, the ground opening at their feet** associated with Aaron • **bull with censer** the Day of Atonement

centaur the complete domination of a being by baser forces; the instincts; brute force; the superior force of the instincts; man torn between good and evil; the unconscious uncontrolled by the spirit; man's lower nature; lechery; drunkenness heresy; death; the sin of adultery; savage passions and excesses; vengeance; heresy; the dual nature of Christ; wisdom; the teachers of the gods; associated with Bacchus, St. Anthony Abbot • **centaur on a font** the overcoming of original sin by baptism • **centaur with bow and arrow** the fiery darts of the wicked • **heraldry** eminence in battle

centaury in flower language: felicity; delicacy

center the connection between heaven and earth; the genitals; going through death to eternity; the supreme being; unity

centipede regression; fragmentation of the psyche

cereal grains the seven gifts of the Holy Spirit

Ceres agriculture • **Middle Ages** the Church • **Ceres with a torch** search for Proserpine • **Ceres with a chariot drawn by dragons** search for Proserpine • **Ceres with a sickle, cornucopia, or wreath of corn** earth's abundance personified

cereus in flower language —*creeping cereus*: modest genius, horror

chaff worthlessness; barrenness; the transitory; the ungodly; lower qualities

chain(s) enthrallment; sin; slavery; binding; imprisonment; authority; legal control; security; strength; matrimony; the link between heaven and earth; attachment of the mind to the lower world; the power of the Devil; the Flagellation of Christ; attribute of Vice personified, St. Peter • **more than one chain** usually indicates punishment, suffering, slavery, hopeless misfortune • **broken chains** liberation; attribute of St. Leonard • **chain and scepter** Joseph's advancement • **golden chain** honor; dignity; respect; wealth; the spirit binding earth to heaven; attribute of Hermes • **person in chains** man enslaved by sin or his earthly desires • **demon in chains** • attri-

bute of St. Bernard, St. Vincent •
heraldry the refusal to be defamed
or humiliated
chair pause; rest; old age; authority;
judgment; sovereignty • **empty
chair** absence of authority; the deceased; undying hope • **occupied
chair** implies the occupant's superior position to those who are standing
• *see also* **throne; cathedra**
chalcedony secret prayer; open righteousness; associated with June
chalice sacrifice; suffering; redemption; the Last Supper; the Eucharist;
intuition; wisdom; prudence; the
source of life; attribute of St. Bruno,
St. Thomas Aquinas, St. Bonaventura, St. Josaphat • **chalice with
bread** the Eucharist; associated with
Melchizidek • **chalice with spider**
attribute of St. Norbert • **chalice on
a closed book, with a stole** ordination • **chalice with staff** attribute
of Chamael • **chalice with serpent**
attribute of St. John • **chalice with
wafer** attribute of St. Barbara; the
sacrifice of Christ upon the cross •
broken chalice attribute of St. Donatus • **woman with chalice** Faith
personified
chalk attribute of an apprentice
chamber *see* **room**
chameleon adaptibility; changeableness; love; attribute of Air personified
chancel the Church Triumphant
chaos incipient creation; the unconscious; the earliest state of creation;
death of religion and morality; man;
absence of love
charcoal a piece of charcoal: an attribute of an apprentice • **Orient**
prosperity; changelessness
chariot war; conquest; authority; the
self; triumph • **four chariots** associated with Zechariah • **fiery chariot** the sun; associated with Phaeton, Elijah, the Ascension of Christ
• **black bearded king carrying off a
maid in his chariot** the rape of Pro-

serpine • **chariot drawn over a
corpse** associated with Tullia •
chariot with a body dragging behind
Achilles' victory over Hector • **chariot bound in cord** associated with
Alexander the Great • **chariot of
cockle shells, drawn by sea horses** attribute of Neptune, Galatea • **chariot drawn by wolves** attribute of
Mars • **chariot drawn by two youths**
Cleobis and Bito • **chariot drawn by
unicorns** attribute of Chastity personified • **chariot drawn by angels**
attribute of Eternity personified •
chariot drawn by an ass attribute of
Silenus • **chariot drawn by cen-
taurs, tigers, or leopards** attribute of
Bacchus • **chariot drawn by dogs**
attribute of Vulcan • **chariot drawn
by dolphins** attribute of Galatea •
chariot drawn by doves, swans attribute of Venus • **chariot drawn by
dragons** attribute of Ceres • **chariot drawn by eagles** attribute of Jupiter • **chariot drawn by elephants**
attribute of Fame personified •
chariot drawn by goats attribute of
Bacchus, Cupid • **chariot drawn by
four horses** attribute of Apollo, Aurora, the sun • **chariot drawn by
four white horses** attribute of Cupid
personifying love • **chariot drawn
by one white horse and one black
horse** Luna, Diana • **chariot drawn
by black horses** (usually two) attribute of Night personified • **chariot
drawn by black horses** (usually three)
attribute of Pluto • **chariot drawn by
horses** attribute of Armida • **chariot
drawn by lions** attribute of Cybele •
chariot drawn by oxen (usually black)
attribute of Death personified • **chariot drawn by peacocks** attribute of
Juno • **chariot drawn by stags** attribute of Diana, Father Time
Chariot (tarot) self control; progress
and victory; triumph; majesty
charity universal love
charoset for Jews; a reminder of their
slavery under the Egyptians

Charybdis desire for immediate fruits of an action as an impedance to moral progress

chaste tree in flower language: indifference; coldness; chastity

chasuble protection; the seamless garment of Christ for which the soldiers cast lots; the vulva (from its oval shape); celebration of the Eucharist; Christian charity (because it covers all other vestments, as charity is the virtue that should preceed all other virtues); attribute of SS Ignatius of Loyola, Martin of Tours, Thomas à Becket, Philip Neri • **the Virgin Mary robing a man in a chasuble** St. Ildefonso

checkers the effort to control irrational impulses by containing them in a given order; duality; reason; intellect

cheek pale   cheek melancholy • **rosy cheek** youth

cherry sweetness of character derived from good works; virginity; merriment; fruitfulness; attribute of Ceres • **cherry in Christ's hand** the delight of the blessed • **cherry stones** used in witchcraft

cherry   blossom(s) friendliness; spring; April; spiritual beauty; feminine beauty; short-lived pleasures; emblem of Japan

cherry tree education; protection against evil; the Great Divine Spirit; good heart; chivalry; manly virtue; emblem of women; associated with Aquarius; attribute of George Washington, and, hence, a symbol of truthfulness in the U.S. (especially when the tree has been chopped down) • **heraldry** humility; riches; hospitality • **flower language** education; *white or winter cherry*: deception

cherub religion; vigilance; "keeper of the threshold"; executor of God's will; messenger of divine wisdom; a guardian; attribute of St. Matthew • **heraldry** dignity; glory; high position; honor

chervil in flower language: **garden chervil** sincerity

chess life; war; conflict; the sexes meeting on equal terms

chest (container) a feminine symbol of containment; related to fertility • **money chest** attribute of St. Matthew • **money chest containing a heart** attribute of St. Anthony of Padua • **money chest with metal bands** an emblem of banking • **buried money chest** booty of pirates • **closed chest** secrecy • **woman placing a coin in a chest** the "widow's mite" • *see also* **casket**

chestnut foresight; sensuality; voluptuousness; obstinate durability; associated with Gemini • **Christianity** chastity; triumph over the temptations of the flesh • **Old Testament** magic • **Roman** associated with the lower classes • **old chestnut** mustiness; something that is hackneyed • **flower language** sweet chestnut: do me justice • **horse chestnut** luxury

cheveril conscience; elasticity

chick emblem of Easter; rebirth • *see also* **chicken; hen; rooster; capon**

chicken cowardice; effeminacy • **China** on a rooftop: ill fortune • *see also* **chick; rooster; hen; capon**

chickweed in flower language: rendezvous • **mouse-eared chickweed** ingenuous simplicity

chicory attribute of Frugality personified • **Jewish** the bitterness of bondage • **flower language** frugality

child the future; innocence; purity; beginning; dawn; spring; unity with nature; conjunction of the conscious and the unconscious; a sign of impending beneficent change; ignorance; ingratitude; forgetfulness; the preconscious; associated with the eternal; attribute of St. Hilary, St. Augustine • **children** attribute of St. Vincent DePaul • **dead child** attribute of St. Zenobius • **naked**

child new life; when issuing from the mouth of a dying person: the soul • **child kissing the hand of a saint** the saint is St. Nicholas of Myra • *see also* **boy; girl; Christ child**

chimera complex evil; cunning; drought; darkness; the underworld; alarm • **Christianity** the spirit of evil

chimere dutiful perserverance

chimney on a house: the joy of giving; peace; life; happiness; contentment • **on a factory** power; industry; commerce

chimney sweep omen of good luck; the work of chimney sweeping is related to fertility

china an attractive woman; delicate beauty

Chinese evergreen long life

chive in astrology: related to Mars

chocolate self-indulgence; sensuality; aphrodisiac

chough prattle

chrism baptism; ordination; conformation; unction; dedication; attribute of St. Catherine of Siena

Christ child attribute of St. Christopher, St. Anthony of Padua

Christmas God's love; renewal of love and hope

chrysalis resurrection; the soul leaving the body; valor; regeneration; balance; transformation; organization; passive and blind obedience to the laws of nature

chrysanthemum regal beauty; constancy; reliability; fruitfulness; long life; abundance; associated with Scorpio; emblem of the sun, Japan, China • **flower language**— *Chinese chrysanthemum*: cheerfulness under misfortune; *red chrysanthemum*: I love; *white chrysanthemum*: truth; *yellow chrysanthemum*: slighted love • **China** autumn; October; September; joviality; the life of ease • **Orient** scholarliness

chrysoberyl patience in sorrow

chrysolite wisdom; unrequited love

chrysoprase eloquence; confidence; sometimes related to Cancer

church faith; the intersection of heaven and earth; the body of Christ • **church on a rock** the whole Church, securely founded on the rock of faith • **church as an ark** the salvation of its members • **church model being carried** an attribute of St. Gregory, St. Jerome; a particular church being carried may indicate that the person carrying it was its founder or first bishop

churning creation

ciborium consecration; Ark of the Covenant; womb of the Virgin Mary; the Last Supper; the Eucharist; the grave of Christ; attribute of St. Oswald, St. Bonaventura • **ciborium as a receptacle** the Eucharist; the Last Supper • **ciborium supported by pillars as a canopy over an altar** the Ark of the Covenant

cicada loquacity; garrulity; chatter; melody; resurrection; worldly grandeur; immortality; metamorphosis; eternal youth; happiness; evanescent worldly glory; restraint of vice and lasciviousness; the discarded lover; cunning; improvidence; negligence; attribute of Apollo, Aurora, Dawn personified, bad poets

cicatrix *see* **scar**

cider rural festivities

cincture chastity; self-restraint; continence; patient suffering; temperance; preparation for service; truth; humility; contempt for the world; the scourging of Christ; attribute of the Virgin Mary • *see also* **girdle**

cinnamon an attribute of the Virgin Mary

cinquefoil (plant) maternal affection; death • **heraldry** hope; joy • **flower language** maternal affection; beloved daughter

Circe enchantment; feminine wiles; desire leading to good or evil

circle perfection; eternity; heaven;

unity; limitlessness; a cyclic process; the ultimate state of oneness; never ending existence; a monogram of God; protection • **two circles intertwined** marriage (from two wedding rings) • **three circles** (especially in a triangle) the Trinity; three persons in one god • **five circles intertwined** the Olympics, and the linking that occurs during them; the five continents: Asia, Europe, America, Africa, Australia • *see also* **circumference**

circumcision sublimated castration; spiritual purification; initiation (into the Jewish faith in particular) • *see also* **castration**

circumference objects contained within are limited, defined, and of the manifest world; viewed from without, the circumference is the defense of the conscious world against the unconscious or chaos • *see also* **circle**

circus *see* **carnival**

cistern a wife who must be guarded to keep pure; associated with Jeremiah

cistus in flower language: popular favor; *gum cistus*: I die tomorrow

cithara or cithern *see* **zither**

citron in flower language: ill-natured beauty

city the feminine principle; mother; the society or the beliefs of the society of which it is a part; manifestation of a particular discipline or principle; loneliness; refuge; lack of spiritual, natural, or emotional contact • **golden city** Babylon • **city with seven gates** Thebes • **walled city** the heavenly Jerusalem; the transcendent soul; associated with Zechariah • **walled city with a sword above it** associated with Zephaniah • **city on a hill** the stability and prominence of the Church

claw greed; ferocity; flattery; degenerate sexuality; tenacity; prowess; the law; ferality • **heraldry** eagle claw: one who preys

clematis emblem of the Virgin Mary • **flower language** mental beauty; artifice; *evergreen clematis*: poverty

cliff attribute of St. Sylvanus

climbing *see* **ascending**

Clio history

cloak the outer bounds of the wearer's personality; mental covering, often revealing the wearer's principles of action, opinions, prejudices, associations, mental state, etc.; superior dignity; protection; concealment; mystery; invisibility; villany; infamy; sleep; righteousness; Christian charity; attribute of a pilgrim, St. Angela Merici • **cloak trimmed with crimson feathers** characteristic fairy dress • **cloak lined with fur** rank • **cloak lined with ermine** attribute of royalty, Charlemagne, St. Ursula • **cloak split in two with a sword** attribute of St. Martin of Tours

clock the universe; order; the march of time; cyclic existence of man, the seasons, etc.; related to the magical creation of beings that pursue their own autonomous existence; attribute of Temperance personified, St. Ursula • **portraiture** implies that the subject has a temperate nature

closet secrecy; the grave; the earth; passage into another existence

clotbur *see* **burdock**

clothes deception; concealment of reality or truth; indication of profession, mental state, beliefs, associations, etc.; intimately related to the owner's personality; distinction in rank, sex, mood; hiding of nakedness, vice • **new clothes** (particularly at Easter) renewal of the owner • **changing clothes** changing personalities, roles, opinions, loyalties, etc. • *see also* particular articles of clothing: **cloak; hat; shoes;** etc.

cloud the intermediate world between the formal and non-formal; the transitory; death; illusion; mystery; fertility; sanctity; chastity; change; storm; evanescence; sleep; betrayal; obscuring of truth; disgrace; providence; benignity; a symbolic messenger • **lightning flash through a cloud** mythology • **hand emerging from a cloud** the omnipotent God • **dark, or storm clouds** portent of evil, trouble • **fleecy clouds** benignity • **green clouds** in China: a plague of insects • **feet emerging from cloud above mountain** Nahum's vision

clove in flower language: dignity

clover the Trinity; good fortune; ease; fertility; abundance; ardent, but humble love; emblem of Ireland, the Irish • **heraldry** sincerity; hope • **four leaf clover** good fortune; sacred to the Druids • **flower language**—*red clover*: industry; *four leaf clover*: be mine; *white clover*: think of me; *purple clover*: provident

clown *see* **jester**

club (bat) brute force; punishment; strength; intrepidity; victory through destruction; brutality; a royal weapon; attribute of St. James the Less, Mercury, Hercules, St. Jude, the betrayal of Christ, St. Gervase, St. Protase, Fortitude personified, the "wild man" of medieval European painting • **Christianity** betrayal; martyrdom • **knotted club** attribute of Cain, St. Jude • **club with spear and/or lance and/or inverted cross** attribute of St. Jude • **fuller's club** attribute of St. James the Less, St. Simon, St. Mark, St. Jude

club (playing card suit) will power; authority; glory; enterprise; energy; reason

coal (ember) *see* **ember**

coal (mineral) repressed energy; the negative side of energy; dirtiness; worthlessness

coat of many colors: attribute of Joseph • **without seams** attribute of

the Passion of Christ • *see also* **cloak; clothes**

cobaea in flower language: gossip

cobbler lust (from the vulva symbolism of shoes)

cobweb *see* **web**

Cockaigne ridicule of poetic bliss or wishful thinking; ridicule of monastic life

cockatrice *see* **basilisk**

cockle evil; wickedness invading the good field of the Church

cockleshell *see* **shell**

cockroach filth; heat

cocoa tree wisdom; love

coconut wisdom; love; fertility; abundance; endless summer; emblem of the South Seas, tropical islands

cocoon the soul

codfish productiveness; fishery; emblem of Massachusetts

coffer the heart; the maternal womb; a secret

coffin death • **man rising from coffin** Lazarus; Christ • **woman rising from coffin** Drusiana and St. John • *see also* **sarcophagus**

cogwheel fate; industry; mechanics

coin(s) the unfavorable aspects of money; avarice; bribery; trade; attribute of Vanity personified • **coins at the feet of a saint** St. Onuphrius • **coins at the feet of an old man** charity to the poor; renunciation of worldly goods • **silver coins** attribute of Judas • **thirty coins** (especially silver) attribute of Judas • **gold and silver coins in a dish** attribute of St. Laurence • **coins in a still life painting** the power and posessions that death takes away

cold (disease) inhibition of psychic powers

cold (temperature) silence; a spiritualized atmosphere; longing, especially for solitude; resistance to all that is inferior; death; lovelessness; sexual frigidity

collar (clothing) insignia of office;

rank; occupation; modesty • **clerical turned collar** humility; meekness • **clerical collar with two tabs** the tablets of the Ten Commandments

collar (for restraint) slavery; restriction of freedom; bondage; restraint

colt *see* **horse**

coltsfoot maternal care • **in flower language** justice shall be done

columbine folly; desertion; inconstancy; marital infidelity • **Elizabethan** compassion • **Christianity** humility; love; the Holy Spirit, especially prior to the 16th Century; with seven blooms: the seven gifts of the Holy Spirit • **flower language** folly; *purple columbine*: resolution; *red columbine*: anxious and waiting

column (architectural) steadfastness; power; phallus; the connection between heaven and earth; the upward impulse; attribute of the Crucifixion; free standing columns especially may represent a sky god or other deity, glory, achievement, honor • **broken column** death; frustrated hope; unfinished work; attribute of St. Titus • **Egyptian column** attribute of Joseph • **tall column** attribute of St. Philip • **woman holding a column** Fortitude personified • **horizontal column** inertia

comb knowledge; sacrificial remains; associated with burials; the sun's rays; entanglement; fertility; rain; vanity; attribute of Venus, the sirens, lamia, mermaids • **iron wool carding comb** attribute of St. Blaise, St. Laurence

comet unrest; impending disaster or change; evil omen of war, famine, plague, earthquake, drought, etc.; a brilliant, but short-lived career • **Christianity** emblem of Christmas

communion rail the separation between the Church Militant and the Church Triumphant

compass guidance; navigation

compasses the act of creation; the beginning of all things; right conduct; astronomy; architecture; navigation; geometry; science; measuring; reason; temperance; knowledge; an attribute of Urania, Euclid, the personifications of Astronomy, Geometry, Maturity, Melancholy, Prudence • **portraiture** may denote an architect, navigator, or artist (the latter especially in renaissance or baroque art)

complexion • **dark complexion** underworld deities; death; sleep; ignorance; villainy; mystery; fertility • **light complexion** heavenly deities; knowledge; wisdom; peace; purity; a hero or heroine

computer *see* **engine**

concealment *see* **withdrawal**

conch shell wealth; learning; the feminine principle; vulva; primitive summons; the spiritual and natural means of development rendered active; attribute of Aphrodite, Triton, and other deities associated with the sea

condor eternity; strength

cone psychic wholeness; phallus; sun; attribute of fertility deities

coney *see* **rabbit**

confetti fertility; a substitute for rice, which see

convolvulus humility; uncertainty; coquetry; emblem of Insinuation personified • **flower language** bonds; uncertainty; *great or major convolvulus*: extinguished hope; *blue, minor, or night convolvulus*: night, repose; *three-colored convolvulus*: coquetry; *pink convolvulus*: worth sustained by judicious and tender affection

coot beauty; courtliness; understanding; wisdom; a common or stupid fellow; something valueless • **chattering coots** warning of a storm

cope (garment) innocence; purity; dignity

copestone contemplation; the head

copper firmness; strength; hardness; low value; money; autumn; harvest; decay; metal of the common people; associated with Taurus, Libra, the planet Venus, Ceres, Aphrodite, Cyprus

coral (sea coral) marriage; good fortune; blood; longevity; protection against evil • coral necklace protection; healing; attribute of Africa personified • China official promotion; longevity

cochorus in flower language: impatient of absence

cord execution; union; bondage; security; force; sin; attribute of the Passion of Christ, St. Lucy • silver cord related to Judgment Day • seven cords associated with Samson • cord of garments chastity; temperance; self-restraint

coreopsis in flower language: always cheerful; *arkansa coreopsis*: love at first sight

coriander hidden worth • flower language concealed merit

cormorant vanity; instability; winter; desolation

corn fertility; germination and growth; development of a potentiality; health; plenty; peace; prosperity; a spermatic image • U.S. emblem of the Midwest, agriculture • flower language riches; *corn straw*: agreement; *broken corn straw*: argument • NOTE: In this citation, and in the U.S., corn is taken to mean maize. Corn is often taken to mean the chief cereal grain of a country, so it may also mean, for example, wheat in England, or oats in Scotland or Ireland. Look under the appropriate citation.

corn bottle in flower language: delicacy

corn cockle in flower language: gentility

corn flower *see* cornflower

cornel tree in flower language: duration

cornelian cherry *see* dogwood

cornerstone foundation; something fundamental, or of primary importance; Christ; remnant of a "foundation sacrifice" (originally a child was used, later, small animals)

cornet attribute of Notoriety personified • *see also* horn; trumpet

cornflower related to the heavens; associated with Cyanus, who was turned into one by Flora; emblem of Germany • flower language delicacy; devotion to an inferior

cornucopia abundance; fruitfulness; liberality; the bounty of God; thanksgiving; associated with Asher; attribute of Ceres, Zephyr, the personifications of Earth, Autumn, Peace, Abundance, Concord, Fortune, Hospitality, Europe, Charity, occasionally Africa, and in the Middle Ages, Justice • old woman and naked goddess with cornucopia Vertumnus and Pomona respectively

coronation achievement; victory; consummation • coronation of a young woman by a soldier the soldier is Alexander the Great • coronation of a youth by a maiden, or vice versa, in a pastoral setting Mirtillo and Amarillis • *see also* crown

coronella in flower language: may success crown your wishes

corpse the personality in its lower aspect; the end of a cycle or idea

corrosion destruction; infirmity; suffering

corset support; protection; society hampering development of the psyche

cosmetics vanity; deceit; disloyalty; trickery; wantonness; foolishness; lust; sorrow; seduction; depersonalization; attribute of a loose woman

cotta innocence; purity

cottage the simple, carefree, country life; the humble life • cottage in a vineyard loneliness

cotton emblem of the South in the

U.S. • **cotton blossoms** happiness; well-being

couch a place for reverie, languor, seduction

courtesan *see* **prostitute**

cow mother (especially a white cow or a heifer); related to most mother goddesses; female sexual desire; procreation; associated with the earth and the moon; attribute of Apollo, Hermes, Zeus, and of many fertility gods • **heifer** a bride; fertility; mother; giver of nourishment; emblem of many mother goddesses; sacred to Hathor, Io, Isis, etc.; sacrifice; wantonness; mildness; a young woman • **red cow** related to the dawn • **white cow** related to many mother goddesses; mother; rain; sacrifice • **hollow wooden cow** the cow Daedelus built for Pasiphae • *see also* **cattle; calf; bull**

cowherd honored in Greece, despised in Britain and Egypt

cowhide fertility

cowslip rusticity; grace; comeliness; pensiveness • **flower language** pensiveness; winning grace; divine beauty; early joys (particularly of youth) • **American cowslip** you are my angel, my divinity

crab aggressiveness; peevishness; regression; grossness; death; regeneration; repulsive sex; emblem of the sea, Cancer; associated with June • **hermit crab** caution; foresight

crab apple in China: perpetual peace, the blossoms signify feminine beauty

crab tree irritability; old, foolish, cowardly people

cradle birth; rebirth; shelter; protection; the coffin; innocence; motherhood; security; the Nativity of Christ; associated with the sibyls Cumana, Samiana • **rocking cradle** the ups and downs of life

cranberry the divine seed present in all lower nature • **flower language** cure for heartache

crane (bird) justice; longevity; the good and diligent soul; vigilance; loyalty; good life and works; good order in monastic life; haughtiness; snobbery; pomp; justice; purity; dawn; happiness; inquisitiveness; lust; a good omen; related to poetry; attribute of the personifications of Religion and Monastic Life; sacred to Artemus, Athena, Apollo, Hermes, Thoth, Theseus • **heraldry** (usually with a stone in its mouth) vigilance • **China** longevity; old age

crane's bill (flower) in flower language: envy

cranium *see* **skull**

crayfish nonchalance; laziness; loss of faith; attribute of the Synagogue as the Jewish faith personified

Creation the days of Creation: • **Sunday** light • **Monday** division of waters • **Tuesday** dry land, pastures, trees • **Wednesday** heavenly bodies • **Thursday** sea beasts, birds • **Friday** land beasts, man and woman • **Saturday** rest

cremation sublimation; purification; resurrection; return to ashes; destruction of what is base to make way for what is superior

crescent sleep; womanhood; the feminine principle in general; the pure soul; emblem of the Virgin Mary and virgin goddesses in general; emblem of Egypt • **heraldry** high honors, especially in the Crusades; change; sciences; hope for greater glory; in modern times: second sons and their families • **crescent and star** paradise; the Islamic world; the Virgin Mary • **crescent and seven-pointed star** attribute of Cybele • **crescent and many stars** God and the Heavenly Host • *see also* **moon**

cress old age; something small or worthless • **flower language** stability; power; *Indian cress*: eclat, warlike trophy • *see also* **watercress**

cresset the Gospel

crest thought; the predominating characteristic of its owner

cricket (insect) summer; courage • chirping twittering women; loquacity; coming rain; coming death

crimson sin; royalty; love; attribute of Pan; shares much of the symbolism of **red**, which see

crocodile fury; evil; fecundity; power; viciousness; dissimulation; knowledge; hypocrisy; the Devil; lust; attribute of St. Theodore • **crocodile with jaws bound** Fasting personified • **Egypt** fury; evil; tyranny; death; voracity; divine reason • *see also* **caiman**

crocus death; cheerfulness; illicit love; hardiness; joy; emblem of the Virgin Mary • **flower language** abuse not; *saffron crocus*: mirth; *spring crocus*: youthful gladness, pleasures of hope

crook (shepherd's) pastoral life; power; divine leadership; sovereignty; attribute of Anubis, Osiris, Apollo, Pan, Argus, Polyphemus, Christ, St. Genevieve, Moses, Abel (especially when shown with lamb), Amos, David; associated with Christmas, the Nativity of Christ • *see also* **crozier, staff**

crosier *see* **crozier**

cross the conjunction of opposites; the connection between heaven and earth; the tree of life; crucifixion; suffering; agony; struggle; martyrdom; the suffering of existence; man's longing for the higher world; finished redemption; faith, especially the Christian faith; the Passion of Christ; the Atonement; attribute of St. Louis of France, St. John Berchmans, occasionally the Hellespontic sibyl, the Cimmerean sibyl • **cross with heart or lily** attribute of St. Catherine of Siena • **cross with monstrance** attribute of St. Clare • **cross with scroll** attribute of Jeremiah • **cross with martyr's palm** attribute of St. Margaret of Antioch • **cross with a saw** attribute of St. Simon Zelotes • **cross above a pome-**

granate attribute of St. John of God • **cross with a chalice** attribute of St. Bonaventura and Faith personified • **flowering cross** the tree of life; attribute of St. Anthony of Padua • **cross with instruments of the Passion** attribute of St. Bernard • **cross with rope on it** attribute of St. Julia • **cross with a lamb** the Crucifixion of Christ • **cross with a winding sheet** the Passion of Christ • **cross with an empty skin** attribute of St. Bartholomew • **cross with a carpenter's square** attribute of St. Philip • **cross made of faggots** attribute of Isaac • **inverted cross** attribute of St. Peter, St. Jude, St. Philip • **inverted cross with lance, club, or halberd** attribute of St. Jude • **cross on three steps** finished redemption (the steps represent faith, hope, and love); Calvary • **cross on an orb or globe** salvation; the gradual enlightenment of the world; the triumph of Christ; triumph of the Gospel • **small cross carried in the hand** attribute of St. Philip • **five crosses** the five wounds of Christ • **knotted cross** attribute of St. Philip • **processional cross** attribute of the Phrygian sibyl; the Church Militant • **processional cross carried by a deacon** the deacon is St. Stephen • **tall cross with book or scroll** attribute of St. Philip • **tall cross alone** attribute of St. Matthias • **pointed cross emerging from a chalice** Gethsemane • **cross with two horizontal arms** attribute of a Patriarch, St. Sylvester, St. Gregory the Great • *see also* **Cross of Lorraine** in this listing • **cross with two horizontal arms and a bar dexter** *see* **Eastern cross** in this listing • **cross with two horizontal arms and a spear** attribute of St. Philip • **Cross of Lorraine** emblem of the Free French in World War II • **Eastern cross** emblem of the Greek Catholic Church; the mercy shown the thief to the right of Christ • **cross with three horizontal arms** the papacy; attribute of St. Peter and of popes with the exception of St. Sylvester, St. Gregory the Great, both of whom have a cross with two horizontal arms as an attribute) • **tau cross** Passover; attribute of St. Anthony the Great • **tau cross on the end of a staff** attribute of St. Philip, St. Anthony Abbot • **Maltese cross** emblem of Freemasons, Germany; the union of male and female; attribute of John the Baptist • **Maltese cross with triangles at the end of each arm** power • **St. Andrew's cross** attribute of St. Andrew, St. Patrick • **St. Andrew's cross with boathook** attribute of St. Andrew • **Greek cross** usually the Church of Christ, rather than Christ or christianity • **Latin cross** the Passion of Christ; the atonement • **Latin cross borne by a woman** St. Reparata, St. Margaret • **Latin cross carried in the hand** St. Philip • **Latin cross made of reeds** attribute of John the Baptist • **Latin cross borne by angels** attribute of St. Helena • **Latin cross with rays on a shield** faith; attribute of St. Paul • **red Latin cross** attribute of St. Ursula, St. George of Cappadocia • **Egyptian cross or ankh** the living; life in general; the tree of life • **Jerusalem cross** the five wounds of Christ

crossroads choice; union; the mother; intersection or conjunction of any binary form: space/time, body/spirit, etc.; the mystic cetner; the union of opposites; meeting place of demons, witches, etc.; a place of magic power

crow chatter; usually an unfavorable omen; death; piracy; a Negro; the negative or occult; solitude; cunning; pride; the Devil; untrustworthiness; a plebian; longevity; a hermit; the isolation of one who lives on a superior plane; a messenger; a prophet; the possessor of mystic

powers; a demiurgic power; associated with the idea of beginning; related to Apollo, Asclepius, Saturn; attribute of Hope personified • **two crows** attribute of St. Vincent • **China** a red crow: the sun • **Orient** an ill omen, although two together represent conjugal fidelity • *see also* **raven**

crowfoot (plant) in flower language: ingratitude (especially celery-leaved crowfoot); *aconite-leaved crowfoot*: luster

crowd the unconscious; discordant actions in the unconscious (when the crowd is orderly, it loses its negative connotations)

crown pre-eminence; success; the sun's rays; spiritual and enlightenment (especially a jeweled crown); rank; sovereignty; victory; recompense; eternal life; at one time a funeral symbol; attribute of royalty, the gods, Christ's kingly office, Deborah, St. Margaret of Antioch, St. Louis of France, St. Catherine of Alexandria, St. Gertrude, St. Helena, St. Josaphat, St. Sebastian; as the attribute of a martyr it indicates victory over sin and death, or that they were of royal blood; reward of the faithful Christian life • **crown in a still life** the earthly power that death takes away • **two crowns** attribute of Liberty personified • **three crowns** attribute of King Arthur, the pope, St. Elizabeth of Hungary • **crown of flowers** attribute of Euterpe, Terpsichore, Flora, Melpomene (when held in the hand), the personifications of Asia, the Golden Age • **crown of corn** attribute of Ceres • **crown of feathers** attribute of America personified • **crown of laurel** attribute of Clio; when held in the hand: attribute of Calliope • **crown of roses** attribute of St. Cecilia, St. Dorothea • **crown of reeds and rushes** attribute of river gods • **crown of olive branches** attribute of

Peace personified, St. Agnes • crown of thorns the misery and humiliation of Christ; attribute of Christ, St. John of God, St. Rose of Lima, St. Joseph of Arimathea, St. Louis IX, St. Mary Magdalene, St. Catherine of Siena, St. Veronica, the Delphic sibyl • crown of laurel attribute of poets, Roman emperors and governors of provinces, Apollo, Homer, Dante, Virgil, Calliope, Clio, Arion (riding a dolphin), St. Paul, the personifications of Victory, Fame (with trumpet), Truth (naked) • crown of stars attribute of Urania, virgin martyrs (usually held in the hand), the Virgin Mary (particularly with lilies) • crown of vine attribute of Bacchus, Gluttony personified • turreted mural crown attribute of Cybele, Earth personified, towns and cities personified • crown and scepter attribute of Christ as king, David, Deborah, Melchizedek, St. Louis of Toulouse (at his feet) • red crown and papyrus emblem of the Lower Kingdom of Egypt • white crown and flowering rush emblem of the Upper Kingdom of Egypt • see also coronation; tiara

crown imperial in flower language: majesty; power

crowsbill (plant) in flower language: envy

crozier authority; jurisdiction; divine power; creative power; faith; power to draw souls to God and to goad the slothful (the hooked end, or crook, is for pulling, and the pointed end is for prodding); the correction of vices; mercy; firmness; an attribute of bishops, abbots, shepherds, St. Sylvester, St. Benedict, St. Giles, St. Bernard, St. Martin, St. Clare, occasionally St. Bernard, St. Martin, St. Clare, occasionally St. Bridget • crozier with fish dangling from it attribute of St. Zeno • crozier with white banner or veil attribute of an abbot or abbess • crozier terminating with a cross with two cross pieces attribute of archbishops, St. Gregory • crozier terminating in a cross with three cross pieces attribute of St. Peter, popes • see also crook; staff

crucible attribute of the Alchemist personified

crucifix the suffering Savior; the Passion of Christ; the Atonement; attribute of St. Frances Xavier, St. Charles Borromeo, St. Francis of Assisi, St. Mary Magdalen, St. Jerome, St. Scholastica, St. Catherine of Alexandria, St. Anthony of Padua (especially with an unclothed Christ) • crucifix with Christ dressed in vestments the Reigning Christ • crucifix with the figure of Christ leaning toward a saint attribute of St. John Gualberto • crucifix between the antlers of a stag attribute of St. Hubert • crucifix held by martyr with a hatchet in his head St. Peter Martyr • crucifix entwined with lilies attribute of St. Nicholas of Tolentino • crucifix entwined with roses attribute of St. Therese of Lisieux • crucifix with dove attribute of St. Scholastica • crucifix with a praying desert hermit usually St. Jerome

crucifixion of lamb Christ

cruet redemption; the Eucharist

cruse • cruse of wine, with napkin attribute of the Good Samaritan • cruse of oil the inexhaustible grace and mercy of Christ; attribute of the Widow of Sarepta

crutch misfortune; temporary handicap; hidden or shameful support; great age; attribute of beggars, Father Time, Vulcan, Saturn, St. Anthony Abbot (especially when it has a bell on it), St. Anthony the Great, St. John Gualberto, St. Romuald, St. Maurus; emblem of those who care for the aged or crippled

crystal transparency; purity; wisdom; intuitive knowledge; the spirit; the

intellect associated with the spirit; simplicity; truthfulness; related to the eyes, water, baptism, ice; tears
crystal ball immortality; divine light; entrance to another world; attribute of fortune tellers
cube the earth; the solidity and persistance of virtues; stability; devotion; truth; cubes suggest artificial or constructed objects; attribute of the personifications of Faith, History • **heraldry** constancy; truthfulness; devotion
cuckoo cuckholdry; usurpation; jealousy; spring; egoism; selfishness; infidelity; foolishness; deception; the frivolous; insanity; the eternal bachelor; the Devil; associated with April; attribute of Hera
cuckoo plant spring • **flower language** ardor
cucumber in flower language: criticism
cudweed in flower language: never ceasing remembrance
cuirass *see* **breastplate**
cup friendship; temperance; renewed spiritual vigor; the moon; the passive element; vulva; consolation; blessing; prize; attribute of Dionysus, Asclepius, Hygeia, Hermes, Chthonius, Artemesia • **overturned cup** (in still life) vanity; the emptiness of worldly things • **overturned cup spilling wine** the spilling of blood; death • **golden cup** virginity • **silver cup** prize • **clay cup** man's life • **broken cup** broken life; attribute of St. Benedict • **cup with a serpent in it** attribute of St. John • **cup in a sack of corn** attribute of Joseph (son of Jacob) • **cup with a heart in it** associated with Ghismonda • **woman drinking from a cup** Sophonsiba; Artemesia • **broken communion cup** attribute of St. Donatus of Arezzo; Christ's agony in Gethsemane • **communion cup with wafer** the Eucharist; attribute of St. Barbara,

Bonaventura • **baptismal cup** attribute of St. Ansanus • **Norse** life token; container of the soul; emblem of the gods • **heraldry** liberality; purity; joy; a bailiff, treasurer, archivist, or holder of the honarary title of royal cup-bearer or meat carver • *see also* **chalice**
cupola a phallic symbol
curlew the good Christian
currants in flower language: you please all (especially when a branch of currants); thy frown will kill me
curtain concealment; protection; veil of the future **dropping a curtain** — the end; death
cuscuta in flower language: meanness
cushion comfort; wealth; authority; ease • *see also* **pillow**
cuttlefish *see* **octopus**
cyclamen the Virgin Mary • **in flower language** diffidence; distrust; voluptuousness
cydippe spiritual values; masculinity; has phallic significance; associated with Mercury
cylinder material thoughts; the mechanistic intellect
cymbal vanity; religious ardor; the dance (especially two cymbals); attribute of Petulance personified
cypress funereal implications; sorrow; death; immortality; mourning; a tree dedicated to infernal deities; occasionally, the righteous man who preserves his faith; sacred to Zeus, Venus, the Furies, the Fates, Dis, Apollo, Artemis, Hercules, and various other nature and fertility deities; attribute of Aphrodite • **cypress of Zion** attribute of the Virgin Mary • **cypress coffin** resurrection • **cypress chest** preservation • **cypress and marigolds** despair; melancholy • **palm, olive, and cypress together** attribute of the Virgin Mary

D

D associated with adversity; material barriers; equity; justice; tolerance; limitation; the supreme being; the square; the geometric; the number four; corresponds to the blood, the planet Jupiter, and the Empress in the tarot deck

dabchick weakness; a sensitive purpose; a parasite; a girl; hiding; a seeker of the wisdom of the deeps

dactyls *see* **fingers**

daffodil unrequited love; herald of spring; courage; dancing; short-lived beauty; death; mourning; spiritual rebirth; gracefulness; associated with Aquarius, the number six; emblem of Wales • **heraldry** chivalry; courage; Wales • **flower language** regard; *great yellow daffodil*: chivalry

dagger danger; treachery; weapon of a traitor or assassin; phallus; protection against a foe; attribute of Hecate, Melpomene (from the 17th Century on), Lucretia, St. Thomas the Apostle, St. Lucia (piercing her neck), Wrath personified • **wooden dagger** attribute of Vice personified • *see also* **knife**

dahlia elegance; the dignity of the lower, or lower-middle class; vulgar obstentation; instability; pomp; health • **blue dahlia** impossibility • **flower language** instability; my gratitude exceeds your care

daisy innocence; virginity; adoration; dissembling; resurrection; the silence of death; youth; the Sun of Righteousness; hope; humility; the innocence of the Christ child; attribute of Christ, the Virgin Mary; related to pearls • **in art** a flower of Paradise • **flower language** innocence; *double daisy*: participation; *field or wild daisy*: considering a suit (particularly in the days of chivalry, when turned in a wreath and worn in the hair by a woman); *garden or small double daisy*: I share your sentiments, I reciprocate your affection (both, especially in the days of chivalry); *Michaelmas daisy*: farewell, an afterthought; *ox-eyed daisy*: a token; *parti-colored daisy*: beauty

dalmatic joy; salvation; justice; because of its shape, it refers to the Passion of Christ; attribute of deacons (although bishops and abbots may wear it under a chasuble), St. Stephen (especially with three stones), St. Laurence, St. Vincent of Sargossa, St. Leonard (with a fleur-de-lys)

damsel the anima • *see also* **woman**

dance, dancing the act of creation; a process; the desire for escape; the passage of time; fertility; release from disagreeable circumstances; war; victory; orgy; grief; joy; gratitude; sex; protection; black magic

dandelion coquetry; grief; bitterness; the sun; wisdom; the Passion of Christ; associated with Saggitarius, Leo, Jupiter; in Elizabethan times, a diuretic called piss-a-bed; the seeds floating free represent gossip • **Jewish** a bitter herb of the Passover; the bitterness of bondage • **flower language** love's oracle; *when blown — all seeds removed*: a lover is faithful; *some seeds remain*: a lover is unfaithful; *many seeds remain*: a lover is indifferent

dangling unfulfilled longing

daphne odora in flower language: painting the lily

darkness spiritual darkness; evil; the Devil; primeval chaos; ignorance; the germinant; undeveloped potentialities; the maternal or feminine; terrible judgment; misfortune; mystery; sin; error; when appearing after light, it represents regression

darnel misfortune • **in flower language** vice

dart sun ray; phallus; evil words; attribute of Cupid • **dark with flaming tip** attribute of St. Teresa (usually piercing her breast) • **dart and egg** male generation and female productiveness

date (fruit) the flight into Egypt • **bunch of dates** attribute of St. Ansanus • **date tree** the Resurrection • **date tree with doves** earthly paradise • **date tree, Near East** the Tree of Life • **date tree, Greece** sacred to Leto; governed by Dionysus

dawn creation; youth; beginning; the unconscious broadening into consciousness; the Advent of Christ; the beginning of salvation • **red dawn** the blood of Christ; sailor's warning; emblem of Chinese communism • *see also* **twilight**

Day of Judgment (tarot) *see* **Judgment**

day star Christ

days *see* **birth; creation; gods; marriages; sneezing; works; zodiac**

deacon deacon with wings: St. Josaphat • **deacon with stones** St. Stephen • **deacon carrying processional cross** St. Laurence

deafness inability to hear the voice of the conscience or spirit; an indication that the person may have a sixth sense or other compensatory power • *see also* **hearing**

death end of an epoch; an escape from unendurable tension; means of gaining immortality • **"little" death** sexual intercourse, specifically, orgasm

Death (personified) an old man or old woman, 90 to 100 years old in particular

Death (tarot) death of the old self (not necessarily physical death); abandonment of earthly desires; transformation; ambivalence; the progress of evolution; dematerilization; melancholy; strength; rebirth; creation; decomposition; destruction

decapitation *see* **beheading**

December gloom; coldness; old age; peace and quiet; associated with Capricorn, Saturn

decoration glorification; sublimation

deepness chaos; hell; abyss • *see also* **abyss**

deer timidity; fleetness; gentleness; the soul; aspiration of the soul (especially a jumping deer); longevity; autumn; vanity; a Christian searching after truth; a catechumen; attribute of St. Francis of Assisi • **doe** timidity; fidelity; wildness • **fawn** flattery; subservience; innocence; defenselessness; attribute of St. Jerome • **Greece** sacred to Artemis • **China** longevity • *see also* **stag; hart; hind**

defile (topographical feature) *see* **gorge**

Deimos panic

deluge awakening of the mind from ignorance and error; the final stage of a cycle; purification; destruction and regeneration • *see also* **rain**

Demegorgon chaos personified; the creative spirit; an evil spirit; an underground demon; a fertility spirit

demon agent of the Devil • **demon underfoot** attribute of St. Norbert, St. Geminianus, St. Catherine of Siena • **demon emerging from victim's mouth** exorcism • **demon whispering in man's ear** the man may be Judas • *see also* **monster**

desert the realm of abstraction, spirituality, truth, purity, ascetic spiritualism; a spiritual and holy place; a vast and unknown desert may represent chaos; desert animals represent evil and the forces of destruction

desk authority • *see also* **writing table**

devastation barrenness and unproductiveness in the spirit

Devil the unrealized dark side of man; evil personified; sin personified the **Devil underfoot** attribute of St. Romuald

Devil (tarot) domination of the soul by matter; black magic; disorder; perversion; regression or stagnation of all that is fragmentary, inferior, or discontinuous; the instincts and desires; the half knowledge of the senses

devouring burial; fear of incest (especially maternal); dissolution of the body after death; fear of castration; fear of death; fear of the Terrible Mother; mystery; assimilation; acquisition of the powers of that which is eaten

dew spiritual illumination; Christ; purity; purification; divine blessing; freshness; delicacy; fragility; youth; transitoriness; fertility; remembrance; related to nightfall, sleep, the moon, dawn

dew plant in flower language: a serenade

diamond (gem) light; brilliance; moral and intellectual knowledge; sanctity; perfection; fortitude; hardness; pride; intelligence; hardness of heart; invulnerable faith; lucidity; frankness; joy; life; dignity and wealth, especially royal; associated with Taurus, April • **Christian** Christ; constancy; love

diamond (playing cards) material force; money; trade; industry; justice; silence

diamond (shape) vulva • **heraldry** merchant; escutcheon of women

Diana the woods; nature; fertility; virginity; the Terrible Mother

dianthus divine love

dice chance; divination; debauchery; vice; falseness; fortune; gambling; fate; attribute of the Three Graces, Fortune personified • **three dice** the casting of lots for Christ's garment • **heraldry** equity; fickleness of fortune

Dido tragedy

digestion mastery; dissolution; assimilation (especially spiritual); good digestion is a sign of congruence with nature, and vice versa • *see also* **eating; devouring**

dill cleansing

dimple love; attribute of attractive children, maidens • **dimple in the cheek** misfortune • **dimple in the chin** good fortune

Diomedes bravery

Dionysus *see* **Bacchus**

diosma in flower language: uselessness

dirt (earth) *see* **earth**

dirtiness accumulation of error, prejudice, sin

disease divine displeasure; malady of the soul; ailment of the psyche; pathway to heaven; natural or spiritual disorder or disharmony

disguise assumption of a different personality; entrance into a new stage of life • *see also* **mask**

dish limitation; the female principle; family; martyrdom

dismemberment being possessed by the unconscious, unconscious mania, or unconscious obsessions; degeneration; destruction; disintegration, especially mental • *see also* **maiming; beheading**

dispersal dismemberment, which see

distaff time; the continuity of creation; weaving; spinning; industry; cosmic time; woman; the domestic role of women; may have sexual significance; attribute of the Fates (especially Clotho), Eve after the expulsion from the Garden of Eden, the Virgin Mary at the Annunciation, St. Genevieve when shown as a shepherdess

ditch pitfall; the grave • **ditch digging** low work

dittany birth; emblem of Juno, when functioning as Lucina "the bringer of light" who took responsibility for mothers and babies during childbirth • **flower language** — *white dittany*: passion; *dittany of Crete* birth, emblem of Juno as discussed above

dividers *see* **compasses**

divorce the apparent or delusive separation of love from wisdom, emotion from reason, or goodness from truth; divorce for the purpose of marrying another is leaving higher nature for lower desire

dock (plant) changeableness; shrewdness; patience; attribute of Affection personified • **flower language** patience

doctor an agent promoting growth of the spirit, or treating its ailments

dodder (plant) in flower language: meanness; baseness

doe *see* **deer; hind**

dog flattery; contempt; impurity; depravity; envy; fury; the Devil; heresy; prowling enemies; scavenger; paganism; war; greed; voracity; irritability; bragging; egotism; folly; faithfulness; the priest; companion of the dead; fidelity; obedience; science; the will; flattery; bootlicking; fertility; cunning; watchfulness; courage; protection; a man 60 to 80 years old; dawn; healing; orthodoxy; married fidelity (especially when shown in a woman's lap or at her feet); emblem of the Great Mother, and the moon goddess; associated with Vulcan; attribute of Asclepius, Tobias, Diana, St. Roch, the personifications of Smell, Fidelity, and sometimes, Envy • **Bible and the East** usually an object of contempt; a thief and a scavenger (although in Christian art in the Middle Ages and after, it represented loyalty) • **dog hair** said to cure dog bite • **dog with a flaming torch in its mouth** attribute of St. Dominic • **black and white dogs** Dominicans • **two dogs fighting** quarreling theologians • **three dogs** (Germany) the Mercy, Justice and Truth of Christ • **four dogs** (Germany) the Mercy, Justice, Truth and peace of Christ •

spaniel a subservient person; attribute of St. Margaret of Cortona • **bull dog** perseverance; stolidity; tenacity; generosity and courage; emblem of Great Britain • **puppy** a male child up to 10 years of age • **heraldry** vigilance; faithfulness; affection

dog rose *see* **rose**

dog star *see* **Sirius**

dogfish the lowest kind of fish

dogsbane in flower language: deceit; falsehood

dogwood faithfulness; durability • **dogwood blossoms** the Crucifixion of Christ • **flower language** duration; durability • **dogwood blossoms alone** Am I perfectly indifferent to you?

doll the soul; an ancestor; fertility; external beauty with no feelings

dolphin woman; mother; womb; fertility; fecundity; love; society; water; sea; swiftness; youth's pleasant wantonness; warning of danger; harbinger of rain; the highest order of fish; resurrection; salvation; bearer of souls to the next world; related to death and homage to the dead; Christ (rare); the Christian faith (used primarily in the early Church); sacred to the moon goddess; attribute of Jonah, St. Matthew, Neptune, Venus, Galatea, and other sea deities, also of Water personified, Arion (usually shown riding a dolphin with a lyre, the personifications of Fortune, Youth (both usually shown riding a dolphin) • **dolphin with anchor or boat** prudence; the Christian soul; the soul of the Church; the Church being guided to salvation by Christ • **dolphin with trident** freedom of commerce; supremacy of the seas • **dolphin speared by a trident** the Crucifixion • **dolphin pulling a chariot** attribute of Galatea • **two dolphins swimming in the same direction** equipoise, or, sometimes merely ornament • **two dolphins swimming in opposite directions** involution and evolution • **heraldry** affection; charity; love of music; provinces of France; sea towns; sea farers; pugnacity • *see also* **porpoise**, with which it was often confused, especially in classical times

dome the canopy of heaven; the love of God

dominoes scholarship; learning; emblem of the medieval period

donkey stubbornness; steadiness

door a feminine symbol; vagina; opportunity; change; Christ; salvation; beginning; death; entrance to heaven; protection; attribute of St. Anne • **closed door** secrecy; prohibition; mystery; barrier • **open door** opportunity; hospitality; *for Jews*: opened on Seder night to allow entrance for Elijah announcing the Messianic Age • **blood on doorposts** the Passover; Atonement • **house without doors** rumor

dove aspiration; gentleness; the cosmic All Mother; truth; wisdom; divination; amorous delight; love; mourning; melancholy; timidity; humility; innocence; purity; simplicity; guilelessness; a dupe; sacrifice; cowardice; simpleton; longevity; peace; a peacemaker; pride; constancy; a girl 10 to 20 years of age; a divine agent; the soul; the Holy Spirit (especially when descending); attribute of Bacchus, Peace and Chastity personified, St. Ambrose, St. Augustine of Hippo, St. David, St. Catherine of Sienna, St. Benedict, St. Gregory the Great, St. John Chrysostom, St. Teresa, St. Thomas Aquinas • **two doves in a dish** attribute of St. Nicholas of Tolentino • **two doves carried by St. Joseph** (sometimes in a basket) the Presentation of Christ at the Temple • **two doves** attribute of Venus, Lust personified, Concord personified (when facing each other); Chastity personi-

fied • **seven doves** the Seven Gifts of the Holy Spirit • **12 doves** the 12 Apostles of Christ • **dove with lily** the Annunciation • **dove embedded in lead** the spirit embedded in matter • **dove with date tree** earthly fertility • **dove with olive branch** the Deluge; peace; eternal life; victory; new life; *in funeral art*: eternal peace • **dove with palm branch** in funeral art: eternal peace • **white dove** a departed soul; the Holy Spirit (particularly when shown descending); associated with John the Baptist • **white dove with changeable tints** chastity fighting and surmounting the passions of life • **white dove with blue wings** celestial thoughts • **purple dove** Christ • **gold and silver plumed dove** the treasures of purity and innocence • **gold and silver dove with many wings** the Church • **dove meat** considered an aphrodisiac • **billing doves, turtle doves** love • **dove with ark** the Deluge; peace; glad tidings • **two-headed dove** attribute of Elisha • **dove on a font cover** regeneration through the Holy Spirit • **dove on a pyx** reservation of the sacrament • **dove on a wand or rod** (the wand or rod may be flowering) attribute of St. Joseph • **dove with a vial in its beak** attribute of St. Remigius • **dove carrying an ampulla** the baptism of Clovis • **dove with a twig** signal of land to Noah on the Ark • **dove on one's shoulder** creative imagination • **dove on the shoulder of an Apostle** divine inspiration • **dove on the shoulder of a saint** divine enlightenment • **doves in a basket** attribute of St. Joachim; the Presentation of Christ at the Temple (usually the basket is carried by St. Joseph) • **dove with three-rayed nimbus or stars around its head** the Holy Spirit • **dove issuing from one's mouth** the soul escaping at death; attribute of St. Reparata • **dove flying over the water** Creation (especially when dove has a three-rayed nimbus around its head) • **dove hovering around a man's ear** attribute of St. Bernardino • **dove drinking from a cup or eating bread** the soul being fed by the Eucharist • **China** long life; good digestion; faithfulness; impartial filial duty • **heraldry** peace (especially when it carries an olive branch); loving constancy; eternal life; simplicity

dragon adversary; evil; the unconscious; a plague or sickness; fear of incest; the enemy of truth; the Devil; sin; idolatry; ignorance; pestilence; the bad element in nature; fertility; wisdom; prophecy; nature; chaos; the instincts; darkness; impurity; heresy; guardian of fertility symbols (jewels, gold, etc.); the Terrible Mother; emblem of China; attribute of Ceres (usually pulling her chariot), St. Theodore, the personification of Strength, Vigilance, Prudence, Error, Heresy, Paganism • **Christianity** heresy; error; paganism; envy; emblem of the Devil • **Orient** attribute of a beneficent deity; associated with the element water • **China** guardianship; vigilance; emblem of China; *five-clawed dragon*: imperial authority; *four-clawed dragon*: lesser authorities • **dragon underfoot** attribute of St. George, St. Margaret of Antioch, St. Bernard of Clairvaux, St. Martha, St. Sylvester, the archangel Michael; paganism or sin overcome • **dragon slain, bound, or chained** paganism or sin overcome • **winged dragon** emblem of astrology, alchemy • **dragon thrown into a pit by an angel** the Apocalypse • **dragon led by a cord** attribute of St. Margaret of Antioch • **woman emerging from the stomach of a dragon** St. Margaret of Antioch • **two dragons drawing a chariot** attribute

of Ceres • **tattoo of a dragon** in the 19th Century: a sailor who had been to China • **dragon biting its own tail** time • **dragon biting the hilt of a sword** emblem of the planet Mars • **dragon's teeth** seeds of dissension; warfare; associated with Cadmus • *see also* **wyvern**

dragon fly male dominance; soul of the dead; regeneration; immortality; summer; instability; weakness; emblem of Japan • **Orient** victory

dragon plant in flower language: snare

dragonwort in flower language: horror

drawbridge defense; repression; regression

dregs the lower instincts that remain unpurified

drilling sexual intercourse

drinking the soul acquiring truth

drought an inert spiritual condition

drowning being overwhelmed by the conscience or subconscious

drugs desire; ignorance; warring against right and truth; escape; running away from reality

drum call to war; warning; primordial sound; thunder and lightning; the mediator between heaven and earth; communication, especially of word or tradition; a vehicle for magic; attribute of Mars • **beating a drum** the passage of time • **muffled drum** death; funeral • **kettle drum** emblem of Denmark

drunkenness religious frenzy; elevation of normal powers; conviviality; loss of control; closely related to fornication as a libido symbol; revelation of inner thoughts or feelings; escape from reality

dryness truth; immortality • *see also* **drought**

duality ambivalence; the physical and spiritual nature of all things

duck connubial love; fidelity; love of knowledge of profound mysteries; freedom from worry; superficiality;

idle chatter; volubility; deceit; lying; its meat was considered an aphrodisiac • **Orient** felicity; *mandarin ducks*: conjugal fidelity • **Egypt** associated with Isis bringing forth the sun • **Jewish** immortality • **heraldry** resourcefulness

dumbness (inability to speak) the early stages of creation; inability to express love from within; sometimes an indication that a person has a sixth sense or other compensatory powers; a prophet; being struck dumb shows regression

dummy (manequin) an image of the soul

dung an equalizer of various classes; worthlessness; offensiveness, especially to ghosts • *see also* **excrement**

dusk death; end of a cycle • *see also* **twilight**

dust the beginning and the end of man; the unstable lower mind; death; mourning; decay; disintegration; return to the primordial state; drought; famine; the passage of time; the great equalizer; something forgotten or neglected • **Egyptian, Jewish** associated with mourning • **dust and ashes** deep humiliation; mourning; penitence

dwarf hidden forces of nature; the Father Spirit; the unexpected; the unconscious; the instincts; ignorance; inferiority; abnormality; possessor of supernatural powers; unpredictability • *see also* **jester**

dynamo power; energy; technology • *see also* **engine**

E

E associated with hope, munificence, logic, intellectual character, energy, excitement, the number five, cataly-sis, the autumnal equinox, the liver, the Archpriest in the tarot deck, Aries, Mercury

eagle height; the father; daring; speed; heroic nobility; imperial power; fertility, especially male; regeneration; longevity; protection of young; pride; dalliance; generosity; carrion eater; occasionally, impotence; Christ; the spiritual principle in general; prayer; resurrection; a divine messenger; new life; the Christian soul strengthened by grace; those who are just; faith; contemplation; the inspiration of the Gospels; sun; fire; day; baldness; thunderbold; the heavens; air; the spirit of prophecy; divine grace descending; the Ascension; attribute of St. John, St. Wenceslas, Jupiter, Odin, Zeus, the personifications of Pride, Power, Strength, Youth, Victory, Geometry, Sight; associated with the gods of war, the south, fire, youth, noon, Scorpio, Cancer, air, the constellation Aquila; emblem of the U.S., Germany, and other countries; sacred to Aphrodite • **eagle holding book and/or pen and/or inkhorn** attribute of St. John • **eagle rising from a cauldron** attribute of St. John • **eagle and globe or orb** consecration of power • **head of an eagle** center point of the universe • **eagle's scream** the Apocalypse; battle; challenge; fury • **eagle and jug** attribute of Hebe • **eagle shown as a bird of prey** the demon that ravishes souls; rapacity; the sins of worldly power and pride • **eagle and wolf** emblem of the elect part of Valhalla • **double-headed eagle** emblem of Czarist Russia, the Holy Spirit, the Holy Roman Empire, the union of the Roman and Byzantine empires, Gemini, creative power; associated with Elisha • **youth borne aloft by an eagle** Ganymede • **eagle with human arms** sun worship (Syria) • **lion-headed eagle** conflict between heaven and hell • **eagle carrying a victim** victory of the superior over the inferior; augury • **eagle carrying a flaming pentagram** the planet Jupiter • **eagle devouring a lion** victory of the evolutive over the involutive • **eagle atop a a ladder** The Way (Gnoticism) • **golden eagle** Babylon; the East; Egypt • **heraldry** a man of action; high position; lofty spirit; wisdom; *eagle's claw*: tenacity, defense of freedom and justice, free hunting rights (in some parts of Germany) • **white eagle** emblem of Poland • **Norse** the north wind • **China** authority • **Egypt** the soul; Horus • **Jewish** God's providential care over Israel • **Greece** emblem of Troy; emblem of Zeus as maker of Thunder • **Germanic** associated with Yggdrasil • **Christianity** baptism; Christ as mediator between God and man; Mary leading people to true light; Christ swooping down to save a soul

ear inquisitiveness; eavesdropping; gossip; advice; temptation through flattery; conception; the betrayal of Christ • **pointed ears** attribute of Pan, fairies • **ear being cut off** defamation; St. Peter at the betrayal of Christ • **ass ears on a human** stupidity; a buffoon • **long ears** associated with an ass; connected with dwarves • **burning or tingling ears** someone is talking about you; evil gossip; *if the left ear only*: your sweetheart is thinking of you; *if the right ear only*: someone is speaking spitefully of you • **pierced ears** blood sacrifice for the protection of a child; *in ancient Israel*: the mark of a freed slave who preferred to stay with his former owner

earring an amulet • **earring of gold** sun worship; protection for sailors from drowning • **earring of silver** moon worship • **an earring falling off** your sweetheart thinks of you

earth (soil) the Great Mother; the passive; the end of material life; the great sepulchre; sustainer of material life; the cycle of existence as a symbol of man's life; the moral opposite of what is heavenly or spiritual; divine will; God's power; associated with the stomach • **Christian** the Church • **handful of earth** death and mortality

earthenware humanity; mortality

earthquake a sudden change in a process; upheaval in the unconscious; the female orgasm; fertility; omen of divine birth, anger, or intervention, death, sacrifice, any sudden cosmic change • **folklore** a man born during an earthquake will be the ruin of a country

earthworm *see* **worm**

east illumination; the future; infancy; spring; the fount of life; dawn; sunrise; the mystic point of reference; wisdom; the right half of the body; Christ; associated with Aries, Leo, Saggitarius • **east wind** an ill omen

eating the acquisition of knowledge; material existence; fertility; equivalent to the sowing of seed; eating the food of another world binds one to that world • *see also* **devouring; digestion**

ebony death; melancholy; gloom; skepticism • **ebony couch** bed of Morpheus • **ebony throne** attribute of Pluto • **flower language** blackness; you are hard

echo thesis and antithesis; many of the same qualities as a mirror, which see

eclipse omen of the death of kings, the end of the world, the start of war or plague • *see also* **devouring**

edelweiss purity; noble memories; ostentatious or feigned mountaineering skill or courage; sentimental, but dangerous good fellowship; emblem of Switzerland

eel slipperiness; enmity; nimbleness;

phallus; augur of a storm • *see also* **serpent**

effigy the psychic aspect of a person; contains a person's powers; has magical properties for warding off evil spirits, for fertility, for placating the gods; an image of the soul

egg immortality; potentiality; creation; the universe; the mother; sanctuary • **Near East** creation • **golden egg** the sun, laid on the waters of Chaos by the primeval goose • **ostrich egg** virgin birth • **still life** resurrection (especially when it has a broken shell) • **egg with broken shell** resurrection • **egg surrounded by serpent** the eternal germ of life encircled by creative wisdom • **egg and dart** male generation and female productiveness • **sulphur and eggs** purification; cure for unrequited love; worship of Isis • **burned eggs** (for Jews) burnt offering; the ancient glory of the Temple • **two infants hatched from eggs** Castor and Pollux • **egg white** tastelessness • **egg shell** worthlessness

eglantine *see* **sweet brier**

Egypt the animal in man; bondage; idolatry; concern with life after death

eight regeneration; baptism; entering into a new state or condition of the soul; circumcision; a twin, or binary, symbol; perfect blending of the conscious and unconscious, knowledge and love, action and reaction, etc.; connection between heaven and earth; inspiration, occasionally spiritual, but more often material and personal; ruthlessness; coldness; opposition; power; wealth; self-destruction; good deeds; justice with mercy; good health; endurance; discipline; discrimination; corresponds to the letters h, q, and z, the planet Mars, violent passions, Scorpio, rose color, abnormal tendencies, material success, self-assertion; related to the gods, the eternal movement of the sea, rain and thunder, solidity, the directions of the winds, health, immortality, punishment; sacred to Poseidon • **kabala** balance; associated with the angel Anael, the color silvery blue • **Jewish** resurrection; atonement; eternity; endlessness • **Egypt, Babylonia, Arabia** sacred to the sun • **folklore** the hours of sleep needed by merchants

eighteen life; associated with the angels Asariel, Sachiel, Gabriel; in the Old Testament, an evil number, but in Christianity, it is a sign of great reward

eight hundred the number of Odin's warriors at Valhalla

eight hundred and eighty-eight the sacred number of Jesus in the Hebrew alphabet

eighty enduring hope; multiplies the values of eight, which see

eighty-one truth (nine), multiplied by itself

elder tree zeal; death; related to witches; compassion; in legend, one of the trees that the cross of Jesus was made of, also the tree that Judas hanged himself on • **flower language** zeal; compassion • **dwarf elder** in Ireland: power; in the Eastern Mediterranean area: royalty (in ancient times)

Electra vengeance

elephant strength; wisdom; memory; moderation; the power of the libido; puissant dignity; eternity; pity; care; caution; the Self; chastity; priestly chastity; the Fall of Man; firmness; longevity; self-restraint; meekness; piety; religion; pride; purity; ponderousness; the earth; insensibility; the rising sun; attribute of the personifications of Fame, Africa, Instinct, Pity, Meekness, Piety, Religion; the mount of kings and deities; associated with Hannibal, the circus, military victory; emblem of Judea, and the Republican

Party in the U.S. • **China** strength; sagacity; prudence • **Christianity** a sinner • **heraldry** power; cunning; sagacity; willingness to be guided; chastity; courage; a person who has made distant journeys • **winged elephant** clouds • **elephant's head** attribute of Africa personified • **elephant in a net** associated with Fabricus Luscinus • **trumpeting elephant** truth • **folklore** an elephant would not kill a virgin, hence, a test for virginity • **pink elephant** popular symbol for delirium tremens • **elephant with trunk drooping** sorrow; failure; defeat • **elephant with trunk held up** cheerfulness; success; victory

eleven transition; excess; peril; conflict; martyrdom; incontinence; balance; unity; surfeit of completion and perfection; associated with the angel Michael; sometimes has an infernal character; the eleven faithful Disciples, the eleven brothers of Joseph, the eleven curtains of the Temple, etc. • **Christianity** sin; transgression; intemperance; transition • **folklore** the hours of sleep needed by wicked people

eleven hundred *see* **one thouusand one hundred**

elf the joys of the natural life; light colored elves are generally favorable to man, dark colored elves are generally unfavorable and may kill babies

elk shares in the symbolism of the deer, which see

ellipse the superconscious • **Egypt** the Universe; the world of the dead

elm patriotism; dignity; longevity; beauty; grace; stateliness; justice; the strength derived by the devout from their faith in Scripture; related to burial places, fertility • **elm in leaf** attribute of St. Zenobius • **elm with vine** the ideal husband and wife relationship; natural sympathy; unity; benevolence; marriage

• **flower language** dignity; *American elm*: patriotism

embalming purification of the soul through faith and trust in the ideal

ember old age; gloom; dying passion; the sun; purification; fertility; anger; warmth; the hearth; vengeance; martyrdom; a concentrated expression of fire, q.v. • **ember held in tongs** associated with Isaiah

embrace copulation; affection; deceit; concord

emerald victory over the flesh; spring; hope; rebirth; immortality; true love; the overcoming of temptation; associated with May, Gemini • **Christianity** faith; purity; chastity; associated with the pope • **heraldry** freedom; happiness; beauty; friendship; health; hope

emperor absolute rule; tyranny

Emperor (tarot) magnificence; energy; power; law; severity; domination; subjection; initiation; thought; reason; temporal power; sterile regulation and power

Empress (tarot) the subconscious; production; growth; fertility; the ideal; sweetness; dominance by persuasion; vanity; seduction; fecundity; the Word

emu emblem of Australia

endive in flower language: frugality

endurance long endurance implies living in concord with God

Endymion youthful beauty; man trespassing in a woman's realm

enemy the forces threatening a person from within

engine the inhumane forces of modern society; a magical invention which has an autonomous existence and will; technological power

entanglement the unconscious; the repressed; the forgotten past; being caught in the universe and being unable to escape by any means • *see also* **bondage**

entombment detention of the spirit in the world

epigonation dignity; attribute of St. Gregory Nazianus and of bishops of the eastern Church

epileptic seizure communion with a god; possession by evil spirits

equinox the point of balance and change reached within the soul's development when a new process is started

Erinyes *see* **Furies**

ermine royalty; honor; purity; nobility; justice; moderation; chastity; attribute of royalty, judges, lawyers, virgin saints (St. Ursula in particular), and the personifications of Touch and Chastity • **portraiture** alludes to the subject's virtue • **heraldry** prudence; courage; cleanliness; dignity; sovereignty

eryngium for Jews: the bitterness of bondage

Esther the Church of the Gentiles

Ethiop *see* **Negro**

Ethiopia a "far away" land

Eucharist attribute of St. Charles Borromeo, St. Ignatius of Loyola • *see also* **Host**

eupatorium in flower language: delay

Euphrates River the great fertilizer; the irreversible process of nature; the fourth river of the Garden of Eden

Eurydice the poet's anima escaping; half formed intuitive vision; undeveloped imaginative or intuitive sensibility

Eve artlessness; guilelessness; beauty; gentleness; pride; the material and formal aspect of life; the inversion of the Virgin Mary; the mother of all things; emotionality; instinctiveness; inconstancy; lower nature; dissembling; that which diverts man from spiritual progress

evening peacefulness; dead quiet; involution; return to chaos; middle or old age; autumn or winter • *see also* **night**

evergreens permanence; eternity; immortality; poverty; used in fertility and funeral rites

everlasting (plant) in flower language: never ceasing remembrance

ewer refreshment; purity • **ewer and basin** purity; innocence; refers to Pilate washing his hands • *see also* **pitcher**

excrement allied with what is highest in value; it was thought to have magical powers over a person; evil; foulness; related to gold • *see also* **dung**

exile banishment of a principle or ideal; purification; ostracism

eye(s) the sun; divine omniscience; knowledge; understanding; judgment; authority; abode of the mind; window to the outer world; guardian of the inner man; the Mystic Center; female genitals; testicles; care; the world; expressive of mood or character • **blue eyes** innocence; sign of being in love; in Elizabethan times: a sign of pregnancy, or, when they had dark rings around them, debauchery; attribute of good fairies, sky deities, northern Europeans • **green eyes** jealousy; hope; untrustworthiness; in Elizabethan times, valued for their rarity • **red eyes** weeping; sorrow; demonic fury; attribute of Bacchus, Charon, the Furies; debauchery • **one eye** divine omniscience; subhumanity; extra human effort devoted to one aim, usually unfavorable; God the Father (especially when in a triangle or above an altar) • **two eyes** physical and spiritual normality; binary functions such as male and female, sun and moon, intelligence and love, etc. • **two eyes on a platter, or carried** attribute of St. Lucy • **two eyes, one opened, one closed** Church and Synagogue, happiness and sorrow • **three eyes** superhuman; divine attribute; attribute of Prudence personified • **four eyes** someone who wears glasses • **multiple eyes** usually associated with evil • **closed eyes** death; avoidance of unpleasantness • **squinting eyes** poor vision; ignorance; meanness; attribute of Envy personified • **winking eye** seduction; joking; secrecy; mockery • **bandaged eyes** blindness; ignorance; slavery; impartiality; attribute of Justice personified • **owl eyes** blindness; ignorance • **eagle eyes** sharpness of vision • **mole eyes** intellectual and spiritual blindness • **right eye** associated with the future • **left eye** associated with the past • **double pupils** attribute of a witch • **eye on a scepter** omniscience; temperance; modesty • **eyes in odd places of the body** clairvoyance

eyebrows defense; the abode of pride • **eyebrows set far apart** cold-heartedness • **eyebrows set close to eyes** gravity • **long eyebrows** attribute of a sage • **bushy eyebrows** attribute of a superstitious person • **eyebrows that meet** deceit; a person who will not live to marry; *Greece*: attribute of a vampire; *Norse*: attribute of a werewolf; *on a man*: hardheartedness; *on a woman*: jealousy

eyelids vigilance; observation; lidless eyes show regression

eyesight mental perception

F

F associated with domestic felicity, protection, responsibility, fire, sun, life, the father, fertility, the feelings, the protection of law and trial, failing (especially in education); corresponds to the number six, the ears and heart, Taurus, Virgo, The Lovers in the tarot deck • **Celtic** associated with the alder tree • **Anglo-Saxon** associated with money

fabric the transitoriness of this world

face mirror (sometimes false) of man's character; the sun; a deity; authority; power • **two faces** Janus; a liar or dissembler • **three faces in the moon** Kore, Artemis, and Hecate • **three faces of the Devil** — *red*: anger; *yellow*: impotence; *black*: ignorance • **shining face** enlightenment; innocence; ingenuousness • **painted face** charm against the evil eye; seduction; depersonalization; vanity; deceit; disloyalty; trickery; foolishness; wantonness; lust; sorrow; attribute of a loose woman • **folklore** The red is wise; the brown trusty; The pale envious, and the black lusty *or*, To a red man give thy counsel; With a brown man break thy bread; At a pale man draw thy knife; From a black man keep thy wife. (Note that the verses above refer to colorings, not to races.) • *see also* **complexion**

faggots when burning: martyrdom by fire • **when formed in a cross** associated with Abraham, Isaac, the Widow of Sarepta

fairy supra-normal powers of the human soul; latent possibilites; personification of stages in the development of the spirit; the lesser spiritual moods of the universal mind • **legendary or forgotten fairies** frustrated acts • **fairy land** escape or regression to childhood; the real joys of natural life

falcon fire; the sun; the hunt; nobility; pride; death; wind; storm; clouds; confidence; modesty; noble servitude; wildness; evil thought or action; an evil person; immortality (especially when spiraling); associated with Saggitarius; attribute of St. Bavo, St. Baldric, St. Julian the Hospitator • **tamed falcon** a holy man; a Gentile convert to Christianity; an attribute of the personifications of Logic, Touch, Taste, Speed • **Egypt** symbol of light gods •

heraldry chivalry; anyone on an eager quest; hunting skill (especially when hooded) • *see also* hawk, with which falcons are commonly confused

fall *see* autumn

Fall of Man the incarnation of the spirit

family qualities in close connection to one another, and attached to a single center

famine mental and spiritual inertia

fan wind; the imagination; the moon; change; femininity; coquetry; fickleness; power; rank; celestial air; purification; separation; related to the phases of the moon

fanlight the rising or setting sun

farm *see* agriculture; farmer

farmer the catalyst of the forces of regeneration and salvation in harmony with nature • *see also* agriculture

fasces authority; controlled power resulting in authority; unity (especially in marriage); attribute of the personifications of Concord, Justice

fasting self mortification; the seeking of favor or forgiveness from a deity; mourning; saintliness

fat (animal fat) affection; love; plenty; riches • fat in a sacrifice the choicest morsel being offered to a deity • covering one's face, heart, or flanks with fat hubris; hardheartedness; presumption

father the masculine principle; heaven; dominion; the conscious; dominion; tradition; wisdom; moral commandments; the supreme deity; the Creator; death; prohibitions • *see also* man

faun lasciviousness; revelry

fawn *see* deer

fear lack of intellectual will

feast a completed period or stage of development

feather the wind; air; purification of evil; pride; ostentation; charity; faith; contemplation; thoughts; the spiritual principle; abundance; attribute of St. Gregory • two feathers height • three feathers light; the end of nurse's training; good thought, word, and deed; emblem of Wales, the Prince of Wales; when passing through a ring: faith, hope, charity; *three feathers in Druidism*: power, light, the Light of the World • white feathers cowardice; sea foam; clouds • crimson feathers cloak trimming for fairies • black feathers sleep; mourning • ostrich feathers distinction • peacock feathers attribute of St. Barbara • feathered serpent duality (good/bad, rain/drought, etc.) • feathered serpent with horns opposite forces in conflict • a feather as a quill poetry; literature; the scribe

feces *see* excrement

feeding dispensing truth and goodness to the mind and soul

feet *see* foot

female *see* woman; maiden; virgin

fennel dissembling; flattery; stimulant; attribute of the Virgin Mary • garland of fennel crown of a victorious gladiator • flower language worthy of all praise; force; strength

fern solitary humility; frankness; sincerity; endurance; confidence; fascination; Christ (although sometimes considered the Devil's plant); associated with snakes; hated by witches and evil spirits; emblem of colonizers • fern leaf victory over death • flower language sincerity; fascination; *flowering fern*: reverie

ferret bloodthirstiness; fiery temper; cunning; restlessness; mischievousness; inquisitiveness for hidden things

ferry attribute of Charon

ferule attribute of the personifications of Grammar, Geometry

fess(e) in heraldry: service in the army; anyone ready to work for the public good; solidity; support; power; strength of character

fetters *see* chains

fever excitement; passion; restlessness; love • **Jewish** punishment for disobedience to God

fibula (clasp or buckle) virginity; restricted virility

ficoides in flower language: your looks freeze me

fiddle, fiddler freedom from care; gaiety

field limitless possibility; fertility; space; freedom from restraint; physical creation; related to death • **field flowers** modesty; the Virgin Mary and the Church

fifteen ascent; progression; the steps of the Temple, mysteries of the Rosary, Gradual Psalms, etc.; generally, an unlucky number; may have erotic connotations; associated with the Devil, the angel Cassiel

fifty expansion to infinity; space; understanding and sympathy; a special rapport with the deity; by multiplication, shares in the powers of five, which see • **Christianity** remission of sins; the Holy Ghost • **kabala** initiative

fig fertility; fruitfulness; abundance; prosperity; luxury; longevity; spring; rejuvenation; truth; peace; fidelity; death; woman; the breasts; sex in general; purgation; attribute of St. Bartholomew • **an opened fig** the vulva • **eating a fig** erotic ecstasy • **flower language** argument; longevity

fig tree fecundity; fruitfulness; fidelity; good works; divine life; attribute of St. Bartholomew • **fig tree and vine** male and female, respectively • **sitting under a fig tree** the peaceful life • **flower language** profuseness; prolificacy

filbert (plant) *see* hazel

file (rasp) refined ideas or expressions; ideas free from superstition

fillet death; sacrifice; related to the gods • **white fillet** attribute of the dead in the Elysian Fields • **purple fillet** victory in sports • **Rome** a slender fillet: a lawfully wedded wife; modesty • **Germany** an unmarried woman

finger(s) the forces of the unconscious that can emerge without warning and hinder efforts of the conscious; they have a phallic significance, especially a single finger extended • **index finger** direction; command; rule; fortunate guidance; delivery from evil; the Holy Ghost; associated with character, materialism, law, order, the vernal equinox, Jupiter (the god) • **index finger when upraised** warning; lesson; Jesus Christ as the one way to salvation; the number one, signifying the best; when the finger is to the lips: silence, a vow of silence • **middle finger** related to the god Saturn, death, humanity, system, intelligence, the summer solstice; as a ring finger; hope of resurrection, the salvation of Christ • **middle finger upraised** coition; penetration; contempt; cuckholdry • **ring finger** associated with truth, economy, energy, Apollo, the autumnal equinox, a sage, betrothal, marriage, the divine nature of Christ • **little finger** related to the god Mercury, inspiration; divination, the phallus, goodness, prudence, the winter solstice, the human nature of Christ • **crooked little finger** you will die rich • **thumb** related to the goddess Venus, Hercules, the will, logic, God the Father; awkwardness; the phallus • **thumb up** yes; mercury; pleasure • **thumb down** no; displeasure; death • **thumb in mouth or between closed fingers** coition; penetration; contempt • **thumb to the nose, or biting the thumb** infancy; regression; occasionally, wisdom • **index and middle finger in a vee** victory; peace • **index and little finger raised** the horns of the moon; aversion of danger or the evil eye; in the U.S.: a bull, and by extension, bull excrement, meaning a lie, or nonsense • **raised hand, vee between the middle and ring fingers** Jewish blessing • **index finger as long as the middle finger** dishonesty • **long fingers** improvidence; musical ability; sometimes, a thief • **crooked fingers** a crabbed disposition • **finger in the mouth** (occasionally the thumb) wisdom • **crossed fingers** the sign of the Cross; hope; untruth (especially when the fingers are hidden) • **extra fingers** the luck of the extraordinary; sometimes a sign of evil • **cutting off a finger** mourning; atonement; ritual castration • **finger snapping** disdain; peremptory command; the beginning or end of an idea, cycle, process • **fingertips** divination; poetic inspiration • **rubbing the fingertips** money; carefulness

fir fervor; power; patience; choice; elevation; constancy; immortality; regeneration; fidelity; purity; regal beauty; pride; fire; sun; hope; the androgyne; the elect who are in heaven; those who excel in patience • **Egypt and the Near East** sex • **Jewish** related to birth, youthful strength, patience • **Greece** related to birth • **flower language** time; elevation (especially the Scotch fir) • *see also* **pine**

fire spiritual energy; the libido; fecundity; creation; destruction; purification of evil; the soul; the creator god; essence of life; the sun; authority; power; spiritual enlightenment and zeal; sexual fertility; martyrdom; regeneration; forbidden passions; war; the torments of Hell; Pentecost; attribute of St. Anthony of Padua, St. Anthony Abbot, St. Agnes, St. Florian (usually extinguishing a fire) • **fire and a serpent** attribute of St. Paul • **fire and brimstone** Hell; the vengeance of God • **circle or wheel of fire** chastity; magic spell; charity; inviolabil-

ity; attribute of Brunhilde • **tunic on fire** attribute of St. Laurence • **arson** regression (especially male) • *see also* **flame**

firebrand life; associated with Melager

firefly summer; a spirit; a memory; a ghost of the dead (especially a dead warrior)

fireworks fertility; warding off of evil spirits; purification; celebration • **U.S.** associated with July Fourth, Independence Day

fish phallus; wisdom; freedom; purity; sexuality; faith; folly; greed; the self hidden in the unconscious; the soul; fertility; fecundity; female genitalia; emblem of woman; sexual coldness; sacrifice; baptism; Christ; Christianity; Christians; attribute of marine deities, Tobias, St. Peter, St. Anthony of Padua, St. Francis of Assisi • **heraldry** Christianity; taciturnity; secrecy; humility; temperance; health; vigilance; free-fishing rights • **China** wealth; regeneration; harmony; connubial bliss • **two fish** the joy of union; a charm to avert evil • **fish in a net** attribute of St. Peter • **fish on a hook** attribute of St. Peter • **fish and wallet** the angel Raphael • **fish and loaves of bread** attribute of St. Jude • **fish dangling from a crozier** attribute of St. Zeno • **fish on a confessional** penitence • **fish with ship and windmill** associated with St. Mary of Cleophas • **man with a fish in his hand** St. Andrew • **fish with a bird's head** (usually a swallow) bringer of cyclic regeneration • **fish swimming into a whale's mouth** unsuspecting souls trapped by the Devil • **two fish** marriage; domestic felicity; sexual indifference; frigidity; emblem of Pisces • **two fish, crossed** baptism; attribute of St. Simon, St. Andrew • **two fish on a hook, with a pitcher** attribute of the Virgin Mary • **three fish** the Trinity; Trin-

ity Sunday; baptism • *see also* specific kinds of fish, **carp; sturgeon**, etc.
fisherman St. Peter; Christ
fishhook perfidy; faithlessness; deceit; means of investigation for esoteric knowledge, or of the unconscious • **heraldry** riches gotten from fishing; honor; patience; virtue; good confidence; important fishing rights • **large fishhook** attribute of St. Andrew
fishing communion with nature; quietness; contemplation; inquisitiveness about the unconscious; searching for deeper wisdom; the act of cuckholding; seeking wisdom; introspection; seeking regeneration or spiritual rebirth
fishnet attribute of St. Andrew, St. Peter (usually has a fish in it)
fist power; resistance; deterrent capability; threat • **fist placed over the heart** tearing out one's heart as an offering • *see also* **hand**
fit *see* epileptic seizure
five spring; growth; organic fullness of life; fecundity; fertility; the erotic; health and love; man after The Fall; marriage; the powers of nature; change; travel; new experiences; new friends; religious interest; freedom; hedonism; changeability; associated with Mercury, God, the angel Anael, David, the color indigo; also associated with good judgment, sympathy, understanding, but these can be perverted • **Christianity** the five lesser sacraments, the five wounds of Christ, the five wise virgins and the five foolish virgins, the five yoke of oxen, the five talents, the five sparrows sold for a farthing, etc. • **Jewish** (ancient) aspiration; hope; optimism • **five hearts** Judah's five sons
flag victory; self-assertion; thought or ideal; identification; nationalism • **lowering or striking a flag** defeat • **dipping a flag** salute • **flag at half-mast** mourning • **flag flown upside down** distress • **white flag**

surrender; truce; peaceful intent • **white flag with red cross** resurrection; victory over death; attribute of the Phrygian sibyl, St. Ansanus; St. George; St. Reparata; St. Ursula • **black flag** pirates; death; execution of criminals; success in battle (especially World War II submarines) • **red flag** danger; revolution; anarchy; socialism; communism • **yellow flag** disease
flagelation initiation; purification; fertility; sexual stimulation; introversion; encouragement against spiritual laxity or inertia • **man being scourged** St. Andrew, St. Laurence • **man scourged by angels** St. Jerome • *see also* **scourge; whip; lash**
flail the harvest; attribute of Suffering personified, St. Jude • **Egypt** emblem of the king
flak trouble; criticism
flame transcendence; the Holy Spirit; wisdom; the soul; the supreme deity; charity; love; religious zeal; martyrdom; attribute of Choler personified, St. Anthony of Padua • **flame on the forehead** attribute of Fire personified • **flame on the head** divine inspiration; attribute of the Apostles at Pentecost, the personifications of Charity, Piety • **flaming mountain** divine inspiration • **flaming pillar or tree trunk** the God of light and wisdom • **flaming sword** sun rays; protection; Old Testament; attribute of the cherubim protecting the Garden of Eden • **woman with flame in her hand** attribute of Charity personified • **flaming tunic** attribute of St. Laurence • **man with flames underfoot** St. Anthony Abbot • **sea of flames** life as an infirmity • **six flames** the six gifts of the Holy Spirit (Isaiah 11:2) • **seven flames** the seven gifts of the Holy Spirit (Revelation 5:12) • **nine flames** the nine gifts of the Holy Spirit (Galatians 5:22–23) • *see also* **fire**

flash attribute of St. Omobuono

flax domestic industry; fertility; simplicity; fate; gratitude • **flower language** industry; fate; I am sensible of your kindness; *when dried*: utility

flea parasite; pettiness; pest; despicability

fleece alluring desire; closely guarded wealth; related to sheep, which see • **fleece hanging from a tree, guarded by a dragon** associated with Jason • **warrior kneeling beside a fleece** Gideon • **fleece with bowl** associated with Gideon • **golden fleece** (also occasionally a white fleece) wisdom; hidden treasure; something elusive; purity of soul; conquest of the impossible; attribute of royalty • *see also* **wool; sheep**

fleur-de-lis the androgyne; purity; the Trinity; the Annunciation; emblem of royalty, especially French royalty, France, Christ, the Virgin Mary, St. Louis of France, St. Louis of Toulouse; purification through baptism • **fleur-de-lis with letters IHC, or IHS** the dual nature of Christ • **fleur-de-lis on a halo or book** attribute of St. Zenobius • **heraldry** France; French royalty; when in red: Florence • **flower language** flame; I burn

flesh lower nature

flight *see* **flying**

flint indifference to insult; everlastingness; hardness of heart • **thrown on a grave** a suicide • **heraldry** zeal to serve

floating regression; return to the womb; passivity; refusal to explore the subconscious; sexual ecstasy (especially female)

flock the disordered or semi-ordered forces of the cosmos; the collapse of a force or objective; a church congregation; often has a negative connotation

flogging *see* **flagellation**

flood punishment, as opposed to complete destruction; rebellion; The Flood

Flora's bell in flower language: you make no pretension

flour truth; goodness; abundant life; the finest extract of something (as opposed to bran); shares in the symbolism of *bread, grain*, q.q.v.

flower spring; transitoriness; beauty; the soul; the work of the sun; festivity; joy; the cycle of life: birth, copulation, death, and regeneration; virtue; purity; goodness; mystery; victory; temptation; deceit; love (especially female); the vulva; virginity; woman; balance; justice; the finest product; the evanescence of life; attribute of St. Elizabeth of Hungary, Flora, Aurora, the personifications of Spring, Smell, sometimes Hope • **in still life** (especially with dew drops) brevity of life; decay • **scattered flowers** joys; pleasures • **Christianity** the result of charity and other good works • **field flowers** modesty • **flowers in a field** the Virgin Mary and the Church • **plucking flowers** innocent joys; sexual indulgence; coition • **basket of flowers and fruit** attribute of St. Dorothea of Cappadocia • **three flowers held in the hand** attribute of St. Hugh of Grenoble • **red flower** love; passion; blood; animal life • **orange or yellow flower** the sun • **blue or golden flower** the impossible • **white flower** innocence; blamelessness; love; coition; death; heroism; attribute of Diana, June, the Virgin Mary, the Great Goddess

flower-of-an-hour in flower language: delicate beauty

flute a phallic and lascivious instrument; dance; love; delight; lust; erotic anguish or joy; wind; fertility; praise; attribute of Dionysus, Apollo, Euterpe, Marsyas, Hermes, Adonis, Flattery personified • **Greece** associated with funerals

fly (insect) pestilence; sin; annoyance; minor trouble; impurity; lust; greed; the Devil; filth; squalor; disease; a dandy; deceit; diminuitive life; sin, leading to redemption; the priest, or other inhibitor of the preconscious who taints innocent joys; Egypt; Egyptians • **painting** in 15th and 16th Century European painting, the fly was often not a symbol, but a superstition that the painted fly would keep real flies from landing on the fresh paint • **Lord of the Flies** Beelzebub • *see also* **water fly**

flying thought; imagination; spiritual elevation; speed; escape

flytrap (plant) in flower language; deceit

foam body moisture, especially milk, semen, sweat, saliva, tears

fog dimness of vision; isolation; transformation; the unreal

font baptism; rebirth; the immaculate womb of the Virgin Mary; attribute of St. Patrick, Faith personified

food truth; the real as opposed to the illusory; the visible form of divine life; eating the food of another world binds one to that world • **sharing food** kinship; friendship; bonding • **red food** (Greece) reserved for the dead • *see also* **eating; digestion**

fool *see* **jester**

Fool (tarot) the irrational; blind impulse; the unconscious; a choice of vital importance; Absolute Zero, from which all proceeds and returns

foot the soul; humility; willing servitude; seat of power; magic power; genitals, especially the phallus • **washing of someone else's feet** humility; penitence; willing servitude • **washing of feet in a basin** attribute of St. Lioba • **bare feet** poverty; humility; direct contact with Mother Earth; attribute of Poverty personified; *Jewish*: mourning, respect, willingness to serve • **flat feet** misfortune • **silver foot** associated with Cletis • **purple foot** associated with Demeter, Hecate • **feet above a mountain** Nahum's vision • **footprints** funereal implications; they leave the magic powers of the maker • **lack of footprints** sign of a fairy • **extra toe** good fortune • **second toe longer than the first toe** sign of a cruel husband • **cloven foot** sin; attribute of the Devil and of "unclean" animals • **heraldry** discovery of an important track, or fact which gains lasting merit • *see also* **sandal; shoe; heel**

footstool the earth; lowest subservience; attribute of El, Baal • *see also* **stool**

forceps attribute of a surgeon • **forceps holding a tooth** attribute of a dentist, St. Apollonia • *see also* **pincers**

ford, fording the dividing line between two states such as consciousness/unconsciousness, sleeping/waking, time/eternity; marks a decisive stage in action, development, etc.

forehead intelligence; the intellect; knowledge; wisdom; reflects character or feelings; piety; related to the head, which see • **high forehead** intelligence; refinement • **low forehead** lack of intelligence; ignorance

forest the female principle; the Great Mother; the unconscious; danger; mistakes; problems; the obscurance of reason; fertility; enchantment; hunting; the home of outlaws, fairies, supernatural beings

forge the brain; thought; poetic inspiration; attribute of Vulcan, a blacksmith, an alchemist

forget-me-not ingenuous simplicity; constancy • **flower language** remembrance; true love; forget me not

fork (implement) spitefulness; torture; a large fork may indicate martyrdom • **two pronged fork** attribute of Hades; death • **three pronged fork** Caduceus; attribute of sea deities • *see also* **pitchfork**

fork (in a road or path) choice; parting of the ways

fornication the primacy of base desires • *see also* intercourse

Fortitude (tarot) *see* Strength

forty the Deluge; fasting; prayer; highest functioning of the intellect; multiplication of the powers of four, which see; probation; trial; the Church Militant; anticipation; purification; expiation; Lent; maturity; castigation; sacred in both Christian and Jewish numerology • kabala transformation

forty-two weakness; being cut off halfway to perfection; creative generation; punishment; trial; expiation; correction

fossil time; eternity; life and death; evolution; threshold; a link between two worlds

fountain rejuvenation; the soul; the life-force; life; spiritual energy; totality; the unconscious; birth; resurrection; divination; wisdom; truth; consolation; refreshment, both spiritual and physical; woman; related to death and future life; eternal life (only when flowing); attribute of St. Clement, St. David; emblem of Christ, the Virgin Mary • sealed fountain the Virgin Mary; the virginity of Mary • three fountains associated with St. Paul • four fountains the four Evangelists

four the earth; the material aspect of life; the terrestrial order; the Elements; rational organization; tangible achievement; justice without mercy; hard work; stability; coldness; disciple; the seasons; order; reason; wholeness; the functional aspects of consciousness: thinking, feeling, sensation and intuition; concentration; double vision; the four corners of the earth; usually a "human" number, but may be associated with divinity; also associated with the square, the mind, the teacher, the taskmaster, reality, Sa-

turn, the angel Samael, the color bright blue • Christianity the four Evangelists, the four Gospels, the four major prophets, the four rivers of Paradise, the four cardinal virtues, the four horsemen of the Apocalypse, etc.; divine equilibrium • kabala completion

four hundred in the U.S.: upper class society (especially in the East) • kabala reward

four o'clock (flower) timidity; rest

fourteen fusion; organization; temperance; justice; delusion; loss; sacrifice; associated with the angel Sachiel, Croesus • Bible a holy number

fox the Devil; base desires or instincts; craft; cunning; intemperance; sensuality; mischief; guile; bucolic lust; thieving; flattery; fertility; sexuality; hypocrisy; a false preacher; solitariness; ingratitude; hiding; carrion eater; a man 40 to 50 years old; a solar animal; Protestantism; attribute of Intemperance personified • China longevity; craftiness; the transmigrated soul of a deceased person; possessor of supernatural powers, such as transformation • Jewish rapacity • meeting a fox good luck • meeting several foxes bad luck • fox fur on a fleece attribute of usurers • fox tail badge of a jester • heraldry slyness; strategic cunning; sagacity or wit used in one's own defense

foxfire a forest spirit; elusiveness; a wild scheme pursued

foxglove youth; a wish; insincerity; associated with Taurus • flower language insincerity; a wish • foxglove and nightshade together pride and punishment

fracture, or fragmentation destruction and disintegration of the spirit; the disabling or altering of whatever the broken object symbolizes; ritual killing

frankincense wisdom; purification of

the mind; divine love; adoration; Old Testament priesthood; Christ's priestly office; attribute of the Nativity of Christ • **flower language** faithful heart • **casket of frankincense** assoc. with Melchior, Magus

fraxinella in flower language: fire

freckles the gods do not obey or see people with freckles; youth, especially bucolic

Friday a day of melancholy, fecklessness; related to Venus • **Rome** a lucky day • **Christianity** an unlucky day • *see also* **days**

fritillary persecution; emblem of Power personified

frog fecundity; fertility; resurrection; lasciviousness; related to the moon, creation; emblem of Isis, the Resurrection; evil; sin; the Devil; the repulsiveness of sin; a heretic; worldly things, and those who indulge in them; heresy; vanity; coldness; attribute of Laziness personified • **Bible** uncleanliness • **Jewish** a neophyte; a lower order aspiring to become higher • **peasants by osiers, changing into frogs** associated with Leto • *see also* **toad**

front the conscious; the right side

frost death; autumn; friendliness • *see also* **ice**

fruit abundance; spiritual abundance; wisdom; heavenly bliss; earthly desires; ripeness; the Virgin Mary • **fruit in a basket** temptation; attribute of Pomona, Taste personified, St. Dorothea of Cappodocia (especially when fruit is with flowers) • **fruit in a cornucopia** attribute of Ceres, the personifications of Abundance, Summer • **fruit in a bowl** attribute of Charity personified, when shown with a fat figure, Gluttony personified

fuchsia taste; gentleness; grace; faithfulness; confiding love • **flower language** taste

fuller's bat the betrayal of Christ; attribute of St. James the Less

fuller's teasel in flower language: importunity; misanthropy

fumitory in flower language: spleen; hatred

Furies anarchy; remorse; guilt turned to destructiveness; guilt turned upon itself to the destruction of the guilty; involutive fragmentation of the unconscious

furnace the mother; spiritual gestation; uterus; creative faculty • **furnace full of inferior metal** Jerusalem • **iron furnace** Egypt as a place of bondage and oppression

furze anger; spring equinox

fusil in heraldry: labor, travel

G

G associated with introspection, mediation, intuition, action, knowledge, Jesus, the number seven, Gemini or Saggitarius, the Chariot in the tarot deck

Gabriel divine messenger; protector of Israel; messenger of the Day of Judgment

Gabriel Hounds omen of death, evil; the lost souls of unbaptized infants

gadfly (insect) a pest; punishment for pride; noisome lust; war; attribute of Bellona

galbanum divine wisdom

gall bitterness; bravery; nerve; misery; punishment; poison words; the bitterness of injustice; seat of vitality; consecreated to Neptune • **wormwood and gall** punishment

gallows sacrifice; disgraceful death; typical execution of lower class criminals, especially thieves

gangrene spiritual decay

gannet in heraldry: one who subsists on virtue and merit without material help • *see also* **duck**

garden the conscious; the soul; nature subdued; feminine fertility; related to Paradise; happiness; salvation; purity; the world; vulva; place of mystic ecstasy; attribute of Spring personified • **garden gate** labia • **walled or closed garden** virginity; emblem of the Virgin Mary

gardener Adam; Priapus; a cultivator or his soul; the farmer (q.v.), raised to a higher or more spiritual plane

gardenia refinement; chastity; femininity • **China** emblem of November

gargoyle the forces of the cosmos; evil forces made to serve good; evil spirits; "scarecrows" for evil spirits; fertility enslaved by superior spirituality; evil passions • **on the outside of a church** evil passions driven out of man by the Gospels

garland fellowship; merit; ephemeral beauty

garlic protection against the evil eye, vampires, snakes, plague, scorpions, colds • **Elizabethan** associated with the lower classes

garment riches; the body; knowledge; evanescence; reflection of the inner man; lack of innocence as a result of The Fall • **rending garments** grief; penitence • **seamless garment** Christ's garment at the Crucifixion, hence: purity, unity, divinity • **white garment** attribute of heavenly beings, important people, festivity, virginity, Egyptians • **multicolored garment** diverse possibilities; disharmony; diverse and wide knowledge; attribute of Israelites, Free Will personified •*see also* clothes, and specific garments (**cloak, trousers,** etc.)

garnet deep affection; associated with January, Aquarius

garters have a sexual connotation • **red garters** attribute of the Devil

gate opportunity; the feminine principle; death; departure from this world; entrance into heaven or hell; a dividing barrier; power; fortification; justice; mercy; praise; salvation; vulva • **closed gate** restraint; expulsion; war; misery; inhospitality; emblem of the Virgin Mary, Ezekial • **open gate** hospitality; peace • **garden gate** labia • **horn gate** entrance for prophetic dreams • **brass gate** entrance to hell • **pearl or gold gate** entrance to heaven, knowledge • **ivory gate** entrance for deceptive dreams • **arched gate** entrance to knowledge, or the way to knowledge • **turreted gate** emblem of the Virgin Mary, Ezekial

gauntlet protection; power; challenge; punishment; attribute of Thor • **heraldry** reward and elevation; justice; challenge and readiness for combat

gavel law; order; discipline; attribute of a judge, chairman, president

gazelle graceful speed; the soul; struggle; gentleness; grace; innocence; the beloved • **Bible** gentleness; grace

geese *see* **goose**

Gehenna hell; punishment; eternal torment

Gemini the dual physical/spiritual, mortal/immortal nature of all things; creative and created nature; thesis and antithesis; opposites; inversion; Castor and Pollux; brotherly love

gems *see* **jewels**

gentian autumn; loveliness

geranium conjugal affection; melancholy; stupidity; foolishness; a bourgeois plant; associated with Aries • **flower language**—*fish geranium*: disappointed expectation; *ivy geranium*: bridal favor, I engage you for the next dance; *lemon geranium*: unexpected meeting; *night smelling or dark geranium*: melancholy; *nutmeg geranium*: an expected meeting; *oak geranium*: true friendship, lady, deign to smile;

pencilled geranium: ingenuity; *pink or rose geranium*: preference; *scarlet geranium*: comfort, stupidity, folly; *silver leaved geranium*: recall; *sorrowful geranium*: melancholy mind; *wild geranium*: steadfast piety

Germans, Germany associated with rashness, subservience to authority, crudity, the drinking of beer

ghost psychic dissociation; disembodied spirit; lack of substance

giant the unconscious; the forces of dissatisfaction; everlasting rebellion; despotism; evil; impending evil; the Terrible Father; Universal Man; the father principle; quantitative simplification; man before The Fall; the id; tyranny; protector of the common people • **one-eyed giant** Polyphemus; cyclops • **giant carrying a youth on his back** Orion • **giant carrying a baby on his back** St. Christopher carrying the Christ child

gibbet disgraceful death

gillyflower natural beauty; sweetness; unchastity; attribute of the Virgin Mary, the Annunciation • **flower language** unfading beauty; bonds of affection

gingerbread a burial or deity offering; Christ's body (especially at Christmas time)

giraffe lofty thoughts; eloquence; gentleness; coquetry; speed; ambition • **Bible** timidity; fleetness • **Renaissance art** often depicted because of its unusual appearance rather than for any symbolic value

girdle (cincture) strength; righteousness; faithfulness; truth; gladness; pilgrimmage; protection; virginity; invisibility; spiritual purity invigorating the soul; attribute of the Virgin Mary, Thor, love and fertility goddesses (Venus, etc.) • **gold girdle** attribute of Jesus • **starred girdle** the heavens; the zodiac • **straw girdle** fertility; aid to childbirth • **red girdle with black clothes** attribute of the Furies • **girdle with locust** attribute of John the Baptist • **girdle with arrows and stones** attribute of St. Thomas • **monk's girdle** the three knots in it symbolize the vow's of poverty, chastity, and obedience • **turning one's girdle** preparing to fight • *see also* **cincture**

girl *see* **child; woman; maiden; virgin**

gladiolus abundance; generosity; the Incarnation; readiness to fight

glass purity; peace; virginity; revelation; brittle, short-lived beauty • **rose colored glass** optimistic or unrealistic view • **blue colored glass** pessimistic view • **drinking glass** the Immaculate Conception • **drinking glass with a snake in it** attribute of St. Benedict • **broken drinking glass with wine running from it** attribute of St. Benedict

glasses (for vision) *see* **spectacles**

glasswort in flower language: pretension

globe wholeness; unity; perfection; imperial dignity; the head; the world soul; the Mystic Center; eternity; the earth; felicity; travel; power; attribute of Apollo, Cybele, occasionally Cupid, Urania (especially when in a tripod), and the personifications of Fortitude, Fame, Abundance, Truth, Justice (especially when accompanied by scales and a sword) • **globe underfoot** attribute of God the Father, Christ, Nemesis, the personifications of Philosophy, Fortune, Opportunity • **person kicking a globe** disdain of the world • **celestial globe** attribute of Urania, Astronomy personified • **black globe** prime matter • *see also* **orb; sphere; ball**

glory (luminous glow around the entire body) the supreme state of divinity; attribute of God the Father, Christ, Christ as Judge • *see also* **nimbus; aureole**

glory flower in flower language: glorious beauty

glove(s) power; protection; have some of the powers of their owners; nobility (especially the left glove); attribute of the pope, cardinals, bishops, but also witches, thieves, and other mysterious characters; attribute of God in medieval plays • **removing a glove** (especially the right) salutation; candor; disarming oneself before a superior • **iron glove** tyranny; attribute of Thor • **raw hide gloves** attribute of a boxer in ancient times • **glove and ring** (or gloves alone) a traditional courting gift • **white gloves** innocence; elegance; good taste; a pure heart; formality; cleanliness • **black gloves** sorrow; grief; mourning • *see also* **hand; finger**

glow worm resurrection; the soul of someone departed; harbinger of mourning; related to the stars, which see

glycine in flower language: your friendship is pleasing and agreeable to me • **China** tender and delicate friendship

gnat torment; irritation; insignificance; triviality; related to slander, sunshine, autumn

gnome a miner; related to miners, which see

goad ox goad: attribute of Cain

goat dishonor; materialism; desires; instincts; passions; evil; repression of one's conscience; lust; fertility; agility; elegance; inelegance; stupidity; freedom; fever; messenger of the gods; associated with Bacchus, Cupid, Jupiter, Pan, Thor, Venus, Athena, Odin, Love personified, Lust personified, witches, tragedy; occasionally shows moral superiority because it is associated with high peaks in its wild state, but more often shows moral inferiority; poor man's "cow" • **billy goat** a male child 10 to 20 years old; *Christianity*: Sa-

tan, carnal love, a sinner, the damned, avarice, the Synagogue • **nanny goat** caprice; vagabondage; lust • **riding a goat** an initiation rite; inversion of the normal order • **Old Testament** fraud; lust; cruelty • **Egypt** a sacred animal • **goat with a spiral tail** Capricorn; December; occasionally; winter • **goat's milk** error; desire; milk of the poor • **scapegoat** vicarious atonement • **heraldry** striving after higher things; a warrior who wins • **half goat/half lion** Pan; duality (love/hate, good/evil, etc.) • shares in the symbolism of **horns** (which see) by cunning, rather than by force

goblet the female principle; the Eucharist; vulva; the human heart (especially when covered); attribute of Ares, Artemesia • **goblet filled with liquid** the non-formal world of possibilities • *see also* **cup**

goblin malice; terror; mischief; evil; Hallowe'en

Godiva (Lady) fertility • **with Peeping Tom** lechery

gods days associated with gods • **Sunday** Sol; Helios • **Monday** Luna; Diana • **Tuesday** Mars; Tiu • **Wednesday** Mercury; Wodan • **Thursday** Thor; Jupiter • **Friday** Freya; Venus • **Saturday** Saturn

Gog and Magog the king and the people

gold solar light; divine intelligence; virtue; superiority, especially on a spiritual plane; pure light; heaven; worldly wealth; idolatry; the sun; the id; divinity; the glory of God; sacredness; revealed truth; marriage; fruitfulness; the glory of faith triumphant; associated with Leo • **golden apple** discord; immortality • **golden ball** the sun; when atop a flagpole: the male and female principle • **golden bough** the rays of the setting sun • **golden casket** the Epiphany; attribute of St. Gaspar, Magus • **golden chain** honor; dignity; respect; wealth; the spirit binding earth to heaven; attribute of Hermes, high office • **golden cup** the Eucharist; the Holy Grail; the Immaculate Conception; prize • **golden egg** the sun (laid on the waters of chaos by the primeval goose) • **golden fleece** conquest of the impossible; spiritual knowledge; supreme strength through purity of soul; wisdom; hidden treasure; something elusive; attribute of royalty • **golden house** the Virgin Mary • **Jewish** divine, mystic power • **heraldry** excellence; intelligence; respect; virtue; nobility; elevation of mind; generosity; dignity

goldenrod precaution; encouragement

goldfinch gallantry; fruitfulness; the Passion of Christ

goldilocks (plant) languishing passion • **flower language** flax-leaved goldilocks: tardiness

Gomorrah carnal passion

gong honor; announcement; associated with the Orient • **Greece** a bronze gong was sounded at the death of a king or the eclipse of the moon

goose earth mother; maternity; fertility; a woman 50 to 60 years of age; the sun; creative energy; inspiration; truth; love; constancy; vigilance; providence; silliness; stupidity; female sexuality; wind; snow; speech; eloquence; soul; winter; conceit; innocence; cowardice; the good housewife; attribute of St. Martin of Tour; sacred to Juno, Venus, Dionysus, Eros, Mars, Mercury, Apollo, Peitho, Isis, Osiris, Isis, Thoth • **goose with flames coming from its mouth** the Holy Spirit • **eating a goose** a sun sacrifice • **China** the yang principle; a pair of geese show conjugal fidelity • **goose pursued around the table by an old man** the man is Philemon (of Philemon and Baucis) • **flock of geese** autumn • **her-

aldry** resourcefulness; vigilance; self-sacrifice • **barnacle goose** the unhallowed soul of a dead person; immortality; augur of trouble or storm • **gosling** a young fool

goose foot (plant) in flower language: goodness; *grass leaved goose foot*: I declare war against you (especially when the stems alone are presented)

gooseberry anticipation; regret; worthlessness; the sun; attribute of Wisdom personified

gordian knot the labyrinth (which see)

gorge the maternal; the unconscious; the forces of evil; danger; inferiority in the face of overwhelming odds; the part of the conscious through which parts of the unconscious may be glimpsed

Gorgon the fusion of opposites; a condition beyond the endurance of the conscious mind; the infinite forms in which creation is manifested

gorse roughness • **in flower language** enduring affection

gosling a young fool • *see also* **goose**

gourd fertility; the creative power of nature; blessing; death; resurrection • **Christian** pilgrimmage; pride; adaptibility; the Resurrection of Christ; attribute of Christ, Jonah, St. James the Greater • **gourd as a rattle** creation; resurrection; rainmaker • **gourd as a cup** the female principle • **gourd and apple** the Resurrection of Christ as an antidote for sin • **gourd with pilgrim's staff and wallet** attribute of the archangel Raphael • **flower language** extent; bulk

graft(ing) artificial interferance with the natural order; there is also a sexual significance

grail the source of happiness; God; spiritual knowledge; mystery; elusive quest; salvation; attainment of perfection; attribute of St. Joseph of

Arimathea; associated with King Arthur and the Knights of the Round Table

grain cultivated higher emotions in the soul; autumn; fertility; abundance; the human nature of Christ; the Eucharist (especially when shown with grapes); attribute of Ceres, Adonis, Osiris, Ruth, Attis, Agriculture personified; the cereal grains are all spermatic images • **seven grains** the seven gifts of the Holy Spirit • **sheaf of grain** attribute of Concord personified • **sheaf of grain shown with a plough** attribute of the Silver Age personified

granite hardness of heart; death; power; intransigence

grapes fertility; sacrifice; the Eucharist (especially when shown with wheat or bread); the spiritual nature of love and wisdom; charity; intoxication; wine; shares in the symbolism of wine, which see; fruitfulness; blood; the blood of Christ; attribute of Bacchus, Moses, Caleb, Joshua, Mithra, St. Vincent of Saragossa, the Tribe of Ephraim • **harvesting of grapes** associated with September • **grapes with wheat** the Eucharist; agriculture; fertility; attribute of Saturn and of various earth goddesses • **birds feeding on grapes** the faithful gathering sustenance from the blood of Christ • **grapes borne on a staff by two men** entry into the Promised Land, Canaan • **twelve clusters of grapes** the Apostles • **grape leaves or vine** Christ • **wild grapes** charity • **workers in a vineyard** the work of good Christians for the Lord

grass humble usefulness; the common people; submission (especially a lawn); surrender of a handful of grass indicates defeat; acquisition of a territory by conquest • **Bible** the fleeting quality of life • **flower language** utility; submission; *mouse-eared scorpion grass*: forget-me-not;

ray grass: vice; *rye grass*: changeable disposition; *vernal grass*: poor, but happy

grasshopper timidity; fear; dotage; meaningless chatter; weakness; carefree life; improvidence • **Christianity** conversion • **Greece** nobility • **Bible** judgment of God • *see also* **locust**

gray discretion; penitence; humility; barrenness; grief; egoism; neutralization; depression; inertia; indifference; the undifferentiated; asceticism; renunciation; vagueness; concealment; clouds; associated with ashes, which see • **pale gray** associated with Virgo • **silver gray** associated with the moon

grayhound speed; hunting; elegance; sharpsightedness; grace; fawning; attribute of the personifications of Lust, Envy, Sickness, Care • **heraldry** courage; loyalty; vigilance • *see also* **dog**

grave *see* **sarcophagus; tomb**

gravestone mortality

Great Priest *see* **High Priest** (tarot)

Great Priestess *see* **High Priestess** (tarot)

Greece reason; intellectual keenness; hedonism • **Jewish** paganism; idolatry • **Roman** the highest culture • **English** cunning; wantonness • **U.S.** sometimes associated with sodomy

green fertility; life; growth; rebirth; immortality; spiritual integrity; victory over the vicissitudes of life; victory over the flesh; youth; hope; spring; regeneration of the spirit; freshness; innocence; liberty; peace; inexperience; sympathy; charity; vegetation; spiritual initiation; expectation; obedience; associated with water in pagan rites; a feminine color; neutrality; passivity; indecision; material decay; decay in general; decomposition; associated with Libra; attribute of Venus, Nature personified • **yellow-green** associated with Virgo • **bluish green** associated with Scorpio • **dark green** associated with the planet Saturn • **China** green clouds: a plague of insects; *green sedan chair*: attribute of a lower government official • **heraldry** freedom; beauty; happiness; health; hope; mildness; a feminine color • **green mantle** attribute of St. Anne, St. John

grey *see* **gray**

gridiron martyrdom; attribute of St. Laurence, occasionally, St. Vincent of Saragossa

griffin invincibility; watchfulness; the relationship between psychic energy and cosmic force; eternal vigilance; victory; attribute of Apollo, Nemesis, Christ • **Christian** the dual nature of Christ; the Incarnation; Christ's kingdom on earth; Christ's omnipotence and omniscience; those who oppress and persecute Christians • **two griffins** enlightenment and wisdom • **griffin with a ball underfoot** enlightenment protecting wisdom; supporter of a water goddess • **heraldry** watchfulness; courage

grill *see* **gridiron**

groom *see* **bridegroom**

grotto associated with Diana and her nymphs

grouse (bird) emblem of Scotland • **heraldry** a forebearer that fought a gallant duel, or was a great hunter • **grouse feather in a hat** challenge to a duel

guard force gathered on the threshold of transition

gudgeon a credulous fool

guelder rose *see* **snowball** (plant)

guillotine martyrdom; terror; the Reign of Terror in France

guinea hen attribute of Artemis; a low woman

guinea pig experiment

guitar the male and female principle

gull foil; victim; gullibility; voluptuousness; usefulness; plaintiveness; versatility; travel; adventure; emblem of the sea; attribute of Aphrodite, Athena, Leucothea • *see also* **bird**

gum (plant gum) related to tears, semen; the seminal substance

gun power; violence; the threat of violence; a phallic symbol; the masculine principle; force

guru *see* **poet**

gypsum initiation; disguise; resurrection; slavery

gypsy primitive man; seer; the footloose life

H

H associated with rise and fall, the number eight, Cancer or Libra, the planet Mercury, Justice or the High Priest in the tarot deck, binary or complementary functions (such as justice and mercy)

haberdasher a person of small wit

hag the Terrible Mother; famine; misfortune

Hagar the Church in bondage; the synagogue; a bondswoman unjustly oppressed

hail divine retribution; the assault of an enemy; destruction; a terrible judgment • **hail destroying crops** falsity destroying truth and goodness • **hail stones** evanescence

hair energy; magical power; the external soul; God's providence; related to fire, sun-rays, sun heroes, rain, love, fertility • **white hair** the Son of Man and the eternity of his existence; *see also* gray hair, below • **gray hair** old age; retrospection; wisdom; relativism; tenderness • **golden hair** the sun's rays; purity; wisdom; virtue; immortality; attribute of love goddesses, sun heroes;

Norse: abundance • **red hair** connected with the underworld; a Venusian, satanic, or demoniacal characteristic; an attribute of Judas • **green hair** attribute of mermaids • **violet hair** attribute of Aphrodite, the Graces, the Muses, Eurydice, goddesses having a spring festival • **body hair** irrational power; the instincts • **hair on the head** spiritual power • **braided hair** profane love; attribute of a courtesan • **curly hair** one who follows the arts; facility with foreign languages • **dark hair** terrestrial energy • **lock of hair** a love fetish • **disheveled hair** involution; bereavement; madness; attribute of underworld deities • **long hair worn by a man** strength; attribute of a hermit • **long, flowing hair** penitence; sexuality; attribute of St. Mary Magdalene, St. Mary of Egypt, St. Agnes; *Christian*: virginity; *Jewish*: a sinner, mourning, a bride, an unmarried woman • **man covered by long hair** St. Onuphrius • **woman covered by long hair** St. Agnes; Lady Godiva • **full, thick head of hair** vitality; sexuality; lust; wildness • **loose hair over brow** attribute of Opportunity personified • **letting normally short hair grow** mourning • **baldness** a syphilitic; a fool • **loss of hair** failure; poverty • **cutting hair** asceticism; purification; disgrace; mourning; substitute for human sacrifice • **cutting the hair of a sleeping man** Samson • **maid cutting her hair with a sword** Ermina (of Tancred and Ermina) • **maid tending a woman's hair amid war preparations** the woman is Semiramis • **wet hair on a goddess** Venus • *see also* tonsure

halberd attribute of Minerva, St. Jude, St. Matthew, St. James the Less, St. Matthias (especially with a book)

halo *see* nimbus; aureole; glory

Hamlet introspection; hastiness; rashness

hammer power; destruction; fertility; immortality; divine vengeance; physical power and strength; persistent thought; manual labor; industry; the blacksmith; the carpenter; creation; fecundation; the masculine principle; phallus; emblem of the Crucifixion; attribute of thunder gods, Vulcan, Anake, St. Eloi, St. Helena (especially with nails) • **hammer and nails** the Crucifixion • **hammer and chisel** sculpture

hand protection; justice; power; authority (especially of the father, emperor, deity, etc.) • **right hand** aggressiveness; associated with the rational, virility, logic, the conscious • **left hand** death; decay; associated with the subconscious, weakness, irrationality, the instincts • **open hand** beneficence; generosity; the slapping and mockery of Christ in the Passion; when fingers are extended: the sun; protections against the evil eye • **closed hand** *see* fist • **black hand** threat; vendetta; impending death • **white hand** spring • **red hand** violence; murder; warning of death; the sun; guilt; in heraldry: rank • **ivory hand** attribute of Fortune personified • **gilded hand** bribery • **golden hand** attribute of Fortune personified • **iron hand** harshness; strength; tyranny • **raising open hands** prayer; swearing truth; voice and song; distress; surrender; death; dismay • **upraised hands with middle finger and ring finger separated** Jewish blessing; on a tombstone: indicates a Jewish priest • **two hands clasped in a handshake** treaty; peace; concord; love; alliance; friendship; virile fraternity; solidarity; mystic marriage; individuation; *on a tombstone*: farewell and welcome • **two hands clasped beneath the hand of God** the blessing of marriage by the Church • one hand clasped between two others swearing allegiance • clapping hands rain making; applause; unwillingness • hands on hips challenge; arrogance; independence; impatience; exasperation • hands loose at sides defeat; resignation • washing hands Pontius Pilate; innocence; attribute of Innocence personified • folded hands composure; obedience; complacence • folded hands with fingers interwoven intransigence • hands clasped behind the back harmlessness; innocence • veiled hands a token of respect • branded hand attribute of a sheep thief • hands laid on the head confirmation; ordination; death; a blessing • hand(s) on one's own head mourning; grief; helplessness • hand on the mouth secrecy; member of a secret cult; a vow of silence • hand flat on the heart pledge; a sage; love; adoration; salutation • hand extended protection; invitation • hand with palm upward invitation; bribe; payment • hand raised over the head victory; seeking attention • hand raised with palm outward peace; a blessing • hands clasped and raised overhead union; victory • hand with straws the drawing of lots for Christ's garment • hand with money Judas' betrayal of Christ; bribery; wealth • hand descending from heaven God the Father • hand with thumb and forefinger touching vulva • hand with thumb and last two fingers touching a blessing; eternity; the grace of Christ; the love of God and Communion with the Holy Spirit • hand pierced with arrows attribute of St. Giles of Provence • hand holding a model of a monastery attribute of St. Gerald of Auriliac • hand holding three flowers attribute of St. Hugh of Grenoble • hand holding flame attribute of the arch-

angel Uriel • Roman soldier with his hand in a brazier Mucius Scaevola • woman with cupped hands before Apollo the Cumean sibyl • heraldry pledge of faith; blessing; protection; power; diligence; concord; innocence; a red hand indicates rank • see also fist; finger

hand flower tree in flower language: warning

handcuffs imprisonment; death; sin; bad habits • broken handcuffs death and sin overcome; release; freedom

handiwork in Elizabethan times, a euphemism for sexual activity

handkerchief seduction; jealousy; flirtation

handsaw see saw

Hanged Man (tarot) mysticism; sacrifice; self-denial; continence; the utopian dream world; teaching; a public lesson; an example; detachment from materialism; a flight to overcome evil; power derived from charity, wisdom, fidelity and other higher virtues; reversal of one's way of life by surrender to higher wisdom; spiritual self-sacrifice; a suspended decision

hanging (execution) an ignominious death; death of a common criminal; sacrifice to a sky god

hanging (suspension) unfulfilled longing; suspense

harbor the mother; the Church; Christ; security; refuge; comfort; eternal life • young man bearing a maiden off to a harbor the abduction of Helen of Troy • see also bay

hare procreation; elemental existence; lasciviousness; fleetness; diligent service; fecundity; resourcefulness; a male figure, generally, but may be a woman of loose morals; vigilance; timidity; cowardice; curiosity; love of learning; madness (especially youthful madness); melancholy; life; fertility; resurrection; lust; associated with witches; emblem of Easter; attribute of Osiris, St. Jerome, the personifications of Lust, Fasting, Vagrancy • **Christian** the rapid course of life; the Church persecuted; a Christian's haste to obtain divine gifts; those who put their hope in Christ • **Jewish** contemplation; intuition • **Greece** emblem of autumn • **China** longevity; a supernatural creature; an auspicious omen; associated with the moon • **Middle Ages** emblem of spring • **heraldry** one who enjoys a peaceful, retired life; hunting skill; speed; vigilance; fertility • **white hare at the Virgin Mary's feet** her triumph over lust • **knight pursued by a hare** timidity; cowardice • **message discovered in a hare's body** associated with Cyrus the Great • **three hares turned so they appear to have one pair of ears** the Trinity

harebell in flower language: grief, submission

harlequin mischievous intrigue; tricks played on others; magic transformations; the discordant elements in life; related to underworld deities, fertility gods, the gods of destiny

harlot *see* **prostitute**

harp a bridge between heaven and earth; contemplation; joy; praise; poetry; music; worship in heaven; sadness; human stress; suffering; religious music in general, the book of Psalms in particular; related to heaven; the mystic ladder to heaven; longing for love or death; soothing of strained nerves; related to blindness in conjunction with cunning or aristocracy; instrument of a harlot; attribute of Terpsichore, David (especially with lion), St. Patrick, St. Alfred, St. Cecilia; emblem of Ireland, sometimes Wales • **heraldry** contemplation; elevation; chastity • **harpist** the death wish; fascination with death • **Aeolian harp** conceit; self-confidence; grand airs; associated with those given to wine, wom-

en, and luxurious living • *see also* **lyre**

harpoon fecundation; destruction; emblem of whalers and the whaling industry

harpy evil harmonies of cosmic forces; vice; guilt and punishment; involutive fragmentation of the subconscious; evil; rapacity; plunder; torment; unregulated appetites of sensation and desire using knowledge to promote their own ends; emblem of Virgo, Music personified • **heraldry** faithfulness and compliance with power and wisdom; ferocity under provocation • **harpy blindfolded** attribute of Avarice personified

harrow (plant) in flower language: rest; obstacle

harrow (tool) tribulation; agriculture; fertility; martyrdom

hart grace; nimbleness; resurrection; the morning star; immortality; piety and aspiration of the soul; persecution of Christians; a substitute for the unicorn, which see; associated with Artemis, Esther, Christ • **Christian** thirst for salvation; the faithful partaking of the waters of life • *see also* **stag; deer; hind**

harvest(ing) associated with Ruth, the months of June, July, August, and the personifications of Summer, the Silver Age

hat thought; personality; related to the head, which see; the color of the hat may reveal the wearer's primary characteristic: see entries for the particular color; a hat that confers invisibility implies repression or regression; attribute of pilgrims, missionaries • **red hat** *see* **cardinal's hat** • **yellow hat** in the Middle Ages, attribute of a Jew • *see also* **cap**

hatchet execution; treachery; attribute of carpenters, woodsmen, St. Matthias, St. Joseph • **American Indians** war; *to bury a hatchet*: peace • **hatchet and cherry tree** attribute of the young George Washington, and hence, truth • *see also* axe, with which the hatchet is often imperfectly distinguished

hawk the evil mind of the sinner; fire; sun; vision; the spirit; nobility; immortality; longevity; vengeance; ferocity; a swindler; brute force; violence; war-monger; freedom; fierce nobility; predation; watchfulness; a wild and intractable woman • **Jewish** the providence of God • **hawk eating a hare** the triumph of the mind over the flesh • *see also* **sparrowhawk**, and **falcon**, with which the hawk is frequently confused

hawkweed in flower language: quick-sightedness

hawsers *see* **moorings**

hawthorn death; purification; sexuality; fertility; indulgence; prudence; associated with the Nativity; attribute of Servitude personified • **heraldry** a Tudor prince • **Rome** attribute of Carnea • **trained over a bench to make a bower** associated with old men, lovers • **flower language** hope; May, May Day in particular

hay buttered hay: deceit; cheating

hazel knowledge; wisdom; poetic art; love and fertility; healing; reconciliation; death; associated with Virgo; attribute of Thor • **flower language** reconciliation; peace; healing; *witch hazel*: a spell • **hazel wand** finds water, buried treasure, murderers, thieves; the caduceus; attribute of Mercury, heralds; *Ireland*: said to make a person invisible

head the mind; spiritual life; wisdom; the sun; kingship; authority; the universe; oneness; virility; the masculine; fertility; the world; the spiritual principle as opposed to the body, which represents the physical principle • **head of Goliath** associated with David • **head of Judas** the Betrayal of Christ • **Christ's head on a cloth** attribute of St.

Veronica • **head with two faces** Janus; sometimes Prudence personified • **head with three faces** Prudence personified • **multiple heads** deterioration; fragmentation, however, it can sometimes indicate a positive intensification • **head wound** attribute of St. Peter Martyr • **sword or knife in the head** attribute of St. Peter Martyr • **heraldry** honor for special services; power; *moor's head*: service in the Crusades, or the East India Company • **severed head** wisdom; life of the soul after death • **severed head held over an urn** Tomyris • **severed head held under the arm** attribute of St. Denis • **severed head at the feet or in the hand** attribute of David, Judith, Julius Caesar • **severed head at the feet of a winged god** Mercury • **severed head being held by a woman with a sword, or being put into a sack** Judith • **severed head, blindfold, on a horse** St. Paul • **severed head on a horse, or on a platter** John the Baptist • **large head held by a youth** David with Goliath's head • **severed head held by a woman before a king** the king is Otto III • **severed head with snakes for hair held by youth** Perseus with Medusa's head • **severed head together with the body** Manlius Torquatus • **severed head pierced by an arrow** attribute of America personified • *see also* **forehead; beheading**

headband *see* **fillet**

healing the spiritual process by which certain qualities are harmonized and spiritualized

hearing intuitive perception of the truth in the soul; reception of divine wisdom • *see also* **deafness**

heart (the organ) love; will power; romantic love; love as the center of illumination and happiness; love of God; the seat of true intelligence; understanding (as opposed to reasoning); emblem of Eros; attribute of St. Bernardino, St. John of God, St. Teresa of Avila, St. Valentine, occasionally St. Augustine • **heraldry** sincerity; reason • **heart of gold** a perfect person • **flaming heart** Christian love; intense zeal; emblem of Venus in the Renaissance; attribute of St. Anthony of Padua, St. Augustine (especially when transfixed with two arrows), Charity personified • **heart pierced with sword** (sometimes the heart has wings) the Virgin Mary • **heart pierced with arrow** contrition; deep repentance or devotion; romantic love; associated with Cupid; an occasional attribute of St. Augustine (usually with two arrows) • **heart pierced with arrow with a woman's head shown on the heart** sin against the 9th Commandment • **heart pierced by an arrow with a coin on the heart** sin against the 10th commandment • **heart with cross and anchor** love, faith, and hope, respectively • **heart with a cross** attribute of St. Catherine of Siena • **heart on a tablet or sun** attribute of St. Bernardino • **heart in a woman's hand** the woman is Charity personified • **five hearts** Judah's five sons • **stake driven in the heart** nailing the soul in a particular place; death for a vampire • **heart crowned with thorns** attribute of St. Ignatius of Loyola; emblem of the Jesuits • **woman gnawing on a heart** Envy personified • **heart pierced by a spear** the Passion of Christ • **missing heart in a sacrificial animal** portent of evil • *see also* **hearts** (cards)

hearth the home; love; filial loyalty; altar for home gods (Penates, Lares, etc.); fertility; hospitality; sanctuary; temperance; conjunction of the masculine (fire) and feminine (hearth) principles • **extinguishing the hearth fire** mourning

hearts (cards) the creative world;

knowledge; friendship; hospitality; emotion • **ace of hearts** family ties

heart's ease (plant) peace of mind • *see also* **pansy**

heat source of life; libido; motivation; vitality; passion

heather humility; solitude; emblem of Scotland; attribute of Venus, Isis • **red heather** mid-summer; when shown with mountains and bees, associated with Cybele • **white heather** protection against acts of passion; in flower language: good luck

heaven spirituality; the masculine principle; spiritual reward; union with God

Hecate the Terrible Mother; the evil side of the feminine principle responsible for madness, obsession, lunacy

Hector bragging

hedge privacy; secrecy; illicit love; prohibition; a privet hedge may indicate a lack of means of enforcement as opposed to a thorn hedge, which does have the means

hedgehog self-defense; rascality; cunning; strong defense; emblem of the sun; the critical aspect that destroys error; related to witches and demonic possession; attribute of the personifications of Touch, Fury, Slander, Gluttony • **heraldry** resistance; provident provider; when surmounted by a crown, Louis XII of France

heel vulnerability; the lower nature of the soul • **light heels, round heels** immorality; unchasteness; loose morals • *see also* **foot**

heifer *see* **cow**

Helen the instinctive and emotional aspects of woman; the transitory, inconsistent; unfaithfulness; dissembling; lower nature; that which diverts man from the path of spiritual progress

helenium in flower language: tears

Helios the sun in its astronomic and spiritual aspect

heliotrope (flower) intoxication with love • **flower language** devotion; faithfulness; *Peruvian heliotrope*: devotion

heliotrope (stone) mourning; devotion; faithfulness; associated with March

hellebore the Nativity of Christ • **flower language** scandal; calumny

helmet courage; lofty thoughts; salvation; protection of the soul from the assaults of passions and desires; wisdom; attribute of a soldier, Hades, Athena, Hephaestus, St. George, the personifications of Faith, Fortitude; the color of the helmet often represents the wearer's thoughts, *see* specific colors (**red, black, blue,** etc.) • **crested helmet** a victor • **winged helmet** flight; swiftness; poetic thought; attribute of Mercury, Perseus • **closed helmet** hidden or suspect thoughts • **soldier pouring water from a helmet on a dying woman** Tancred and Clorinda • **heraldry** martial prowess; surety in defense; wisdom; lofty thoughts; *surmounted by a fleur-di-lis*: salvation; *surmounted by a wolf's head*: courage supplanted by astuteness; *surmounted by any kind of strange crest*: imagination, restless exhiliaration • *see also* specific colors as noted above

helmet flower in flower language: chivalry; knight errant

hematite vivacity; wifehood; associated with Pisces

hemlock death; punishment for unpopular beliefs; evil; weakness; emblem of Fragility personified; attribute of Socrates • **flower language** you will be my death

hemp the rustic life; narcotic; attribute of Recognition personified • **flower language** fate

hen maternity; providence; the female; maternal care; a woman 40 to 50 years old; idle chatter; attribute of Grammar personified; associated with death • **hen with chicks** protection; providence; the solicitude of Christ • **hen on its nest** perseverance • **hen crowing** in China: the ruin of a family • *see also* **chicken; chick; rooster; capon**

henbane opiate; emblem of Imperfection personified • **flower language** defect; fault; imperfection

hepatica the liver • **flower language** confidence

Hephaestus *see* **Vulcan**

Hera *see* **Juno**

herb natural forces; magic; healing; primitive desires and ambitions aroused by the senses; nobility; rural life; appetizer; poor man's food • *see also* specific herbs, **dill, sage,** etc.

Hercules strength; the quest for immortality; nobility; the fight against the Terrible Mother; the fight against the unconscious; the individual fleeing himself in the quest for immortality; expiation of sins through heroic striving and heroism; related to the Emperor in the tarot deck • **Elizabethan** a ridiculous, brawny, boisterous tyrant

herd when orderly: coordinated desires and emotions working for the evolution of the soul; prosperity; rural tranquillity • **when disorderly**: loss of unity; disintegration; degeneration; regression

hermaphrodite totality; integration of opposites; Oneness; intellectual activity; androgynous self-creation; Adam before Eve was created out of him; the productive powers of nature; fertility; loss of the sense of separation of the personality • **man's head on a woman's body** solid and profound judgment

Hermes *see* **Mercury**

hermit solitude; contemplation; asceticism

Hermit (tarot) tradition; study; reserve; patient and profound work; tedium; taciturnity; wisdom; good; morality; meticulousness; the successful union of personal will with cosmic will; prudence; solitary vigilance; emblem of Diogenes; related to Leo, Uranus, Neptune

hermitage attribute of St. Giles

heron morning; generation of life; regeneration; parental providence; longevity; silent memory; danger overcome; indiscretion; melancholy; duality; the Christian who turns away from false doctrine; the unfavorable aspects of the priesthood; sacred to the Muses; attribute of February personified; usually, a good omen • **heraldry** prudence in danger; possession of free and rich fishing rights

Hesperides treasure hunt; death

hexagon the six attributes of God (power, wisdom, majesty, love, mercy, justice); partakes of the symbolism of the number six, which see

hibiscus short-lived glory • **flower language** delicate beauty

hiding the period of life before and after its involution as matter, or before and after the manifest life of appearances

Hierophant *see* **High Priest** (tarot)

High Priest (tarot) external religion; traditional teaching suitable for the masses; bondage to convention; information; philosophy; proof; religion

High Priestess (tarot) a balance between initiative and resistance; unrealized potential; duality; hidden influences; sanctuary; the law; knowledge; woman; the mother; the Church

hill aspiration; constancy; stability; place of worship, meditation, innocent pleasures, freedom from care; eternity; fertility; female emblem; entrance to Valhalla • *see also* **mountain**

hind (deer) grace; elegance; acute hearing; timidity; cowardice; innocence; purity; charity; one's own wife; motherly love; sure-footed-ness; wisdom; low birth; search for immortality; emblem of dawn; attribute of Juno, Diana • **running hind** associated with Naphtali • **hind shot with arrow** attribute of St. Giles • *see also* **deer**

hippocampus attribute of Neptune, Galatea, sea deities in general

hippogryph a spiritual mount; combines the favorable aspects of both **horse** and **lion**, q.q.v.

hippopotamus insensibility; duality; strength and vigor; impiety; craft; hate; intellectual pride; the mother principle; gross materialism; attribute of the personifications of Impiety, Behemoth • **Classical** murder; impudence; violence; injustice

hobby horse folly; drudge; a loose woman

hoe diligence; agriculture; fertility; election of the chosen; attribute of a farmer, Adam after the Fall, Spring personified • **heraldry** a right to part of the common ground

hog *see* **swine**

hold (of a ship) the unconscious; experience on the lower plane

hole the feminine principle; the female genitals; the passage between worlds or existences; the Mystic Center

Holland *see* **Netherlands**

hollow (topographical feature) the abode of the dead; memories; the past; the unconscious; the mother; abstract form of a cave, which see; inverse form of a mountain, which see

holly a holy tree; mid-winter; the second half of the year; eternal life; hospitality; harvest; domestic happiness; good will; prickliness; related to Saturnalia, the Green Knight, Christmas; emblem of the Crucifixion (said to have been the tree of the Cross, as were the aspen and other trees); Christ's crown of thorns; occasional attribute of John the Baptist, St. Jerome • **heraldry** truth;

penitence • **flower language** foresight; Am I forgotten?

holly oak the Great Spirit; in classical times: longevity

holly thorn see **hawthorn**

hollyhock ambition; fruitfulness; fecundity • **flower language** fruitfulness; fecundity; *white hollyhock*: ambition, especially female

Holy Grail see **grail**

holy oil see **oil**

holy water see **water**

honesty (plant) in flower language: honesty; sincerity; fascination

honey wisdom; food of the gods; food from heaven; eternal bliss; the Eucharist; poetic ecstasy; spiritual wisdom; eloquence; sweetness; abundance; honor; chastity; virginity; flattery; deceit; lust; slumber; initiation; the spiritual exercise of sole-improvement; Paradise; the work of God; Christ and his work; religious eloquence • **honey and apples** for Jews: eaten on the New Year to symbolize the hope for sweetness and joy, respectively

honey comb labyrinth; confusion; foresight; attribute of John the Baptist

honey flower in flower language: sweet and secret love

honeysuckle love; fraternal love; emblem of the South in the U.S.; associated with Aries; related to the lotus, which see • **flower language** generous and devoted affection; *coral honeysuckle*: the color of my fate; *French honeysuckle*: rustic beauty; *monthly honeysuckle*: (woodbine) bond of love, fraternal love, I will not answer hastily, domestic happiness; *wild honeysuckle*: inconstancy in love

hood repression; invisibility; death; detachment from the material world; spiritual blindness; regression; mysticism; shares in the symbolism of the head and hat, q.q.v. • **pointed hood** associated with Joel •

black hood attribute of an executioner • **heraldry** falcon hood: hunting prowess

hoof cloven hoof: mark of the Devil; separation; treachery

hook related to love, the male • **hooked grill** attribute of St. Vincent

hoopoe parental care; ostentation; vanity; poverty; filth; attribute of royalty, Baseness personified

hops beer; mirth; injustice; passion; overwhelming pride; trust • **flower language** injustice

horehound in flower language: fire

horn (animal) power; strength; virility; abundance; fertility; dignity; protection; defense; phallus; salvation; immortality; madness; rage; intelligence; the outside shape is phallic, the hollow inside is feminine; attribute of Asher, Satan, Pan, satyrs, Erythraea, Delphica, cuckholds • **horn of oil** associated with David • **horn of milk** associated with the sibyl Cimeriana • **ram's horn** see **shofar** • **four horns** associated with Zechariah • **seven horns** entry into Jericho

horn (musical) call to arms; invocation of help; attribute of Melpomene, the Tritons, Fame personified; melancholy • **hunting horn** attribute of St. Hubert • *see also* **trumpet**

hornbeam in flower language: ornament

hornet evil; viciousness • **Bible** plague; punishment

horse lust; fertility; selfishness; fidelity; vanity; stubbornness; stupidity; the unconscious; the self; war; the sun; the blind forces of primeval chaos; the instincts; the baser forces in man; a funereal animal; the Ascension of Christ; sometimes credited with clairvoyance; attribute of kings, nobles, warriors, Europe personified, Dionysus, Pluto, Neptune, Odin, Boreas, Mars, Castor, Pollux, Jupiter, Helios, the Muses, St.

George, St. Eustace, St. Hubert, St. Martin • **heraldry** readiness for action; Master of the Horse; a white horse in an emblem of the Hanoverian family • **colt** friskiness; wantonness • **white horse** innocence; intellect; reason; celestial knowledge; the Divine Word; the conquering Christian; the pure and perfect higher mind; the hero's steed; imagination; dawn; manhood; an emblem of the Hanoverian family • **white horse with flaming mane** the sun • **horse without any white** viciousness • **black horse** famine; error; false knowledge; death; steed of a villain • **gray horse** the Devil; dissolution • **red horse** war; the mind energized by the spirit; associated with Zechariah • **grazing horse** peace and freedom • **horse's head** emblem of Carthage • **double horse head** protection • **winged horse** Pegasus; poetry; the flight of the imagination; imagination itself • **horse with sword coming from its mouth** the Apocalypse • **three-legged horse** attribute of the Devil, of Death personified in time of pestilence • **horse with its leg removed for shoeing** attribute of St. Eloi • **horse attacked by a man with a club** the attacker is Hercules • **wooden horse** the Trojan War; a ruse • **horse, chariot, and rider falling from the sky** the rider is Phaeton • **hobby horse** folly; a drudge; a loose woman • *see also* **horseman; mare**

horse chestnut (buckeye) the sun; emblem of Ohio • **flower language** luxury

horse leech unending greed • *see also* **leech**

horseman the ego trying to control the id; bearer of immortality of prophecy; Christ • **horseman with white banner** St. James the Greater • **horseman on a winged horse** Perseus; Bellerophon • **soldiers on horseback in the sky** Old Testament: portent of war; New Testament: revelation • **four horsemen charging** the Apocalypse • **headless horseman** the Devil; death • **nude woman on a horse** Lady Godiva; Cloelia (not always nude) • **New Testament** — *horseman on a white horse*: the word of God, Christ's spiritual conquest, Christ; *horseman on a red horse*: war as a punishment of God; *horseman on a black horse*: starvation; *horseman on a pale horse*: death • *see also* **horse**

horseradish Jewish: the bitterness of bondage

horseshoe protection; vulva; good fortune (since the exposed genitals were supposed to bring good luck); related to a horse's vitality and sexual potency; emblem of the blacksmith

hortensia in flower language: you are cold

Host (Eucharist) the sacrifice of Christ upon the Cross, especially when shown with a chalice; the body of Christ; breaking the Host symbolizes the death of Christ's body

hound seeker of truth; inquisitiveness; intelligence; the hunter; pursuit; male desire; attribute of Artemis • *see also* **dog; Gabriel Hounds**

hourglass the transciency of life; time; inversion; evanescence; creation and destruction; perpetual inversion of the upper and lower worlds; death; night time as opposed to the sundial which symbolizes daytime; attribute of the Grim Reaper, Father Time, Saturn, the alchemist, Temperance personified • **heraldry** mortality; evanescence • **hourglass with wings** the fleeting quality of time

house tradition; one's life; the feminine aspect of the universe; shelter; security; hospitality; the body, with the roof and attic corresponding to the mind, the basement to the unconscious, the kitchen as a place of transmutation, the windows and doors as body openings, etc. • **house on a rock** the Church securely founded on the rock of faith • **cedar house** incorruptibility • **clay house** evanescence • **golden house** Nero's Palace of the Sun

House of God (tarot) the power of the heavenly over the earthly; spiritual truth breaking down ignorance; involution; materialism struck down by spiritual light to render regeneration possible; the dangerous consequences of over-confidence; the sin of pride; megalomania; wickedness; the wild pursuit of fanciful ideas; small-mindedness; sudden subversion

housefly *see* **fly**

houseleek vitality; attribute of Printing personified • **flower language** vivacity; domestic economy • *see also* **leek**

houstonia in flower language: contentment

hoya in flower language: sculpture

humble plant in flower language: despondency

hummingbird gaiety; courage; jealousy

hunchback sins of the past; nature perverted; regression

hundred *see* **one hundred**

hunter action for its own sake; repetition; pursuit of the transitory; the Devil; killer; pursuer; searcher for truth • **hunter restrained by nude woman** Adonis • **hunter turning into a stag or observing a nude woman** Actaeon • **hunter grieving over a woman shot by an arrow** Cephalus and Procis • **hind protected from a hunter** attribute of St. Giles • **huntress** Diana

hurricane regeneration; fecundation; a hole through which one may pass out of space and time

husband and wife mind and emotion, respectively

husk lower qualities

hut shelter; related to both house and tree symbolism, q.q.v. • **Jewish Feast of Sukkoth**; a reminder of the time in the wilderness

hyacinth (flower) sorrow; sport; game; play; diversion; resignation; faith; resistance to adversity; love and its woes; prudence; wisdom; kindliness; associated with Capricorn, April; attribute of the Virgin Mary, Benevolence personified • **Middle Ages** mourning • **flower language** sport; play; *blue hyacinth*: constancy; *white hyacinth*: unobtrusive loveliness

hyacinth (gemstone) Christian prudence; peace of mind; the desire for heaven

Hydra multifarious evil; the prolific nature of heresy, sin, false doctrine

hydrangea remembrance; frigidity • **flower language** a boaster; heartlessness; you are cold

hyena falseness; fickleness; avarice; ghoulishness; evil; the Devil; cowardice; one who thrives on false doctrine; derisiveness

hyssop cleanliness; freshness; penitence; humility; innocence regained; purgation; winter; decency; baptism • **hyssop and reed** associated with the Passion of Christ

I

I the axis of the universe; associated with the number nine, the winter solstice, the liver, indestructibility, tolerance, sympathy, sensitivity, travel, Leo, Neptune, the Hermit or Wheel of Fortune in the tarot deck

IHC from the first three letters of Jesus' name in Greek; *see* IHS, below

IHS an adaptation of IHC (which see, above) that came into use as Latin became the dominant language of the Church; the understanding was that it meant *Iesus Hominum Salvator* (Jesus, savior of men) or *In haec salus* (In this [cross], salvation). Usually placed at the center of a cross to symbolize that God's love for humanity is revealed in Christ's death on the cross • IHS on a tablet or sun attribute of St. Bernardino of Siena

INRI Latin initials for *Iesus Nazarenus Rex Iudaeorum* (Jesus of Nazareth, King of the Jews), a title originally given by Pontius Pilate

IX the Greek initials for Jesus Christ, often shown with the I bisecting the X

ibis wisdom; perseverance; aspiration; morning; protector; dawn; spiritual awakening; occult art; regeneration; gratitude; a favorable omen; associated with Isis, moon goddess • Greek, Christian carnal desires; filth; laziness

Icarus the limitation of ideas; the intellect in the merely technical and non-spiritual sense; man's questing intellectual spirit; the danger of going to extremes; the intellect trying to escape the world; intellect rebelling against the spirit • the wings of Icarus functional insufficiency

ice winter; death; smoothness; feminine chastity; the rigid dividing line between the conscious and the unconscious, or any other dynamic levels; stultification of potentialities; latent truth; inertness; the coldness of ice implies resistance to all that is inferior

ice plant in flower language: rejected addresses; your looks freeze me

Iceland moss in flower language: health

icicle chastity; frigidity

idol apostasy; paganism; the heathen world; Mammon worship; Solomon's apostasy; fixed ideas which bar the way to truth; outward observances regarded as true spiritual exercise • shattered idol associated with Hosea, St. Philip • fallen idol associated with the Flight into Egypt • idol underfoot denial of paganism; paganism overcome

illness *see* disease

imperial montague in flower language: power

incendiarism *see* arson

incense homage to a deity; dawn; morning; spiritual goodness; prayer; fumigant to scare off evil spirits; sacrifice for thanksgiving or for a favor; atonement; flattery; purification by fire; inspiration; transmutation of the physical into the spiritual; related to the Phoenix; associated with the Virgin Mary

incest longing for union with one's own self; individuation; corruption or perversion of the natural order

Indians (American Indians) the darker side of the personality; base forces; the instincts; natural men; emblem of early America, the American West

indigo (color) associated with Taurus, Saturn, later, Jupiter; night; evil • *see also* blue

infant new beginning; new era; innocence; helplessness; hope • infant in a cradle attribute of St. Vincent DePaul, St. Anthony of Padua • infant in the arms of Mercury Bacchus • infant in a tree trunk Adonis • infant suckled by a woman, with another infant nearby attribute of Charity personified • infant suckled by a goat Jupiter • infant suckled by a wolf Romulus

(Remus is often represented with him) • **infant fed by a satyr** Bacchus • **infant discovered by shepherds** Paris • **infant in the path of a plow** Hercules • **infant held by the ankle over a river** Achilles • **infant held by a judge or king** the judge or king is Solomon • **infant eaten by an old man** the old man is Saturn • **infant holding a snake in both hands** Hercules • **infant with wings** the soul; Cupid • **infant placed before a king and offered two dishes** the infant is Moses • see also **Christ child; child**

inkhorn attribute of authors, St. Augustine, St. Matthew and other evangelists (often the inkhorn is held by an angel in the latter cases)

inn place of freedom, conviviality, protection; power without pomp

inn keeper see **tapster**

insanity a disordered condition in the soul

insect short life; a reduced primeval monster; semen; in swarms they have a negative connotation, such as forces in the process of dissolution, or plague • see also specific insects, such as **mosquito, moth**, etc.

intercourse union of the male and female principles • see also **fornication**

intersection conjunction; communication; choice; the point at which change is sought or induced; a point of special power • see also **crossroads**

intestines the lower qualities; intuition; compassion; affection

intoxicant the libido; fornication

invisibility regression; repression; that which is repressed; dissociation; death

iopode see **centaur**

Ireland associated with drunkenness, laziness, superstition, querulousness

iris (flower) hope; light; purity; power; royalty; eloquence; sacred to Hera; attribute of the Virgin Mary,

the Passion of Christ, the Immaculate Conception (especially in Spanish art) • **flower language** my compliments; I have a message for you; *German iris*: archer, flame; *yellow iris*: flame, passion

iron war; strength; machinery; mental power; the mind; hardness; durability; constancy; cruelty; bondage; patience; force; punishment; attribute of the god Mars; associated with Aries, Scorpio, the Father-Spirit archetype • **Bible** solidity • **China** strength; firmness; determination; integrity; justice

irrigation the bestowing of truth upon the lower qualities

island isolation; solitude; death; refuge from the unconscious; the conscious; stability; superiority; refuge from mediocrity or the passions; consciousness and will as refuge from the unconscious; the synthesis of consciousness and will

Issachar agriculture

itching desire, especially sexual • **itchy palm** mercenary intent • **itchy elbows** joy

ivory purity; moral fortitude; hardness; resistance; wealth; Christ (in reference to the incorruptibility of his body in the tomb); attribute of the Virgin Mary • **ivory tower** retreat from the world, especially by an intellectual or academic; shutting one's eyes to reality; the Church; emblem of the Virgin Mary • **ivory quiver** attribute of Atlanta • **ivory scepter** attribute of Jove, Aeetes

ivy longevity; despondency; dependence; trustfulness; wedded love; fidelity; immortality; tenacity; friendship; death; love; tenacity of memory; ambition; lyric poetry; parasite; intoxicant; ingratitude; attachment; undying affection; sacred to Bacchus; associated with Capricorn; attribute of satyrs, Industry personified • **heraldry** strong and lasting friendship; constant love • **flower**

language friendship; fidelity; matrimony; *ivy sprig with tendrils:* eagerness to please

J

J associated with leadership, an elevated station, gain, intellect, culture, the Wheel of Fortune in the tarot deck, the number one, especially in a magnified sense (multiplied ten times); corresponds to the lungs, Virgo, Capricorn; symbolically the same as the letter "I," which see (this is especially true in any but modern times)

jackal death; intellect; keenness of smell; cowardly service

jackdaw ignorance; vanity; empty conceit; stupidity; a thief; shares the unfavorable symbolism of kites and crows, q.q.v.

Jacob's ladder (plant) in flower language: come down

jade power; purity; immortality; virtue • **China** emblem of the emperor, and of China itself; eternity; strength; perfection; excellence

jail *see* **prison**

Janus wholeness; the past and the future; history and prophecy; the desire to master all things; priest and monarch; all pairs of opposites

japonica in China: married happiness

jar a feminine symbol of containment; rain charm; source of plenty; still movement; burial attribute • **jar of ointment** attribute of Mary Magdalene • *see also* **vase; jug; urn; amphora**

jasmine delicate beauty; love; grace; fragrance; elegance; amiability; memory; separation; divine hope; heavenly felicity; attribute of the Virgin Mary • **China** the blossom indicates sweetness, and is an emblem of woman • **palm and jasmine** adoration of God • **flower language** deception; despair; a lie; *cape jasmine:* transport of joy, I am too happy; *Carolina jasmine:* separation; *Indian jasmine:* I attach myself to you; *Spanish jasmine:* sensuality; *white jasmine:* amiability; *yellow jasmine:* grace and elegance

jasper joy; wisdom; praise; friendship; second sight; associated with Aries, Libra • **red jasper** associated with Aries

jaundice envy; jealousy

javelin kingly force; martial readiness • *see also* **lance**

jawbone of an ass: Samson; the slaying of Abel by Cain

jay generally unfavorable; loose or flashy woman; simpleton; bumpkin

jelly human fear; spinelessness

jerkin ambiguity of thought

Jerusalem freedom; heaven; the Church • **Jerusalem with a sword above it** associated with Zephaniah

Jesse tree the human or royal genealogy of Jesus

jester the inversion of the king; a sacrificial victim; willful involution; inversion of the normal order; repressed unconscious urges; absolute innocence; related to seers, the abnormal, the unformed; a critic of Church and Establishment practices; may personify Folly

Jesus Christ religion; Christianity; the Church • *see also* **Christ child**

jet (mineral) mourning; wisdom

Jew avarice

jewels spiritual knowledge; the transience of earthly possessions (especially in a still life); may have infernal implications; attribute of the personifications of Vanity, Asia, Profane Love • **jewels guarded by a dragon or by other obstacles** the difficulty encountered in obtaining spiritual knowledge • **jewels hidden in caves**

or **underground** the intuitive knowledge of the unconscious • **woman casting off her jewels** Mary Magdalene • **jewels offered to a woman at a well** the woman is Rebecca • *see also* specific stones **diamond; ruby**, etc.

Job the faithful Christian; patience

Jonah precursor of the resurrection of Christ; resurrection; the Resurrection

jonquil in flower language: desire; from the 19th Century on, I desire a return of affection

Jordan River the River of Life; the flow of life essence from heaven to earth

journey adventure; the desire for adventure or change; spiritual pilgrimmage; search for the lost Mother; flight from the mother for fear of incest; aspiration; unsatisfied longing; evolution; seeking; enquiring; studying; desire to undergo profound spiritual experience • **journey into Hell or caverns** exploration of the unconscious • **journey abroad** may represent the cutting of family ties

Joy (tarot) *see* **Sun** (tarot)

Judas tree in flower language: unbelief, betrayal

judge restorer of natural balance; oracle

Judgment (tarot) the mystery of birth in death; awakening; renewal; personal consciousness starting to blend with the universal; healing; illumination; regeneration; hot headedness; Dionysian ecstasy

jug of water: cleansing of the soul; attribute of Penitence personified • **jug with water flowing from it** attribute of the Sea, personified • **eagle and jug** attribute of Hebe • *see also* **vase; jar; urn; pot; amphora**

Julian (Saint) bounty; liberality

juniper resilience; longevity; remembrance; immortality; soporific; protection from evil; associated with the Furies • **flower language** succor; protection; asylum

Juno wisdom; jealousy; the Terrible Mother

Jupiter (the god) superconsciousness; the intuition of the supernatural; judgment; the will; the king

Jupiter (planet) associated with reason, understanding, expansion, bulk, benevolence, the number five, the thighs, Saggitarius, Capricorn, Pisces

justica in flower language: the perfection of female loveliness

Justice (tarot) spiritual justice; balance of opposites; active administration of law; harmony; firmness; strict and correct behavior, restriction, pettiness, craft

K

K associated with personal magnetism, the number one in a magnified sense, also the number two, force, strength, sensitivity, cooperation, martial qualities, theater, nervousness, vitality; corresponds to the nerves, Leo, Mars

kangaroo gregariousness; peacefulness; sportiveness; lack of intelligence; emblem of Australia

katydid *see* **cicada**

keel stability; the lower instincts and desires

kennedia in flower language: mental beauty

kerchief on the head: sickness, a housewife • *see also* **handkerchief**

kestrel Christ's image in the world

kettle magic vessel of rejuvenation; restorer of lost youth; the underworld; realm of rebirth; the womb; inspiration; in cartoons, attribute of cannibals • *see also* **cauldron**

kettle drum emblem of Denmark

key authority; mystery; secrecy; discretion; wardenship; release; knowledge, especially forbidden knowledge; scholarship; education; enigma; the door to the underworld or heaven; a task to be performed and the means for carrying it out; the threshold of the unconscious; spiritual power; attribute of Janus, Hecate, the Church, Mithra, the pope, the Terrible Mother, St. Peter, St. Genevieve, Faithfulness personified • **bunch of keys** attribute of the Virgin Mary, St. Martha (usually attached to her girdle), St. Hippolytus, St. Peter, Adam, Cybele, Fidelity personified • **two keys crossed** home rule; the keys of Parliament on the Isle of Man; attribute of St. Peter; confession and absolution; excommunication and restoration • **two keys, one of silver, one of gold** heaven and earth; the power of the Church to bind and to loose • **two keys, one of gold, one of iron** attribute of St. Peter, the gold key opens heaven's gate, the iron key locks it • **gold key** philosophical wisdom; the key to the gate of heaven, or superconsciousness; the authority or material power of the Church; perfection • **silver key** psychological knowledge; material power; discernment; understanding; power of the subconscious • **diamond key** the power to act • **iron key** the key that locks up the gates of heaven *see also* **keyhole** • **antique key** associated with Hades • **angel holding a key, descending into a pit with a dragon** the Apocalypse • **finding a key** the stage prior to finding treasure • **Jewish** power; trust • **heraldry** trust; guardianship; violence; dominion; faithfulness; readiness to serve; attribute of chamberlains, masters of the cellar, etc.

keyhole vulva; a place for the entrance of demons, witches, etc., which can be guarded by filling it up or leaving an iron key in it

Khamsin God's punishment • *see also* "east wind" under the heading **wind**

kidney bodily constitution; venery • **Old Testament** sacrifice; seat of feelings

king universal and archetypal man; the grandeur of universal and abstract man; stability; self-control; dalliance; protection; divine right; supreme consciousness; elegance; the father; seat of life, energy and power; the supernatural; a concentrated father and hero image; the nation; the ideas of a nation • **crowned king** the consummation or victory of the supernatural • **aged king** the collective consciousness; world memory • **sick king** sterility of the spirit; the negative aspect of man; punishment for sins • **king and queen together** the union of heaven and earth, the conscious and the unconscious, the male and female principles

kingcup in flower language: ingratitude; childishness; desire for riches

kingfisher quiet; connubial faith; mourning • **China** gaudy raiment; beauty

kiss idol worship; peace; power to break a spell; usually has more to do with nutrition than with sex • **kissing a snake's head** fellatio

kite (bird) pride; scavenging; death; cruelty; senseless killing; cowardice; meanness; despicability; a false servant

kite (toy) venture; theory; experiment; idle recreation

kitten playfulness; wantonness; helplessness • *see also* **cat**

knee, kneeling moral strength; prayer; submission to the laws of order; reverence; respect; humility; petitioning; progress by restraining the lower qualities

knife vengeance; death; sacrifice; circumcision; phallus; the instinctive forces in man; a base, secret weapon, the inversion of the sword, which is an heroic weapon; attribute of Abraham, Isaac, the archangel Zadkiel, St. Bartholomew, St. James the Less, St. Lucy • **flaying knife** attribute of the satyr Marsyas, St. Bartholomew (especially three flaying knives) • **pruning knife** attribute of Pomona • **sacrificial knife** attribute of Abraham, the archangel Zadkiel • **knife in the hand or the head** • **attribute of St. Peter Martyr** • **knife with starry blue shield** emblem of Abraham • *see also* **dagger**

knight the spirit controlling the instincts and desires; a spiritually developed or chivalrous person; chivalry • **green knight** an apprentice or squire • **red knight** virility; passion; blood; wounds; sublimation; the ability to overcome all trials and baseness through sacrifice • **white knight** purity; innocence; illumination; gladness; the hero; the one chosen to conquer; open heartedness • **black knight** sinfulness; expiation; involution; penitence; the hidden; sorrow; reclusiveness • **knight errant** one who has not completed his spiritual development • **knight riding a goat** superiority; a saint

knitting related to weaving, spinning, q.q.v.

knock, knocking aspiration; death; birth; copulation; heartbeat

knot an unchanging psychic situation; interdependence; intimate relationship; intermingling streams; virginity; binding; agreement; an individual's existence; marriage; love; infinity; difficulty; entanglement; enclosure; protection; union • **China** longevity; a sign of Buddha; the "mystic," or endless knot • **Gordian knot** the labyrinth, which see • **knot interlaced with initials** marriage • **three knots in the cincture of a friar's habit** a member of

the Franciscan order (the knots represent faith, hope, and love)

kukui tree popular emblem of Molokai Island, Hawaii

L

L associated with success, popularity, versatility, intuition, activity, beauty, violent death, the divine Word; corresponds to the number three, the throat, Libra, Uranus, the Hanged Man in the tarot deck

laburnum in flower language: forsaken; pensive beauty

labyrinth the world; the underworld; divine inscrutability; the wind; pain; mental torture; fury; vulva; the unconscious; the loss of the spirit in the process of creation, and the consequent need to find it again; the difficulty uniting oneself with one's spirit and with God; error; remoteness from one's spirit and from God

ladder ambition; the gradual acquisition of knowledge; the ceaseless striving of man; the connection between heaven and earth; conjunction of heaven and earth; the Ascension of Christ; surmounting the difficulties of the material world; attribute of the Crucifixion, St. Benedict, St. Angela Merici, St. John Climacus, Jacob (especially with angels on the ladder) • **ladder to heaven, or monks in white habits on a ladder** associated with St. Romuald • **soldiers scaling city walls on ladders, nuns observing** associated with St. Clare • **people climbing up ladders against a house** associated with St. Andrew • **eagle atop a ladder** in Gnosticism: The Way

ladle attribute of St. Martha, housewives

lady slippers in flower language: fickleness, capricious beauty

ladybird see ladybug

ladybug good fortune; associated with red (which see), in the beneficial sense; connected with the scarab, which see • **Middle Ages** associated with the Virgin Mary

Lady's bed straw (plant) associated with the manger of Christ

lady's mantle (plant) in flower language: fashion

lagerstraemia in flower language: eloquence

lake prime matter; the occult; the mysterious; giver of fertility; uterine waters; source of creative power; transition of life and death, often in a destructive sense; the unconscious • **reflection of the lake** the conscious; revelation; self-contemplation

lamb sweetness; forgiveness; meekness; docility; weakness; innocence; sacrifice, sometimes unwarranted; temperance; Christ; God's love; frolic; purity; pure thought; the just man; attribute of St. Agnes, St. Catherine of Alexandria, St. Colette, St. Joachim, St. Agatha of Sicily, St. Francis of Assisi, sometimes St. Clement, John the Baptist as the forerunner of Christ, and the personifications of Innocence, Gentleness, Patience, Humility, Phlegmatic Man • **heraldry** patience; gentleness • **China** filial piety • **lamb with nimbus** Christ, often shown on a hill (which represents the Church) with four streams running down it (which represents the Gospels) • **lamb with cross** Christ; the Crucifixion; see also the "lamb with nimbus" entry, above • **slain lamb** the Passover • **lamb on an altar as a sacrifice** associated with Abel • **lamb lying down** the suffering of Christ; Christ carrying the sins of mankind • **lamb standing up** the triumphant, risen Christ • **lamb**

with white flag with a cross on it the body of Christ, that is, the Church (if the flag is on a cruciform staff, it indicates the way in which Christ died and thus redeemed mankind) • see also **sheep, fleece**

lameness a weak or corrupt soul; defect in the soul or spirit

lamia the Terrible Mother; cruelty; infanticide; an evil woman

lamp intelligence; learning; the word of God; immortality; guidance; light; goodness; vigilance; purity; virginity; love; piety; charity; beauty; self-sacrifice; attribute of Florence Nightingale, Hestia, Vesta, Psyche, Isis, the Persian sibyl, St. Lucy, the personifications of Night, Vigilance • **oil lamp** intelligence; learning; the Word of God • **seven lamps** the seven gifts of the Holy Spirit (see entry under flame); the Holy Spirit • **ten maidens with lamps** the five wise and five foolish virgins • **sanctuary lamp** in Catholic and Anglican churches: the presence of the Reserved Sacrament • **naked maiden with a lamp, standing over a sleeping god** Psyche standing over Cupid • **old man with a lamp** Diogenes • **abbot annointing a boy's lips with lamp oil** the abbot is St. Nilus • **genie issuing from a lamp** a magic source of wealth; male masturbation and its objectified emotional consequences • see also **lantern**

lamprey phallus; voracity; ingenuity; evil; sin; the debilitating effect of sin • **alone, or entwined with a snake** adultery

lance war; a kingly weapon; an earthly weapon as opposed to the spiritual implications of the sword; truth; discretion; phallus; attribute of the hunter, Diana, the Passion of Christ, St. Barnabas, St. Matthew, St. Jude, St. Longinus • **lance with three stones** attribute of St. Matthias • **broken lance** attribute of

St. George of Cappadocia • **lance with broken sword** attribute of Micah • **lance with spear and arrows** attribute of St. Thomas • **lance piercing a heart** the Passion of Christ • **heraldry** courage; martial readiness; defense of honor; speed; freedom

lancet attribute of a doctor, St. Cosimas, St. Damian • **doctor cutting a patient's forehead with a lancet** a quack operation for "stones in the head"

lantana in flower language: rigor; sharpness

lantern transitory life in the face of the eternal; transitory truth; distraction; individual light (as opposed to cosmic light); attribute of Judas and the betrayal of Christ, Persica, a hermit, St. Christopher, Diogenes • *see also* **lamp**

lap (human) procreation; protection; flirtation; euphemism for female genitalia

lapis lazuli nobility • **Rome** related to love, and to Venus • **Christianity** chastity; part of a bishop's ring

Lapland land of witchcraft and sorcery

lapwing royalty; craftiness; deceit; a stupid, conceited fellow, who thinks he knows better than his elders; treachery; an ill omen

larch impregnability; stability; independence; boldness • **flower language** audacity; boldness

lark dawn; gaiety; recklessness; activity; joy; wisdom; a disguise for Athena; natural art; visionary inspiration; the humility of the priesthood; treason; connected with heaven, love, spring

larkspur in flower language: swiftness; lightness; levity; *double larkspur*: haughtiness; *pink larkspur*: fickleness

larvae in Rome: evil souls

lash slavery; punishment; attribute of Hecate • **lash with bricks** Israel's

Old Testament captivity and forced labor • *see also* **scourge; whip; flagellation**

lasso knowledge; attribute of a cowboy in the American West

latch especially on a door, the ability to resist change

laurel inspiration; victory, especially in a spiritual sense; achievement in poetry, song, and the arts in general; fecundity; glory; merit; reward; joy; peace; death; mourning; protection; truce; perfidy; winter; chastity; emblem of Apollo; associated with the Muses • **portraiture** implies that the subject was a literary or artistic figure • **laurel sprouting from the arms of a maiden** Daphne • **laurel grove** Parnassus • **flower language** glory; reward of merit; the Arts; I change but in death; *common laurel*: perfidy; *ground laurel*: perseverance; *mountain laurel*: ambition, glory; *spurge laurel*: coquetry, desire to please • *see also* **bay**

laurestina in flower language: a token; I die if neglected

lavabo cleansing; purity

lavender (color) associated with the planet Neptune

lavender (plant) virtue; industry; acknowledgment; precaution; associated with Gemini • **French lavender** emblem of Distrust personified • **sea lavender** sympathy; *see also* flower language entry below • **flower language** distrust; associated with the asp that killed Cleopatra, also with the English viper; *sea lavender*: dauntlessness

laver of brass: Old Testament worship

lawn (grass) submission; emblem of suburbia

lead gravity; weight and density; especially in a spiritual sense; a base metal; stubbornness; ignorance; inertness; death; torture; hypocrisy; matter; associated with Capricorn, the planet Saturn • **dove embedded in lead** the spirit embedded in matter

leaf happiness; transitoriness; a true fact or idea; people coming and going • **dead leaf** sadness; death • **green leaf** nobility; sound judgment • **yellow leaf** old age • **girdle or leaves** attribute of St. Onuphrius • **oak leaf** bravery • **branch with green leaves** friendship; protection; a tavern

Leah the active life

leather resistance; lack of sympathy; stupidity; insensitivity; faithlessness • **a leather medal** farcical award for stupidity or inferiority

leaven spiritual nature permeating lower nature; the Kingdom of Heaven; the Word; Christian influence; increasing corruption; malice; wickedness • *see also* **yeast**

lectern in a Christian church: • **lectern with eagle** the Gospel taking flight • **lectern with pelican feeding her young** the atoning work of Christ • **double-headed lectern** the Old and New Testaments; the Law and the Gospels; the Epistles and the Gospels

leech avarice; intemperance; grandiloquence; emblem of a physician • **horse leech** unending greed

leek emblem of Wales; liveliness; attribute of St. David • *see also* **houseleek**

lees the lower instincts of man that remain unpurified

left side associated with the past, the sinister, the repressed, the illegitimate, the abnormal, involution, death, the unconscious, introversion, the magical, the moon, clumsiness, awkwardness

leg firmness; nobility; elevation; erection; founding; motion; speed; energy; victory; support of the soul; euphemism for genitals; supremacy (especially when bestriding something) • **very long legs** stirring

emotions; love of excitement • **short legs** often a characteristic of sun deities • **crossed legs, right over left** prayer; the position of Christ's legs on the cross; *in art*: the posture of Crusaders, Knights Templar, kings, noblemen • **youth's severed leg restored** associated with St. Anthony of Padua • **patient with one black leg and one white leg** attribute of SS Cosmas and Damian • **horse's leg removed for shoeing** attribute of St. Eloi

lemon fidelity (especially in love); grief; mockery; enthusiasm; pleasant thoughts; discretion; barrenness; failure; defeat; emblem of the Virgin Mary; occasionally the fruit of the Tree of Knowledge • **flower language** zest; *lemon blossoms*: fidelity in love; discretion

lemur (spirit) *see* **ghost**

Lent suffering and sacrifice, particularly of Christ; austerity; penance

lentil humbleness; poor man's food

Leo associated with reproduction, vital forces, solar power, the will, feelings and emotions, fire, clear judgment, perception, the spiritual beginnings of man

leopard ferocity; valor; stealth; bravery; destruction; fraud; jealousy; dark force; lust; sin; cruelty; the Antichrist; the Devil; the opinionated lower mind full of errors that are mingled with truth; attribute of Artemis, Bacchus, Fury personified • **heraldry** a valiant warrior who has engaged in hazardous undertakings; power and pride; freedom; cunning • **Egypt** Osiris; the dignity of the High Priest • **China** bravery; ferocity • **Middle Ages** Christ • **leopard with Christ and the Magi** the incarnation of Christ was necessary for the redemption of sin • **leopard lying with lamb or kid** peace • **crouching leopard** jealousy • *see also* **panther**

leper the lower mind troubled with

conflicting emotions, desires, and confused ideas

leprosy rotting of the spirit from lack of moral progress; divine punishment, especially for pride; punishment for eating tabooed food

Lethe oblivion; forgetfulness of the past

letter (epistle) communication; an ill omen

lettuce temperance • **Jewish** return of spring; resurrection; redemption; characteristic food of feasts • **flower language** coldness; cold-heartedness

level (tool) equality; temperance

Levi priest; priesthood without land

Leviathan envy; the waters of Chaos; rebellion against the creator; God's playfulness; duality; Evil personified • *see also* **whale**, with which it shares much symbolism

Libra associated with cosmic and psychic equilibrium, legality, justice, harmony, communication

lichen hardship • **flower language** dejection; solitude

licking flattery; subservience; affection

licorice (plant) in flower language: I declare against you

light the spirit; virtue; intellect; creative force; cosmic energy; the Word; purity; moral value; knowledge; wisdom; evolution; the masculine principle; creative force; optimism; the past; discovery; understanding; divine revelation; divine love • **Christian** belief; grace; charity; Christ

lighthouse safety; vigilance; watchfulness; religion; the Final Port; warning of danger; man's remoteness and solitude; Christ; salvation; the Word of God; the Bible; refuge

lightning manifestation of a deity's power; divine message; phallus; fecundity; the male orgasm; brevity; an act of God; attribute of Jupiter • **lightning through clouds** mythology • **lightning striking a tree**

near a monk the monk is St. Philip Benizzi

Lightning Struck Tower (tarot) *see* **House of God**

Liguria lying; deceit; abnormal sexual intercourse

lilac (color) friendship; fraternal love; sometimes, male homosexuality

lilac (plant) youth; first love; spring; fastidiousness; mourning; associated with Libra • **flower language** — *field lilac*: humility; *purple lilac*: the first emotions of love; *white lilac*: purity, modesty, youthful innocence

Lillith the Terrible Mother; temptress; the discarded mistress taking revenge

lily purity; virginity; the purified soul; heavenly bliss; connubial chastity; majesty; queenly beauty; grace; immortality; chastity; showiness; fertility; phallus; the masculine principle; desire; repentance; grief; sorrow; emblem of Upper Egypt, Easter, the Annunciation, the Immaculate Conception; attribute of virgin saints (especially in the early Church), the archangel Gabriel, the Erythraean sibyl, Christ, the Virgin Mary, St. Joseph, St. Clare, St. Dominic, St. Anthony of Padua, St. Louis of France, St. Louis of Toulouse, St. Scholastica, St. Gertrude, St. Euphemia, St. Francis of Assisi, St. Francis Xavier, St. Thomas Aquinas, St. Joachim, St. Catherine of Siena (usually surmounting a cross), St. Philip Neri (usually he is praying before an image of the Virgin Mary) • **lily with a dove** the Annunciation • **lily with carpenter's square** attribute of St. Joseph • **lily entwined around a crucifix attribute of St. Nicholas of Tolentino** • **lily with IHC in a triangle** the dual nature of Christ • **Jewish** attribute of Gabriel; trust in God; emblem of Judah • **flower language** majesty (especially the imperial lily); *day lily*: coquetry; *yellow lily*: falsehood, gaity; *white lily*: purity, sweetness • *see also* **water lily; lily of the valley**

lily of the valley daintiness; sweetness; humility; return of spring; return of happiness; modesty; attribute of the Virgin Mary, Christ, the Immaculate Conception, Advent; emblem of Israel; associated with Gemini • **flower language** the return of happiness

lime tree (genus Tilia, not the citrus tree) *see* **linden**

linden gentleness; modesty; sweetness; a "feminine" tree; hospitality; judgment; protection; associated with Sagittarius, Baucis in Greek mythology • **heraldry** (often the leaf only) tenderness; charm; grace • **leaf** lightness • **flower language** conjugal love; *American linden*: matrimony

linen purity; destiny; homage; divine truth; priestly dress; ultimate reality; wisdom; goodness; love; related to music, burial shrouds • **linen thread** attribute of the Fates • **woman in linen** a virtuous woman as opposed to a loose woman dressed in silk

linnet courtship; motherly love

lint (plant) in flower language: I feel all my obligations

lion the king; the sun; the masculine principle; the spirit; continual struggle; victory; an index of latent passions; the danger of being devoured by the unconscious; gold; blood; earth; fertility; the underworld; time; nobility; royal dignity; Christ as king; rarely, the Devil; valor; virility; strength; health; compassion; generosity; gratitude; an avenging god; wildness; ferocity; price; rage; ambition; melancholy; a sinner; a man between 30 and 40 years of age; male sexual desire; courage; associated with Leo, July, the Resurrection; attribute of Hosea, Samson, David, Daniel, St. Jerome, St. Mark, St. Adrian, St. Euphemia, St. Thecla, St. Mary of Egypt, St. Onuphrius, love goddesses, Rhea, Hecate, Ops, and other earth goddesses, Cybele, the personifications of Africa, Pride, Wrath, Choler, Victory; emblem of the tribe of Judah, Great Britain, England • **heraldry** courage; valor; a soldier • **Middle Ages** watchfulness; the Resurrection • **Christianity** emblem of contemplation • **two lions** attribute of St. Onuphrius, St. Paul the Hermit • **two lions back to back** sunrise and sunset • **lion skin** attribute of Hercules, Fortitude personified, sun heroes • **roaring lion** occasionally, the Devil • **lion being devoured by an eagle** victory of the evolutive over the involutive • **man wrestling with a lion** Samson, David, Hercules • **woman wrestling with a lion** Fortitude personified • **lion and harp** attribute of David • **lion with four wings** (Egypt) the south wind • **lion's body with human head** (Egypt) union of the intellect with physical power • **lion's body with human head and hands** the Beast of the Second Coming • **half lion/half goat** Pan; duality (love/hate, good/evil, etc.) • **lion at the feet of saints and martyrs** magnanimity • **lion eating straw** peace • **lion lying with calf, lamb, or kid** peace • **unharmed man in lion's den** David • **man attacked by a lion, hands trapped in a tree trunk** Milo of Croton • **lion with wings** emblem of St. Mark, Venice; attribute of Venice personified • **lion scratching out graves in the desert** associated with St. Anthony the Great, St. Paul the Hermit, St. Onuphrius, St. Mary of Egypt • **lion cub** Judah • **old lion** the setting sun • **young lion** the rising sun • **victorious lion** the exlatation of virility • **tamed lion** the subjugation of virility • *see also* **lionness**

lioness female sexual desire; protection; the Great Mother; maternity

lips associated with sexuality, language, the Word, eloquence, desire for knowledge • **art** the wind • **sealed lips** repression • **thin lips** cruelty; frailty • **thick lips** crudity; grossness

lisping infanthood; voluptuousness; homosexuality; associated with royalty, nobility, and upper classes in Spain

liver seat of passion, the soul; lust; strength; power; feeling; the baser qualities of the personality • **vulture pecking at someone's liver** divine punishment

liverwort in flower language: confidence

livery subservience; the body

lizard evil; piety; religion; spring; health; security; inactivity; immobility; regeneration; guardianship; divine inspiration; wisdom; military strategy; the Word; idolatry; impiety; malice; shyness; disrespect for elders; the power of evil; the illuminating influence of the Gospel; attribute of the Virgin Mary, the personifications of Logic, Affection • **Egypt** kindliness; benevolence; fecundity; devouring heat

lobelia in flower language: malevolence

lobster an unfeeling, grasping monster; bigotry; chaos; lechery; escape; attribute of Inconstancy personified • **Orient** longevity

lock *see* **padlock; latch**

locomotive sexuality; the libido; unconscious forces that threaten to overrun the conscious • *see also* **train**

locust (insect) scourge; force of destruction; wisdom; heathen; heretic; false prophet; seduction; divine wrath; the judgment of God; attribute of John the Baptist • **locust held by Christ** the conversion of the nations to Christianity • **horde of**

locusts divine wrath; a nation without Christ • similar to **grasshopper**, which see

locust tree in flower language: elegance; *green locust tree*: affection beyond the grave

lodestone attraction of any kind; guidance; emblem of the sun

lodge retreat from the world; solitariness; melancholy

loincloth of leaves: attribute of St. Onuphrius, St. Paul the Hermit and other anchorites

loins procreation • **girding of the loins** the restraint of passion and the turning toward the spirit

loitering spiritual inertia

London pride in flower language: frivolity

longevity implies living in concord with God

loom industry; the mysterious strands of life woven into one span; fortune; chance • **spider's web with woman at loom, or woman weaving watched by the goddess Minerva** Arachne • *see also* **weaving**

lords and ladies (plant) *see* **arum**

loss guilt; death; spiritual bankruptcy

lote tree in flower language: concord

lotus the sun; spiritual evolution; Nirvana; life; immortality; the supremely sacred flower; the soul transcending the flesh; the Christian; the Mystic Center; resurrection; human rebirth; the heart; purity; creative power; fire; light; repose; fecundity; the feminine principle; the sexual prison of marriage; attribute of Osiris, Isis • **Egypt** royalty • **China** summer; fruitfulness; offspring; July; a sacred flower • **mythology** dreaminess; indolence • **lotus blossom** beauty; self-fructification • **five petalled lotus** birth; initiation; marriage; retirement; death • **thousand petalled lotus** final revelation • **flower language** eloquence; *flower alone*: estranged love; *leaf alone*: recantation

louse (insect) a pest; filth; disease; love

love-in-a-mist in flower language: perplexity

love-in-a-puzzle in flower language: embarassment

love-lies-bleeding in flower language: hopeless, not heartless

Lovers (tarot) the right choice; moral beauty; integrity; uncertainty; temptation; antagonism; equilibrium; union; harmony of inner and outer life; human love; the tension between sacred and profane love; antagonistic but complementary forces creating an equilibrium

lozenge (shape) the mother; the female genitals; attribute of the Virgin Mary • **heraldry** an unmarried woman; a widow; noble birth; justice; honesty; constancy

lucerne in flower language: life

Lucifer pride

lunacy, lunatic *see* **insanity**

lupin sensitivity; endurance; generosity; associated with the underworld • **flower language** voraciousness; imagination

lute marital bliss; friendship; instrument of lovers, troubadors, divine praise; lasciviousness; the androgyne; scholarliness; attribute of the personifications of Music, Hearing, the Lover; occasional attribute of Apollo, Orpheus, Polyhymnia • **lute with a broken string** discord

lycanthrope *see* **werewolf**

lychnis in flower language — *meadow lychnis*: wit; *scarlet lychnis*: sunbeaming eyes

lying (down) safety • **lying prone** mourning; humility

lynx ferocity; deceit; ingratitude; forgetfulness; cleanliness

lyre the relationship between heaven and earth; the harmonious union of cosmic forces; poetry; song; concord; emblem of conjugal love; attribute of Apollo, Mercury, Orpheus, Erato, Poetry personified, Arion (usually riding on a dolphin), occasionally Terpsichore • **heraldry** poetry; contemplation • **Grecian lute** triumph of the intellect; realism • **seven-stringed lyre** the seven planets known to the ancients; the seven note scale in music, etc. • **twelve-stringed lyre** the zodiac, the twelve note scale in music, etc.

M

M associated with strength of character, orderliness, concentration, enlightenment of the soul and spirit, work, nobility, indomitability, transformation, change, the number four, the planet Saturn, Death in the tarot deck, masculinity when printed angular, femininity when printed rounded • **as a monogram** the Virgin Mary (especially when shown with a crown) • **as a brand on a thumb** a murderer

M.A. monogram of the Virgin Mary (especially when shown with a crown)

M.R. monogram of the Virgin Mary (especially when shown with a crown) • **on a shield** attribute of the archangel Gabriel

macaroni foolishness; flashiness; insolence; lying; immorality

mace royal office; divine office; annihilation or destruction as opposed to simple victory; the subjective assertive tendency in man; authority, especially of the state; battle weapon of medieval bishops; attribute of Hercules • **Egypt** the creative Word • *see also* **club; scepter**

machines their symbolism derives from their particular shapes, functions, or other dominant characteristics; they commonly have ingestive, digestive, reproductive, or sexual meanings; they commonly have infernal implications, or are connected with soulless technology

madder (plant) talkativeness • flower language calumny

madwort in flower language: tranquillity

Maenad *see* Bacchante

magenta associated with the planet Mars

maggot immortality; death; decomposition; filth

magic inner and unobserved processes within the soul by which the lower qualities are raised to a higher level (especially in white magic); black magic has infernal implications

magician *see* sorcerer

Magician (tarot) personal will in union with the Divine; gifts of the spirit; occult wisdom; consciousness; inquiry; man in his struggle with occult powers

magnet *see* lodestone

magnolia magnificence; fecundity; love of nature; feminine sweetness and beauty; beauty; love; perseverance; pride; power; the lofty soul; sensuousness; emblem of the South in the U.S. • China magnolia blossoms: feminine beauty, May • flower language love of nature; *laurel-leaved magnolia*: dignity; *swamp magnolia*: perseverance

magpie mischief; chattering; thievery; indiscretion; destroyer of vermin and insects; a woman 20 to 30 years old; dissimulation; attribute of Dionysus, St. Oda, Dissimulation personified • China good luck emblem; an impending visitor

maiden virginity; innocence; any new start, dawn, spring, etc.; grace; gentleness • maiden slaughtered by tyrant fertility conquered •

maiden killed by a natural calamity flood, frost, etc. • maiden abducted by a black bearded king in a chariot Rape of Proserpine • maiden abducted by a white bull rape of Europa • maiden abducted by a young man, toward ships in a harbor the abduction of Helen of Troy • two maidens, with two soldiers on horseback the two soldiers are Castor and Pollux • *see also* woman; virgin

maidenhead secrecy

maidenhair fern pubic hair • in flower language discretion

maidwort *see* madwort

maiming a weakness or defect in the soul; revenge for maiming shows some vestige of moral strength remains • *see also* mutilation

maize *see* corn

malachite prosperity; longevity; health; success in love

male *see* man; boy

mallow beneficence; rankness; attribute of Benevolence personified • China associated with September • flower language mildness; *marsh mallow*: beneficence; healing; *Syrian mallow*: consumed by love, persuasion; *Venetian mallow*: delicate beauty

maltese cross *see* cross

Mammon avarice; temptation

man the conscious; the spirit; heaven; fire; the imagination • old man the father; the master; tradition; contemplation; justice; old and/or tired ideas; the setting sun • young man the governed; the hero; subversion; boldness; intuition; the primitive mind; new ideas; the rising sun • muscular and/or hairy man energetic and strong mental qualities • man with wings St. Matthew (especially with book and/or pen, especially with an angel dictating or pointing toward heaven) • man's head on a woman's body solid and profound judgment • twelve men (often each with a sheep) the Apostles • **old man with wings carrying off a naked girl** Boreas • **old man with serpent tails for feet** Boreas • *see also* **boy; wild man**

manchineal tree in flower language: hypocrisy; falsehood; duplicity

mandorla perpetual sacrifice and regeneration; perfect blessedness; birth into the next world; spiritual glory

mandrake the soul in its negative and minimal aspects; the Virgin Mary; associated with magical powers; thought to grow under the gallows of murderers • **flower language** horror; rarity

manger ignorance from which wisdom rises; humility from which charity rises; envy; attribute of the Nativity of Christ, the sibyl Cumana • **manger with enthroned lamb** the humiliation and exaltation of Christ, respectively

mani in China: richness; benefaction; the Buddhist trinity (Buddha, his Word, the priesthood)

maniple spirituality; purification; good works; vigilance; penitence; strength; endurance; the order of subdeaconship; the bands that held the wrists of Christ in the Garden of Gethsemane, when he was scourged, and when he was dragged through the streets

manna goodness; truth; spiritual sustenance; God's word; poetic inspiration; the Eucharist; the Bread of Life; a free and valuable gift; God's grace

mantelleta worn as a sign of limited jurisdiction or authority, red for a cardinal, purple for a bishop

manticore a storm demon; the personification of a Sirocco; a beastly rationalist • **heraldry** a soldier

mantis courage; persistence; voracity; cruelty and greed camouflaged by a hypocritical attitude of prayer or religiosity; female viciousness

mantle (clothing) attribute of Elijah, Elisha • **cast off mantle** attribute of Hosea • **mantle enveloping a deity** the unrevealed aspect • **black mantle** attribute of Night • **green mantle** attribute of St. Anne, St. John • **yellow mantle** attribute of St. Joseph, St. Peter • **russet mantle** attribute of Dawn • *see also* **cloak**

manure fertility; fertilization • *see also* **excrement; dung**

maple retirement; conjugal love; earthly, bourgeois happiness; reserve • **in the autumn** past happiness; transitoriness • **maple leaf** emblem of Canada; also associated with New England in the U.S. • **flower language** reserve

marble cold beauty; death; authority; inflexibility; durability; eternity

mare fertility; witchcraft; erotic madness; the Terrible Mother; the Mother; the mother as protector • *see also* **horse**

marguerite (flower) emblem of the sun; innocence

marigold the sun; constancy; endurance in love (especially of women); grief; misery; mercy; incorruptibility; innocence; comeliness; despair; associated with Leo; attribute of the Virgin Mary, Despair personified • **heraldry** devotion; piety • **marigolds and poppies** in the Orient: soothing of grief • **marigolds and cypress** despair and death, respectively • **flower language** grief; sorrow; pain; chagrin; despair; *African marigold*: a vulgar mind; *corn marigold*: comeliness; *French marigold*: jealousy; *fig marigold*: idleness; *garden marigold*: uneasiness; *prophetic marigold*: prophecy; *small cape marigold*: omen, presage; *marigolds mixed with roses*: the sweet sorrows of love; *marigolds mixed with red flowers*: the varying course of life

marjoram grief; marriage • **flower language** beneficence; blushes

mark(ing) *see* tattoo(ing)

maror for Jews: a reminder of the bitterness of their history

marriage the union of the conscious and the unconscious; the union of the male and female principles; the urge to unite what is in fact discrete • days associated with marriage Monday for wealth / Tuesday for health / Wednesday the best of all / Thursday for crosses / Friday for losses / Saturday, no luck at all

marrow manly prowess; semen; lust; the center of being

Mars war; action; destruction; objective evil; the idea that there is no creation without sacrifice; associated with things martial, the driving force, iron, bloodstone, asbestos, brimstone, the number three, Tuesday, tigers, panthers, wolves, sharks, the head, the genitals, Aries, Scorpio

marsh mallow (plant) *see* mallow

martin (bird) domestic happiness; a dupe

martlet in heraldry: the fourth son of a family; cunning; alertness; good reputation; subsisting on merit and virtue

marvel of Peru (plant) in flower language: timidity

Mary (mother of Christ) *see* Virgin Mary

mask dissimulation; ambiguity; equivocation; possesses a magic quality; indication of what the wearer would like to be; protection; hypocrisy; hollowness; attribute of the personifications of Deceit, Vice, Night • mask with a frown tragedy; from the 17th Century on, attribute of Melpomene • mask with a smile comedy; from the 17th Century on, attribute of Thalia • *see also* disguise

mason *see* stone mason

mast aspiration; belief; the connection between heaven and earth; the Tree of Life; the world axle; pride; energy • mast on a ship the androgyne • lowered mast a change in belief or opinions • broken mast submission; defeat

mat the unrolling of a mat signifies the unfolding of life

match (fire) uprightness; hope

matron the domineering mother; protection; the Church; personification of a city

mattock toil; attribute of Adam after the Fall

matzoh for Jews: suffering; affliction; hope

mausoleum *see* sarcophagus

maypole the Tree of Life; the world axis; union of opposites; the phallic-reproductive powers of nature together with the vulva-circle regulation of time and motion

maze *see* labyrinth

meadow ill fortune; sadness; peace; humbleness; patience; dreaminess; gladness; limitation; uniformity; lust; connected with the river (of life)

meadowsweet in flower language: uselessness

measuring with a line: associated with Zechariah • with a rod and a line associated with Shamash

medal honor; glory; victory; prize • leather medal a farce; a reward for stupidity or inferiority

Medusa the Terrible Mother; primal sexuality; sin; the dangerous female

melody *see* music

Melusina intuitive genius • heraldry virginity; motherly love; seafaring ancestors • *see also* mermaid

men *see* man

menhir the masculine; world axis; vigilance; protection

menorah (seven branched) emblem of Judaism; the Tree of Life; Old Testament worship; the Church; an attribute of the Temple in Jerusalem; the seven gifts of the Holy Spirit, the seven Patriarchs of Mankind, the seven Righteous Men, the seven celestial spheres, etc.; the six days of creation, with the center light the sabbath • *see also* **seven**

menorah (eight branched) emblem of Judaism; Chanukah (especially when displayed in the home or synagogue)

Mephistopheles craftiness; cynicism; the negative aspect of the psychic function which has broken away from the spirit to acquire independence

merchant avarice

Mercury (god) manly grace; messenger of heaven; the Holy Spirit; conscience; intellectual contemplation; intellectual energy; potentialities; occasionally, intelligence; conductor of the souls of the dead; Reason, Eloquence, personified

mercury (metal) speed; adaptability; inconstancy; uncertainty; the unconscience; the dominant female principle; the feminine; associated with Gemini, Virgo, the planet Mercury

Mercury (planet) associated with the intellect, the nervous system, the stomach, Gemini, Virgo, communication, the number four, intuition, duality, free will

Merehim pestilence

Merlin enslaved imagination

mermaid sensual pleasure; fatal allurement; the unconscious; the dual nature of Christ; the power of song-magic; the power of seduction; attribute of St. Christopher, St. Margaret • **heraldry** eloquence; sea-faring ancestors • *see also* **Melusina**

merman similar in most respects to mermaids, which see

mesembryanthemum in flower language: idleness

metal wealth; war; the senses; eternity; the libido; energy solidified • **base metals** associated with the flesh, the desires • **precious metals** associated with the spirit • **molten metals** conjunction of opposites: fire/water, solid/liquid, etc. • **metal worker** *see* **blacksmith** • *see*

also specific metals, such as **gold; silver; copper, lead,** etc.

meteor generally, an unfavorable omen

meteorite heavenly creative fire; revelation; seed; spiritual messenger; spiritual life that has descended to earth

mezerion in flower language: the desire to please

midnight gloom; solitude; mortification; the witches' hour

mignonette in flower language: your qualities surpass your charms

milfoil *see* **yarrow**

milk the elixir of life; regeneration; abundance; fertility; nourishment; wisdom; concord; kindness; truth; semen • **milk and honey** abundance; heavenly food; Canaan • **horn of milk** attribute of the sibyl Cimeriana • **goat's milk** error; desire • **mother's milk or cow's milk** higher nature; innocence • *see also* **breast**

milkmaid robust, but not too discriminate love; disguise of Loki

milkvetch in flower language: your presence softens my pain

milkwort associated with hermits

Milky Way the pathway to heaven

mill the Gospel; fertility; the revolving heavens; time; greed; habitual and uncreative thinking; logic as a feeble protection against passion; the Church • *see also* **water mill**

miller associated with the mill, which see

millet a sheaf of millet: attribute of Preservation personified

millipede regression; fragmentation of the psyche

millstone heavy burden; hardness; punishment; gravity; martyrdom; attribute of St. Vincent of Saragossa, St. Florian, St. Christina • **heraldry** determination; going one's own way • **two millstones** mutual converse of human society • **ass with a millstone** Obedience personified

mimosa sensitiveness; fastidiousness; exquisiteness; associated with Sagittarius; emblem of Australia, South Africa • **flower language** sensitivity; bashfulness; delicate feelings

minaret a torch of spiritual illumination

miner extraction of spiritual values; related to Mars; shares in much of the symbolism of the blacksmith, which see

Minerva *see* **Athena**

minnow insignificance

minotaur *see* **monsters**

Minstrel (tarot) *see* **Magician**

mint (plant) virtue; attribute of the Virgin Mary • **Jewish** the bitterness of their bondage • **flower language** virtue

mirror imagination; thought; unconscious memories; consciousness; self-conciousness; self-realization; the ego; introspection; truth; wisdom; fertility; love; the soul; virginity; reflection of one's inner self, feelings, or emotions; attribute of the personifications of Truth (especially a hand mirror), Prudence, Pride, Vanity, Sight, Lust; attribute of Venus; feminine pride; seduction; retrospection; prophecy; door or hole to the "other side"; thesis and antithesis; magical in that it may remember what it sees • **old man and child with mirror** Socrates • **two lovers in a mirror** Rinaldo and Armida • **mirror and serpent** attribute of Prudence personified • **spotless mirror** the Immaculate Conception; attribute of the Virgin Mary • **mirror with the image of the Virgin Mary in it** attribute of St. Germinianus

mist things indeterminate; illusion; the intermediate world between the formal and non-formal; care; associated with the distant past, memory; related to clouds, which see • **rising mist** the female principle in nature, desiring the male

mistletoe fertility; regeneration; life; protection; immortality; atonement; good will; reconciliation of opposites; witchcraft; paganism; sacred to the Druids; associated with Christmas • **flower language** I surmount all obstacles

mitre the flame of the Holy Spirit; Pentecost; the two rays of light that came from the head of Moses when he received the Ten Commandments; Old Testament priesthood; attribute of St. Sylvester, popes, cardinals, bishops, occasionally abbots • **white mitre** now worn by bishops, but once also worn by cardinals and some abbots (an abbot's mitre was usually unadorned); an occasional attribute of St. Benedict • **three mitres on the ground** attribute of St. Bernardino of Siena, St. Bernard of Clairvaux • **triple mitre** attribute of the pope • **mitre and censer** attribute of Melchizedek • **mitre lappets** (fanons) the letter and the spirit of the Old and New Testaments

mock orange in flower language: counterfeit; brotherly love

mocking bird mimicry; courage

moistness falsity

mold (tool) nature; mother

mold (plant) decay

mole (animal) blindness; idolatry; lies; avarice; timidity; industry; keen hearing; wisdom from the underworld; destruction; death; attribute of Avarice personified

molehill insignificance

Monday *see* **days**

money in two hands: Judas • **woman giving money away** St. Elizabeth of Hungary • **dish of money** attribute of St. Laurence

money bag attribute of Judas, St. Cyril, St. Laurence, St. Nicholas of Myra, Avarice personified, occasionally St. Matthew • **money bag with thirty pieces of silver** attribute of Judas • **three money bags** attribute of St. Matthew • open money bag(s) charity to the poor

monk solitude; contemplation; saints represented as monks include St. Anthony of Padua and St. Anthony the Great • monk with claw or cloven hoof showing from under the habit the Devil in his temptation of Christ • monks in white habits on a ladder assoc. with St. Romuald

monkey sexual desires; imitation; maliciousness; unconscious activity; the baser forces; pettiness; the sanguine temperament; lasciviousness; flattery; hypocrisy; melancholy; pride; idle foolishness; attribute of the personifications of Idolatry, Dissimulation, Inconstancy, Avarice • China trickery; ugliness; said to have the power to drive away evil and, hence, bring success, health, and protection

monkshood (plant) in flower language: chivalry; knight errant

monolith resurrection; eternal life; unity counterbalancing multiplicity; primitive life; associated with Osiris; related to the solar, masculine, and procreative principles

monster primordial life; cosmic forces one step removed from chaos; the libido; the unconscious; the instincts that hinder man in his search for truth; an unbalanced psychic function; predominance of the baser forces in life being fought by the spiritual forces (often in the form of a knight) • fighting a monster the struggle to free the conscious from the unconscious • monster ravaging the countryside a bad king • man-eating monster the unconscious threatening to devour the conscious • aquatic monster a cosmic or psychological situation at a deeper level than land monsters

monstrance attribute of St. Clare, St. Hyacinth, St. Thomas Aquinas, St. Norbert (usually with spider); the Eucharist

moon the feminine principle; resurrection; abode of the dead; inconstancy; a regenerating receptacle of the soul; the mutable; the cyclic; the transitory; potential evil; serene loveliness; chastity; virginity; imagination; regulator of water, rain, the fecundity of women and animals and the fertility of plants; passivity; the maternal; the soul; the psyche; the unconscious; lunacy; magic; death; silence; coldness; isolation; opposing values (male/female, constancy/inconstancy, etc.); the physical nature of Christ; the Church reflecting the light of Christ, however, sometimes the Synagogue, with the Church represented as the sun; associated with femininity, emotion, the number two, the sea, Pisces, Scorpio, Cancer; attribute of Rachel • crescent moon chastity; the female; Islam; the Islamic world; attribute of Diana, Luna, the Virgin Mary; *on an outhouse door*: use reserved for females • full moon and the sun surrounded by twelve stars Jacob's wife, Jacob, and their twelve sons, respectively • moon and sun in scenes of the Crucifixion allusion to the convulsions of the heavens • red moon indication of the activity of witches • "blood" on the moon augur of disaster • moonlight distorted truth

Moon (tarot) intuition; imagination; magic; reflection; objectivity; error; arbitrary fantasy; imaginative sensitivity; upward progress of man; the descent of the life force from the heavens; involution; regression in order to make a fresh start; the rejection of reason

moonwort in flower language: forgetfulness

moonstone thoughtfulness

moorings the higher self; God; the Church; the attachment of the physical and spiritual, or spiritual and instinctual

morning childhood; youth; any propitious time; pristine happiness; Paradise; renewal of love; bringer of health, freshness, wealth; release of treasures locked in darkness or myth; new beginning • **red sky at morning** an ill omen • *see also* **dawn**

morning glory associated with Virgo • **flower language** affectation

mortar and pestle pharmacy; pharmacology; attribute of St. Cosmas and St. Damian

moschatel in flower language: weakness

mosquito unrest; disquietude; wickedness; rebellion; annoyance • *see also* **insect**

moss humility; service; friendship; boredom; parasite • **flower language** maternal love; *Iceland moss*: health; *mosses gathered together*: ennui

moth corruption; parasite; decay; destruction • *see also* **insect**

mother the life principle, indifferent to individual human suffering; destiny; wisdom; material life; the unconscious; the collective unconscious; strength; the feminine principle; can have either a benevolent or destructive connotation • *see also* **woman; stepmother**

motherwort in flower language: secret love; concealed love

motor *see* **engine**

motorcycle often has a sexual connotation • *see also* **vehicle; steed**

mould *see* **mold**

Mount Ararat the second cradle of humanity; the "navel" of the world

mountain loftiness of spirit; spiritual elevation; the connection between heaven and earth; realm of meditation; communion with the spirit, deities, wisdom; solitariness; resurrection; world axis; freedom; peace; majesty; attribute of St. David • **mountain peak** meditation; achievement; victory; Oneness • **twin mountain peaks** duality •

snow covered mountain nobility; cold reasoning; abstract thought • **two brass mountains** the gates of heaven • **interior of a mountain** sometimes the abode of the dead • **mountain with temple on top of it** associated with Micah • **mountain with feet above it protruding from a cloud** Nahum's vision

mourning bride (plant) in flower language: unfortunate attachment; I have lost all

mouse timidity; poverty; humility; insignificance; domesticity; untidiness; madness; silence; cleverness; vanity; gratitude; fecundity; decay; passing time; destruction; evil; associated with the Devil, especially in the Middle Ages; occasional attribute of St. Fina • **coat or cloak of mouse skin** humility

mouth creation (as in speech); destruction (as in devouring); the creative Word; a "door" • **open mouth** the female • **closed mouth, or with tongue sticking out** the male

moving plant (plant) in flower language: agitation

mozzetta a non-liturgical garment worn by popes and cardinals when not in Rome, and by bishops, archbishops, and abbots within the limits of their jurisdiction

mud the emergence of matter; a nascent state; evil; primordial slime; excrement; the opposite of marble, which see • **sinking in mud** fear of maternal incest; devouring

mugwort ingredient in love potions; beer flavoring • **flower language** tranquillity; happiness

mulberry tree kindliness and sharpness combined; slowness; wisdom; tragic love; related to silk, war (especially the juice) • **China** industry; the comforts of home; a mulberry staff indicates mourning for a mother

mule perversity; stubbornness; pride; hypocrisy; heresy; sterility;

mutual help among underdogs; durability; a faithful worker; mount of a king or cardinal • *see also* **ass**

mullein in flower language: white mullein — good nature

mullet lasciviousness; stupidity; swiftness

multiplicity disintegration; regression; loss of unity

mum *see* **chrysanthemum**

mummy life; magic beyond the grave; ancient Egypt; a curse; attribute of Joseph, Jacob

murder to remove an idea or principle from one's mind, or from existence

mushroom suspicion; the ephemeral; bad news; a wanderer; related to fairies; emblem of Bohemians in the U.S.

music order; harmony; a general restorative; related to fertility; harmony arising from chaos; the harmony of the unvierse; will; mockery; generally indicative of the prevailing atmosphere (chaotic, erot, somber, etc.) • **music written on a scroll** attribute of St. Ambrose, St. Gregory the Great, St. Cecilia

musical instruments attribute of St. Cecilia • **stringed instruments** usually associated with joy • **metal instruments** usually associated with warriors, nobles, pageantry, war • **wooden instruments** usually associated with the common folk • **Note**: instruments also derive a great deal of their significance from their construction and their sound • **angels with instruments** praise of God • *see also* specific instruments (**drum; flute**, etc.)

musician the fascination with death; harmony with divine nature; the mind which fosters higher emotions

musk female sexuality; attribute of the Virgin Mary

musk plant in flower language: weakness

mustard (plant) fertility; abundance; patience; faith; the Church; indifference; great growth from small beginnings

mutilation fertility rite; proof of courage at puberty; mourning; grief; covenant of friendship • *see also* **maiming**

myrobalan in flower language: privation; bereavement

myrrh a sacred ointment; embalming; purification; chastity; gladness; higher qualities; peace; bliss; truth; logic; natural good and wisdom; attribute of the Nativity of Christ, the Virgin Mary, Nicodemus • **casket of myrrh** attribute of Balthazar, Magus • **myrrh and aloes** the Passion of Christ; martyrdom; sorrow; pity; Christ's priestly office • **flower language** gladness

myrtle love; victory; amiacability; constancy; immortality; humaneness; virginity; messianic promises; everlasting love; conjugal fidelity; supplication; life; nature; happiness; peace; triumph; justice; prophecy; pastoral poetry; purity; mastery of impulses; connected with the underworld, death, immortality, resurrection; attribute of the Virgin Mary, Venus, the three Graces, Dionysus, the Gentiles who were converted by Christ, Academy personified • **myrtle with sleeping soldier** Scipio the Younger • **burnt myrtle** envy

N

N associated with alertness, inconstancy, imagination, water, the ash tree, the number five, entrance, initiation, physical existence, the liver, the nerves, Saturn, Aquarius, Scorpio, and Temperance in the tarot deck

naiad oracle; prophecy

nails (body) attribute of a seductress, an evil being, an aristocrat, the leisure class • **nail clipping** purification • **nail clippings** magically charged; part of the soul • **white specks on nails** sign of lies

nails (for wood) phallus; world axis; tenacity; support; attribute of Christ's crucifixion (early use was four nails, later, three nails became the customary number); attribute of the Hellespontic sibyl, St. Helena, St. Joseph of Arimathea, St. Bernard, St. Louis IX • **heraldry** suffering • **iron   nails** protection against evil • **finding a nail** (especially rusty) good luck • **nails protruding from fingers** St. Erasmus

nakedness see **nudity**

name the soul; key to power; renaming a ship is unnatural, or bad luck, occasionally this belief is carried over to other objects or beings

napkin with Christ's likeness on it: attribute of St. Veronica • **napkin with cruse of wine** attribute of the Good Samaritan

Narcissus grace; self-consciousness; self love; the death of youth; egotism; introspection

narcissus (flower) attribute of the Furies, Revenge personified; shares in the symbolism of Narcissus in mythology, which see, above • **Christian** triumph of divine love over worldliness and the triumph of sacrifice over selfishness • **narcissus fumes** madness • **flower language** egotism; *poet's narcissus*: egotism; selfishness; self love; *yellow narcissus*: disdain

nasturtium in flower language: patriotism; trophy of war

navel origin; midpoint; the mystic center; world axis; fertility; order; peace; the point on the mental plane midway between higher and lower nature; euphemism for vulva; related to prophecy

navigator conductor of the soul

Nazareth a point of progress on the path to perfection

Nebuchadnezzar (tarot) see **Wheel of Fortune**

neck purified emotions; strength; stubbornness; execution; has a sexual and phallic connotation • **wound on the neck** attribute of St. Lucy • **three wounds on the neck** attribute of St. Cecilia

necklace unification of diversity; order from chaos; fertility; riches; light; protection; rank office; a cosmic and social symbol of ties and bonds; an erotic bond (especially on females); attribute of sky goddesses (Aurora, Diana, etc.) • **Rome**-*gold necklace*: attribute of a foreign soldier; *silver necklace*: attribute of a soldier who was a Roman citizen • **broken necklace, with scattered beads** psychic dismemberment

necktie cohesion; social bonds; phallus

nectar the soul's entire service to the highest ideals

needle marriage; the intellect; repression; phallus; attribute of a tailor, housewife • **being pricked on the finger by a needle** an ill omen

Negro child of darkness; the primitive and emotional self; the collective unconscious; the Terrible Father; the baser passions; the darker side of the personality; the instincts; the soul before entering on the path of spiritual evolution • *see also* **complexion**

neigh(ing) an expression of lust, pride, bragging

Neptune (god) the negative aspect of the spirit and of humanity; the regressive and evil side of the unconscious

Neptune (planet) associated with intuition, spiritual aspirations, extrasensory perception, treacherous tendencies, the deepest layers of the soul, the number nine, the feet,

Pisces, regeneration, the subconscious, the cosmic conscience, wholeness, the Bronze Age, the god Neptune

nerve in Rome: euphemism for phallus

nest heaven; haven for growth of the spirit; home; protection; comfort

Nestor justice; eloquence; wisdom

net the Church; entrapment; death; fertility and love; snare; craftiness; repression; entanglement (which see); attribute of a supreme deity • **fishnet** searching the waters of the unconscious; attribute of St. Andrew; associated with fishing, fisherman, q.q.v. • **drag net** the Church; the police • **lovers under a net** Venus and Mars

Netherlands associated with sailing, drinking, gluttony, stinginess, rudeness, the Renaissance

nettle annoyance; distress; envy; slander; cruelty; death; repentance; danger; an aphrodisiac • **flower language** cruelty; *stinging or burning nettle*: slander; *nettle tree*: concert, plan

night the unconscious; the feminine principle; death; evil; winter; germination; potentiality; darkness; passivity; involution; precursor of creation; the subconscious; the lustfull female; feminine fertility; the womb

night blooming cereus in flower language: transient beauty

nightingale harmony: exclusiveness; passion; unrequited love; night love; worldly love; herald of spring; wakefulness; purity; poetic escape or ecstasy; the Devil's deceit; the tragic victim; rape; superstition; betrayal

nightjar (bird) an ill omen; the soul of an unbaptized child

nightmare the longing of man for God; an ill omen; the unconscious threatening the conscious; sexual repression, especially of incest

nightshade death; darkness; witchcraft • **deadly nightshade** (belladonna) death • **nightshade and foxglove together** punishment and pride, respectively • **flower language**—*deadly nightshade* (belladonna): silence; *enchanter's nightshade*: sorcery, witchcraft, skepticism, dark thoughts; *woody or bittersweet nightshade*: truth

Nike strength; progress; freedom; triumph; courage

nimbus holiness; saintliness; sanctity; attribute of Mithras, Apollo, Helios, deified Roman emperors • **in the East** sanctity • **in the West** power • **circular nimbus** attribute of the Virgin Mary, sacred persons, the personifications of the cardinal virtues (Faith, Hope, Charity, etc.) • **square or rectangular nimbus** attribute of a person honored while still living • **triangular nimbus** sometimes God the Father • **cruciform or cross within a circle** used only for Christ • **nimbus around the entire body** see glory • **three-rayed nimbus** used for members of the Trinity • **hexagonal nimbus** used for a figure considered one degree below a saint; attribute of the personifications of the cardinal virtues (Faith, Hope, Charity, etc.) • **polygonal** sometimes used for allegorical figures • **black nimbus** (usually polygonal) attribute of Judas • *see also* **aureole; glory**

nine a mystic number; truth; perfection; completion; spiritual achievement; associated with karma, the occult, philosophy, culture, fine arts, humaneness, Neptune, hidden factors, angels (especially Lumiel), the color violet, the letters I and R, the moon, the Great Goddess, the underworld, Hell, motherhood, fertility, the three worlds (corporal, intellectual, spiritual) • **kabala** achievement • **Christianity** the Nine Choirs of Angels, the Nine Gifts of the Holy Spirit, etc.

nineteen good fortune; associated with the angel Michael

ninety divine discontent; striving toward perfection; reflection; the close of a cycle; multiplies the qualities of the number nine, which see • **kabala** disappointment

noise punishment; chaos; associated with Hell

noon the opposite of darkness; corresponds to summer, to middle age in man

noose knowledge; the captive; death by hanging

north winter; coldness; old age; the new moon; the home of the gods; night; barbarianism; the furthest bounds of the universe • **facing north** posing a question • **reading the Gospel from the north end of a church** the desire to convert the barbarians

North Star the "unmoved mover"; a "hole" in space and time

nose inquisitiveness; meddling; snobbery; clarity; the phallus • **hooked nose** attribute of the White Goddess

nosegay *see* **bouquet**

nostril(s) seat of the breath of life, anger, passion

nothingness annihilation; chaos

nudity shame; protest; related to madness, the dead • **nuditas naturalis** the natural state of man • **nuditas virtualis** purity; innocence; sinlessness • **nuditas temporalis** lack of worldly goods, especially when abandoned in service to God; penitence; contempt for worldly things • **nuditas criminalis** lust; vanity; the absence of all virtues; lasciviousness • **a god naked to the waist** the top half represents the sky, the bottom half the earth

number the farther a number is from one, the more deeply involved it is in the world. The first ten numbers refer to the spirit; repetition of a number stresses its quantitative power, but detracts from its spiritual dignity • **even numbers** associated with the soluble, ephemeral, feminine, earthly, negative and passive principles • **odd numbers** associated with the insoluble, masculine, celestial, positive, and active principles • **China even numbers** associated with night, cold, winter, earth, the color black • **odd numbers** associated with clay, fire, heat, sun, the color white • *see also* specific numbers

nun contemplation; the higher virtues; chastity • **nuns watching soldiers scale city walls** associated with St. Clare

nunnery Elizabethan euphemism for a whorehouse

nurse a promoter of spiritual growth

nursing *see* **breast**

nut hidden wisdom; fertility; hidden riches; testicles; the soul; reincarnation; mystery (especially a hazel nut) • **Christian** Christ (especially a split walnut): the outer casing being his flesh, the hard shell the wood of the Cross, and the kernel his divine nature • **nut cracking** coition, especially between a small man and a large, overbearing woman • *see also* specific kinds of nuts

nutmeg thought to have been an aphrodisiac, an abortive

nymph the unconscious; license; lawlessness; soulless beauty; pleasure of the world; temptation; transitoriness; multiplicity and dissolution; the independent and fragmentary characteristics of the feminine unconscious; guardian of chastity; associated with the fertility of nature • **nymph with St. John** his victory over worldly temptations • **nymphs as companions of a god** expression of the god's ideas

O

O associated with the cosmos, material responsibility, balance, intellect, the home, business, children, affection, restriction, fertility, perfection, eternity, the number six; corresponds to Virgo, the liver, the heart, the Fool in the tarot deck

oak strength; longevity; liberty; hospitality; fertility; thunder; majesty; endurance; eternity; force; virtue; forgiveness; fire; world axis; turning point; faith; courage; a door; durability; steadfastness; great growth from a small beginning; a tree of the first rank; emblem of Druidism; ruling deities (such as Jupiter); associated with Sagittarius • **heraldry** pride; beauty; power; *oak leaves*: military distinction • **Christianity** Christ; the Virgin Mary; the endurance of the Christian against adversity; forgiveness; eternity • **oak leaf** bravery; regeneration (because it has eight lobes) • **bishop with foot on fallen oak** St. Boniface • **flower language** hospitality; *live oak*: liberty; *white oak*: independence; *oak leaf*: bravery, humanity

oar creative thought; the Word; navigation; progress; punishment; slavery; attribute of river gods, Noah, St. Julian the Hospitator, Saturn • **steering oar** the skill, knowledge, and/or bravery of the wielder • **oar with saw or battleaxe, or two oars crossed** attribute of St. Simon

oats food of the lower classes; youthful excesses • **flower language** music; the bewitching soul of music

obelisk aspiration; regeneration; eternal life; fertility; phallus; a sun ray; a penetrating spirit; solar ascension; finger of a god; support of the sky; protection against evil spirits

oboe plaintiveness; phallus; the masculine principle

ocean grandeur; dynamic force; universal life; immense illogic; the generative source of life; the collective unconscious; the mother; woman; separation of the nether world and heaven; unbounded desolation; death and regeneration; the Abyss; primordial creation; related to sexual desire, amniotic waters, longing for adventure, spiritual exploration, conscience, time, eternity; liberty; untamable wildness; loneliness; purification; the mediating agent between life and death • **salt water** suggests sterility • **ocean swells, or a stormy sea** activity or disturbance in the unconscience • **sea of flames** life as an infirmity • **return to the sea** to die • *see also* **waves**

ochre deceitfulness; earth

octagon regeneration; baptism • *see also* **eight**

October associated with harvest, resowing, autumn

octopus existentialism; malignancy; craftiness; the unfolding of creation; attribute of Aphrodite; shares in the symbolism of the whale and the dragon, q.q.v.

odor *see* **smell**

Odysseus *see* **Ulysses**

odyssey *see* **journey**

offering sacrifice of lower values for higher ones

ogre prehuman savage life • **male ogre** the Terrible Father • **female ogre** the Terrible Mother; fear of incest

oil divine love; the grace of God; consecration; riches; light; preservation against corruption; joy; peace; cunning; dedication; incentive; calmness; healing • **oil in a cauldron** attribute of St. John • **horn of oil** attribute of David • **olive oil** the grace of God • **cruse of oil** the inexhaustible grace of Christ • *see also* **chrism**

ointment love; divine love; coition; purity; heroism; hospitality; luxury;

the burial of Christ, St. Cosmas, St. Damian, St. Mary Magdalene, St. Mary of Egypt, St. Mary of Bethany

old man *see* **man**

oleander danger

olive courageous love and faith

olive tree or branch reconciliation between God and Man; Christ's peace, healing, faith, and beauty; the Christian church; Gesthemane (especially a gnarled olive tree); emblem of Mercury, Athena • **olive branch** peace; deliverance; concord; charity; prosperity; wisdom; fertility; faith; righteousness; victory; dedication; annointment; beauty; the new year; attribute of Noah, the archangel Gabriel, St. Agnes, the personifications of the Golden Age, Peace, Concord, Wisdom • **dove arising with an olive branch in its mouth** a soul that has made its peace with God • **wild olive** bitterness • **palm, cypress, and olive trees together** Gethsemane • **flower language** peace

one reason; the cosmos; related to the Creator; shows moral purpose; existence; the active principle; spiritual revelation, unity; light; paradise; the infinite; the Mystic Center; the phallus; unity; associated with the masculine, the sun, intellectual power, will power, change, travel, domination; selfishness, ruthlessness, the angel Raphael, the color orange; has the value of letters A, J, S • **Jewish** the life force; the power and will of the universe

one hundred perfection; plentitude; an indefinite number • **kabala** perfection

one hundred and eleven plentitude

one hundred and fifty-three in ancient times, the number of all the types of fishes in existence

one hundred and forty-four a good omen

one hundred and ten a canonical number; the perfect age to die

one hundred and twenty a magical number • **Jewish** a large crowd

one-legged man *see* **cydippe**

one thousand absolute perfection; eternity; multiplications and additions to one thousand are intensifiers

one thousand, one hundred betrayal; caddish behavior

onion unity; the cosmos in equilibrium; a deity emblem; light; protection against evil spirits

onyx dignity; clearness; quarrel; reciprocity; promotes happiness in marriage and friendship; protects against nightmares and evil spirits; curbs passions; strengthens spiritual thoughts

opal good fortune; emblem of October; associated with Scorpio; gives hope, self-confidence, prophetic powers; increases faithfulness, tenderness, happiness in love; purifies thoughts; drives out grief; protects innocence; prevents heartache, fainting, evil affections

ophrys spider ophrys: associated with Arachne • **flower language** — *bee ophrys*: error; *frog ophrys*: disgust; *spider ophrys*: adroitness; skill

oppressors prejudices; opinions that oppose truth

orange (color) fire; the Holy Spirit; pride; ambition; heat; lust; marriage; hospitality; benevolence; health; vigor; passion tempered by earthly wisdom; endurance; flame; attribute of Buddha; associated with Leo, the House of Orange, Gemini, the sun, protestants in Northern Ireland • **heraldry** endurance; strength; worldly ambition • **ancient East** associated with a convicted criminal • **red orange** associated with Taurus • **yellow orange** associated with Cancer • **impure orange** malevolence; egoism; cruelty; ferocity; the Devil; desperation

orange (fruit) life; fecundity; fertility; generosity; jealousy; love;

purity; chastity; the world; the feminine; an occasional substitute for the apple as the fruit of the Tree of Knowledge; attribute of the Virgin Mary • **orange in the hand of the Christ child** alludes to him as the future redeemer of mankind from original sin • **orange in representations of Paradise** the fall of man and his redemption • **China** an imperial sacrifice to heaven • **cinnabar orange** good fortune; immortality • **orange tree** generosity • **flower language** the blossoms: chastity; your purity equals your loveliness • *see also* **mock orange**

orant prayer

orb the world; sovereignty; completeness; perfection • **orb with a cross on it** Christian dominion over the world; recognition of God's ultimate dominion over the world; salvation; gradual enlightenment of the world • **orb with a spread eagle** devotion • **orb with an orrery on it** sovereignty at sea • **orb with wings** spiritual evolution • **orb with snake around it** sin encircling the earth; when shown at the feet of the Virgin Mary, it indicates her role as the second Eve • *see also* **globe**

orchard death • **orchard of pomegranates** attribute of the Virgin Mary

orchestra activity of the corporate whole; cooperation of the discrete toward a given end

orchid luxury; love; beauty; nobility; labia; associated with Aquarius • **China** refinement; fragrance; love; beauty; fecundity; the perfect or superior man • **purple orchid** euphemism for phallus

orchis in flower language: a beauty; a belle; *bee orchis*: industry; *butterfly orchis*: gaiety; *fly orchis*: error

organ (instrument) the universe; the praise of God from the Church; harmony; attribute of St. Cecilia, Polyhymnia, the personifications of Music, Hearing

orgasm a voluntary return to primordial chaos from which life proceeds

orgy regression; involution; the invocation of primordial chaos; escape from Time to Pre-Time

Orient illumination; the fount of life

Orion the hunter

Orpheus song; music; Christ

orrery on an orb: sovereignty at sea

osier freedom; sincerity without finery or dissimulation • **flower language** frankness • *see also* **willow**

osmunda in flower language: dreams

osprey sovereignty; cause of sorrow

ostentorium the Eucharist

ostrich cowardice; shame; forgetfulness; lack of understanding; justice; cruelty; intemperance; inconstancy; heresy; sinful man; hypocrisy; man deserted by God; one who trusts in God; speed; stamina; foolishness; a monster of Chaos • **heraldry** endurance (often with a horseshoe in its mouth) • **ostrich feathers** knightly dignity; justice; distinction; fertility; attribute of Osiris, Anat • **three ostrich feathers** emblem of the Prince of Wales

otter transitory fertility; Christ's descent into Hell; playfulness; free spirit • **heraldry** prudence; free fishing rights

Ouroboros the continuity of life; cosmic unity; time and eternity; self-fecundation; the self-sufficiency of nature

oval the female; vulva; earth; suggests a natural (biological) object

oven a mother symbol; the womb; lust; unrevealed sorrow; a crucible; pure spiritual gestation

owl death; night; cold; passivity; knowledge; wisdom; ingratitude; darkness; vigilance; prophecy; loneliness; solitude, and hence, associated with hermits; despair; object of ridicule; an unbeliever; lack of nobility; related to witches; mourning;

desolation; associated with Christ in that he gives "light to them that sit in darkness" (Luke 1:79); perjorative emblem of the Synagogue; attribute of Minerva, the Devil, the personifications of Night, Wisdom, Sleep, Avarice • **Bible** a good omen • **heraldry** vigilance; acute wit; the retired life • **screech or squinch owl** an ill omen; disaster; misfortune

ox suffering; sacrifice; patience; labor; agriculture; wealth; submissiveness; stolidity; cosmic forces; the moon; the Jewish nation; strength; humility; those who labor for the good of others; associated with the nativity of Christ; Christ's sacrifice (especially in the Early Church); Christ; attribute of St. Lucy, St. Ambrose, St. Thomas Aquinas, St. Sylvester, the personifications of Sloth, Patience • **heraldry** valor; magnanimity; *ox head alone*: power guided by reason • **ox with wings** emblem of St. Mark • **ox yoked with ass** attribute of Hercules • **ox with an eagle, lion, and angel** St. Luke, St. John, St. Mark, St. Matthew, respectively • **China** spring; agriculture • **black ox** death • **brass ox** attribute of St. Antipas • **lion-headed ox** abundance and earthly power • **ox head with crown** regeneration • **ox skull** death; mortality (but when adorned and shown with horns: immortality) • **coat or cloak of ox skin** fertility

ox-eye (plant) in flower language: patience

oxlip (plant) boldness

oyster silence; stupidity; lust; vulva; the world; folly; imbecility; the lowest form of animal life; considered an aphrodisiac • **oyster maid** the lowest trade

P

P associated with preservation, precaution, foresight, intellect, curiosity, ego, potential for good and evil, prudence, success followed by ruin, the shepherd's crook; corresponds to Mars, Capricorn, the brains, the House of God in the tarot

padlock silence; security; virginity; prudence; secrecy

pain mental or spiritual disharmony or disorder • **a sudden unaccountable pain** a portent

painting a painting of the Virgin Mary: attribute of St. Luke • **painted face** vanity; deceit; disloyalty; trickery; foolishness; wantonness; lust; sorrow; seduction; protection against the evil eye; attribute of a loose woman • *see also* **picture**

palace the Mystic Center; authority; riches; honor; the "unmoved mover" • **palace of mirrors, crystal, or glass that suddenly appears by magic** ancestral memories of mankind; unconscious memories; primitive awareness of the Golden Age • **secret chambers in a palace** the unconscious • **treasures hidden in a palace** spiritual truths; fertility • *see also* **castle**

paleness fear; maidenhood; lovesickness; envy; sickness

palette art; attribute of painters, St. Luke

pall when used as a cover for a chalice: the linen in which the body of Christ was shrouded

pallium crucifixion of Christ; papal authority

palm (hand) oily or wet palm: wanton disposition • **itchy palm** avarice; bribery • **palm held up** peace; friendship; innocence • **palm held out** bribery; payment; demand for possession

palm (tree) victory; military victory; fecundity; Christ's victory over death; martyrdom to attain heaven, and frequent attribute of Christian martyrs; elevation; exaltation; abundance; joy; prosperity; associated with Christ's triumphant entry into Jerusalem, Leo; attribute of the anima, Asher, the archangel Gabriel, St. Barbara, St. Sergius, St. Bacchus, St. Peter, St. Paul the Hermit, and others, Nike, the personifications of Chastity, Abundance, Abstinence, Victory, Fame, Asia, also of the Virgin Mary • **heraldry** (after 1500) victory; royal honor; life; fecundity; wisdom; generosity; justice; friendship • **Egypt** life in the abstract; the residence of the gods • **palm, cypress, and olive** the Virgin Mary • **palm and jasmine** adoration of God • **garment of palm leaves** attribute of St. Apollonia, St. Catherine of Alexandria, St. Clare of Assisi, St. Euphemia, St. Justina of Padua, St. Justina of Antioch, St. Laurence, St. Margaret of Antioch, St. Stephen, St. Vincent, St. Paul the Hermit, sometimes also St. Onuphrius and other desert hermits • **loincloth of palm leaves** attribute of St. Paul the Hermit, sometimes also St. Onuphrius and other desert hermits • **children holding palms** the Holy Innocents • **woman with seven children holding palms** St. Felicity and her children • **palm tree staff** attribute of St. Christopher • **date palm tree** resurrection

Pan nature; the vitality of base forces; base or involutive life

pancake emblem of Shrove Tuesday

Pandora, Pandora's Box the wicked temptations besetting mankind; the irrational; the wild tendencies of the imagination; female masturbation and its objectified emotional consequences; rebelliousness against divine order

pansy remembrance; meditation; revery; marriage; man; trinity and unity; the sun; humility; thought; a homosexual; associated with Capricorn • **flower language** thoughts

panther night; martial ferocity; bravery; rejuvenation; luxury; maternity; emblem of Dionysus • **heraldry** similar to the leopard, which see; a beautiful woman, normally tender, but fierce in defense of her young • **China** bravery; ferocity • **hart and panther** opposites • **panther skin** the overcoming of low desires • see also **leopard**, with which the panther is frequently imperfectly distinguished

paper transitoriness; lack of durability; emblem of bureaucracy

papyrus knowledge; omniscience; love; the hidden; the occult; emblem of the god Amon • **rolled papyrus** knowledge; progress; omniscience; efflorescence • **unrolling papyrus** the unfolding of life • **papyrus with red crown** emblem of the Lower Kingdom of Egypt

paradise the Mystic Center; heaven; union with the spirit

parasol world axis; a solar wheel; sun emblem; protection; authority; dignity; irradiation; emblem of divinity, royalty; dome of the sky • **China** a state umbrella: authority; respect; dignity • see also **umbrella**

park beauty; fertility; wealth; paradise • see also **garden**

Parnassus excellence

parrot prophecy; foolish chatter, laughter; verbosity; greed; docility; attribute of the personifications of Eloquence, Docility • **heraldry** far travels • **China** warning to women to be faithful to their husbands

parsley fecundity; death; promiscuity; spring; hope of redemption • **Rome** victory in sports • **Greece** worn on the head, it was thought to increase cheerfulness and appetite •

flower language feasting; useful knowledge; festivity; *fool's parsley*: silliness

partridge lasciviousness; deceit; cunning; disloyalty to one's own kind; the Devil, in a general sense, sometimes, however, the Church, truth; theft; deception; parental affection; the hopelessness of worldly endeavor

pasque flower *see* **anemone**

Pasiphae the deliberate flouting of natural and divine law; the overthrow of reason by animal passion

passion flower the Passion of Christ (specifically, the 10 petals are said to represent the 10 apostles who did not deny or betray Christ, or the 10 apostles who fled; the rays within the flower represent the crown of thorns; the five stamens represent the five wounds; the three styles represent the nails; the leaf represents the spear; the tendrils represent the cord used to bind Christ; the ovary represents the hammer; and the central column represents the pillar before the Praetorium); Christ's suffering • **flower language** belief; susceptibility; Christian faith; religious superstition

paste *see* **mud**

paten the dish used at the last supper; the Eucharist

path life; experience; learning

patience dock *see* **dock**

pavement humility; foundation

pea love; respect • **flower language** — *everlasting pea*: an appointed meeting; lasting pleasure; *sweet pea*: departure, delicate pleasures

peace union or conjunction of the higher and lower planes

peach immortality; marriage; longevity; vulva; the feminine principle; luxury; the fruit of salvation; the silence of virtue; perfection; attribute of the Virgin Mary, the personifications of Silence, Truth • **peach with leaf attached** the heart and tongue • **China** immortality

peach tree associated with Aquarius • **China** spring; immortality; longevity; marriage • **peach blossom** emblem of February • **flower language** I am your captive; your qualities, like your charms, are unequalled

peacock immortality; the incorruptible soul; the apotheosis of princesses; resurrection Easter; eternal life; Christ; the ever-vigilant Church; royalty; vanity; pride; attribute of St. Liborius, St. Barbara, Juno, the personifications of Pride, Transitoriness, Disobedience • **China** beauty; dignity; the tail feathers were used to indicate official rank • **heraldry** power and distinction; a troubador; royalty; pride of nation • **feather** attribute of St. Barbara

peafowl *see* **peacock; peahen**

peahen a woman 30 to 40 years old • **dancing peahen** dawn

pear the human heart; generosity; affection; Christ's love for mankind; occasionally used as the fruit of the Tree of Knowledge; attribute of Affection personified, occasionally of the Virgin Mary

pear tree • **China** longevity; *pear blossoms*: emblem of August; *wild pear tree*: wise administration; good government • **flower language** affection; comfort; *prickly pear*: satire

pearl the human soul; innocence; purity; genius in obscurity; tears; the Mystic Center; parthenogenesis; faith; esoteric wisdom; wealth; health; self-sacrifice; salvation; euphemism for clitoris in Victorian times; in large numbers they lose their favorable significance and become mere beads; attribute of Cleopatra, Christ, the Virgin Mary, St. Margaret of Antioch, the personification of Eloquence; associated with Cancer, the moon • **China** purity; beauty; obscure genius; protection against fire • **heraldry** (usually on a ring) high grace

peasant ignorance; often used as a personification of Sloth

pebble justice; eloquence; attribute of St. Liborius; thrown on the graves of suicides • **white pebbles** not guilty; a graveside gift to provide resurrection or rebirth • **black pebbles** guilty

Peeping Tom lechery (Lady Godiva symbolized fertility)

Pegasus poetry; poetic inspiration; intellect and morality; the poet; heightened natural forces; the imagination; fame; innate capacity for changing evil into good and for spiritualization; Fame personified • **heraldry** energy leading to honor; poetry; the Inner Temple of the Inns of Court

pelican loneliness; melancholy; parental love and sacrifice; gregariousness; greed; an allegory of Christ and his atonement on the cross (especially when feeding its young with its own blood); the suffering Christ; the Eucharist; resurrection; proof of the possibility of virgin birth (so considered at one time); attribute of Penitence personified • **heraldry** (usually with wings spread) filial devotion; Christian readiness to sacrifice

pelt attribute of John the Baptist • *see also* **skin**

pen (writing instrument) attribute of writers, scholars, Doctors of the Church, St. Matthew, St. Mark, St. Luke, St. John, St. Augustine, St. Bernard of Clairvaux, St. Ambrose, St. Cyril of Alexandria, St. Isidore, St. John Chrysostom, St. Leander of Seville • **pen with three books** attribute of St. Hilary of Poitiers

penance aspiration which implies discontent with the worldly conditions to which one is bound for a time

pendulum time; balance of judgment

Penelope faithfulness

pennyroyal in flower language: flee

pentagon heavenly wisdom; guidance

Pentagon (building) the U.S. military establishment; the U.S. military-industrial complex; war; military force

pentagram magic; protection against sorcery; the five wounds of Christ • **eagle carrying a flaming pentagram** emblem of the planet Jupiter

Pentecost descent of the Holy Spirit to the Apostles in particular, and mankind in general

peony healing; shame; feminine loveliness; anger; indignation; spring; regal power; affluence; prosperity; stability; associated with Leo • **China** love; affection; feminine loveliness; *tree poeny*: the yang principle, spring, good fortune, emblem of March • **flower language** shame; bashfulness

pepper satire; temper; aphrodisiac

peppermint wealth • **flower language** warmth; cordiality; the combination of the coldness of fear with the warmth of love

perfume memories; emotions; nostalgia; reminiscences; amorousness

peridot happiness; emblem of a thunderbolt; associated with Virgo, Leo, Pisces, the month of August

periwinkle love; aphrodisiac • **crown of periwinkle** death • **flower language** — *blue periwinkle*: pleasures of memory, early friendship; *red periwinkle*: early friendship; *white periwinkle*: pleasant recollections, pleasures of memory

Persephone the spring; the earth

persicaria in flower language: restoration

persimmon wisdom; joy • **flower language** bury me amid nature's joys

pestle phallus • **mortar and pestle together** attribute of St. Cosmas and St. Damian

Peter (Saint) betrayal; inversion

petrel presage of a storm

petrification detention of moral progress

petticoat emblem of woman • **red petticoat** in Elizabethan times, attribute of prostitutes

Phaeton aspiration beyond ability

phallus nature's regenerative forces; penetration; world axis; the self; the libido; sexuality; active power; the perpetuation of life; the propagation of cosmic forces; related to oaths or covenants; attribute of sun heroes

pheasant vigilance; activity; resurrection; the sun; beauty; luxury; motherly love; lasciviousness; Christianity; attribute of the personifications of Simplicity, the Christian • **China** occasionally used as an emblem of beauty and good fortune • **heraldry** hunting

pheasant's eye (plant) *see* **adonis**

phial *see* **vial**

phlox in flower language: unanimity

Phobos fear

Phoenix resurrection; immortality; eternal youth; eternity; chastity; temperance; royal succession; faith; constancy; augur of a storm; Easter; the cycle of destruction and recreation; the power to overcome death, change, or tragedy; attribute of the personifications of Justice, Chastity (usually on a shield), occasionally Perseverance • **China** a harbinger of peace; associated with the sun, warmth • **Early Christian** Christ's suffering and the Resurrection • **Middle Ages** the Crucifixion; attribute of Chastity personified

photograph has magical powers of access to the soul of the subject

Phrygia love; fertility; liberty; wisdom; eroticism in a superior form

phrygian cap a phallic symbol; obsessive eroticism; sacrifice; self-immolation, or that of others

physician *see* **doctor**

picture has magical powers of access to the soul of the subject • **picture falling off the wall for no apparent reason** ill fortune • **picture of Saints Peter and Paul** attribute of St. Sylvester • **picture of Christ on a cloth** attribute of St. Veronica • *see also* **painting**

Pierrot the male principle still in a state of innocence

pig a pig skin bag is an attribute of a tinker • *see also* **swine; boar; sow**

pigeon purity; aspiration; gentleness • **modern urban use** a nuisance; a low bird • **China** long life; good digestion; faithfulness; impartial filial duty • **wood pigeon** monotonous chanting; victim of the cuckoo; a cuckhold; vanity • *see also* **dove**, with which the pigeon shares much symbolism, and is frequently confused

pigeon berry in flower language: indifference

pilgrim man in his journey toward salvation; the lover; the human being on earth, traveling toward the Mystic Center; the human soul; renunciation; Christ at Emmaus, St. James the Greater, St. Bridget, and St. Roch are often portrayed as pilgrims • **ragged pilgrim** may be St. Alexis, or the archangel Gabriel

pilgrimage the journey toward salvation; the process of spiritual evolution and growth

pillar the connection between heaven and earth; power; world axis; support of heaven; phallus; the male principle; strength; attribute of the Passion, Samson, St. Sebastian, St. Simon Stylites, the personifications of Fortitude, Constancy • **two pillars** attribute of Samson; the point at which the sun god re-enters the inhabited world; *when shown apart*: Jachin and Boaz; *when shown together*: binary combinations such as love/knowledge, beauty/strength, justice/mercy, etc. • **two pillars of**

Enoch the brick pillar is proof against fire; the stone pillar is proof against water • **three pillars** the Trinity; any triad, such as goodness/wisdom/power, etc. • **four pillars** the supports of heaven; the points of the compass • **seven pillars** wisdom; sanctity; extreme riches • **12 pillars** creation; the planets; the months of fertility; the tribes of Israel • **silver pillars** attribute of Styx's house • **broken pillar** death; broken faith; defeat; attribute of Samson, Strength personified • **flaming pillar** attribute of St. Hecla • **flaming pillars as the legs of an angel** the Apocalypse • **soldier sleeping by a pillar, a woman kneeling beside him** Rinaldo and Armida

pillow security; mercy; comfort; trust; hospitality; peace; love; anguish; luxury; mute audience of confession • *see also* **cushion**

pimpernel fruitfulness; childhood • **flower language** assignation; change; cheerfulness

pin love; marriage; restraint; excitement (often sexual); something of value up to the middle of the 18th century, something valueless after

pincers attribute of St. Agatha • **pincers with a tooth** attribute of St. Apollonia • **doctor holding a stone with a pincers** a quack operation for "stones in the head" • *see also* **tongs**

pinching wantonness; return to reality or wakefulness; connected with fairies, death, and night symbols such as the owl, cat, mouse, etc.

pine immortality; longevity; virility; victory; grief; endurance; pity; philosophy; gloominess; punishment; associated with Saturn, Capricorn • **China** faithfulness; emblem of Lao Tzu • **fallen pine** a man fallen in misfortune • **flower language** — *black pine*: pity; *pitch pine*: time, philosophy; *spruce pine*: farewell, hope in adversity • *see also* **fir; evergreens**

pine cone fertility; spiritual fertility; phallus; conviviality; healing • **wand tipped with pine cone** attribute of Bacchus, satyrs

pineapple emblem of the Hawaiian Islands • **flower language** perfection; you are perfect

pink (color) sensuality; the emotions; the flesh; feminity; effeminacy; homosexuality; joy; youth; good health • **Gnosticism** resurrection

pink (flower) associated with Sagittarius • **flower language** boldness; *carnation pink*: woman's love; *Indian single pink*: aversion; *Indian double pink*: always lovely; *mountain pink*: aspiring; *pink pink*: newlyweds; *red single pink*: pure love; *red double pink*: pure and ardent love; *variegated pink*: refusal; *white pink*: ingenuity, talent

pipe smoking a pipe: monotony; idle filling of time

pipe (musical) allurement; a religious instrument; peace; phallic symbol, especially when played by a male lover; lust; attribute of Bacchus, Euterpe, Mercury, shepherds, Marsyas and other satyrs, Vice personified • *see also* **syrinx, flute**

Pisces associated with defeat; failure; exile; seclusion; the final stage of a cycle

pismire *see* **ant**

pit Hell; euphemism for vulva; associated with Joseph

pitch (pine pitch) evil; punishment in Hell • *see also* **caulking**

pitcher (vessel) refreshment; recognition; election; something of low value; the female principle; attribute of Hebe, Aquarius, St. Florian, Temperance personified • **pitcher overturned** the emptiness of worldly things, especially in still life • **pitcher overturned with Naiads embracing a youth** the youth is Hylas • **pitcher overturned with corpse entwined by a serpent** Cadmus •

woman watering plants from a pitcher Grammar personified • **water pitcher and sword** emblem of Levi • **pitcher with basin** attribute of Pilate • **pitcher with light** attribute of Gideon • **pitcher with rays above** attribute of St. Bede • **pitcher with loaves of bread** attribute of Obadiah • **pitcher with dish and two fish** attribute of the Virgin Mary • *see also* **ewer**

pitchfork typical implement of a man; attribute of the Devil, farmers; weapon of rebellious peasants • *see also* **fork**

plague marriage; vices; God's judgment • **"love's plague"** pregnancy; children

plaid associated with the planet Mercury, Scotland

plain (geographic feature) the land of reality, truth

plait intimate relationship; intermingling streams; interdependence

plane (tool) attribute of St. Joseph, Melancholy personified

plane tree charity; firmness of character; moral superiority; the charity of Christ; regeneration; protection; friendliness; grandeur; magnificence • **flower language** genius; cultivation of the mind; associated with the Greek philosophers

plant life; usually connected with fertility deities such as Osiris, Adonis, Demeter, etc.; the healthy growth of plants signifies cosmic, spiritual, material fecundity • **withered plant** death • **aquatic plant** creation arising out of the primordial waters; the nascent character of life • **"cold" plant** blooms in the early part of the year, or is an annual • **"hot" plant** blooms in the late part of the year, or is a perennial

plantain morning; the food of the pilgrim, of the multitude seeking Christian growth or salvation

plate containment; sacrifice; the female principle

platinum associated with Aquarius

playing cards gambling; idle pastime; attribute of Vice personified

playwright the demiurge

Pleiades completeness; order; since there are seven of them, they share in the symbolism of that number, which see • **rising of the Pleiades** start of the navigation season; the early or spring harvest • **setting of the Pleiades** new sowing; fall

plough *see* **plow**

plover greed • **golden plover** the soul of a Jew who crucified Christ and is doomed to forever lamenting the act; warns sheep of approaching danger; its song is a death omen

plow fertility; fertilization; agriculture; the male principle; the earthly side of man's consciousness; peace; abundance; diligence; labor; attribute of Cincinnatus, Cain, the personifications of Lust, the Silver Age • **heated plow** martyrdom; lust; attribute of St. Cunegunda • **plow drawn by both an ox and an ass** attribute of Hercules • **two wheeled plow** emblem of consecrations; royal dignity; has divine associations

plowman obeyer of natural law; provider of society; Christ; the Christian community • **plowman approached by Roman soldiers** Cincinnatus

plum prize; a valuable object or situation

plum tree fertility • **China** emblem of winter, January • **Orient** emblem of Confucius • **plum blossoms** spring; chastity; fidelity • **flower language** keep your promises; *Indian plum tree*: privation; *wild plum tree*: independence

plumb bob *see* **plummet**

plummet righteousness; justice; punishment

Pluto (planet) associated with the negative aspect of the spirit, Scorpio, elimination or destruction, renewal, regeneration, explosive forces, unpredictability, zero, providence, invisible forces, actors, the will to exercise power

poet a spiritually advanced person capable of leading others to higher qualities

poinsettia Christ's nativity; Christmas; fertility; eternity

point unity; center; origin; that which has no magnitude

pointing an ill omen; an affront

poison ivy ridicule; yearning

pole creative energy

Pole Star the ideal; throne of the Supreme Being; eye of heaven; world axis; the hole between space and time; constancy; Christ

policeman the censorious super-ego inhibiting forces of the pre-conscious

polyanthus in flower language: pride of riches; *crimson polyanthus*: the heart's mystery; *lilac polyanthus*: confidence

polyp collector; cunning; cruelty

pomegranate fecundity; royalty; Christ; autumn; womb; the female principle; emblem of the High Priest; sanctity; unity; concord; love; truth; frankness (usually shown open); love; God's gifts; the Church; the return of spring; rejuvenation of the earth; sometimes the fruit of the Tree of Knowledge; attribute of the Virgin Mary, the personifications of Sufficiency, Victory • **China** (blossoms only) June • **heraldry** the perfect kingdom • **bursting pomegranate** resurrection; Easter; the fertility of the Word • **pomegranate surmounted by a cross** attribute of St. John of God • **pomegranate flower** hope; immortality • **flower language** foolishness; foppishness; *the flower alone*: mature elegance

pond corruption; stagnation; reflection; a wife • *see also* **pool**

poniard *see* **knife**

pool (body of water) wisdom; cosmic knowledge; universal consciousness • **youth gazing into a pool** Narcis-

sus • **man in pool reaching up for dangling pool** Tantalus • **lovers in a pool** Hermaphroditus • **nymphs bathing observed by soldiers** Rinaldo and Armida • *see also* **pond**

poor people *see* **poverty**

Pope (tarot) *see* **High Priest**

popinjay amusement; wantonness

poplar the tree of life; sympathy; lamentation; tremulousness; victory; the duality of all things • **heraldry** a flourishing family; firm faith; aspiration; emblem of Lombardy • **black poplar** despair; associated with Hercules • **flower language** – *black poplar*: courage; *white poplar*: time

poppy sleep; rest; peace; fecundity; fertility; death; chastity; extravagance; ignorance; indifference; consolation; heavenly sleep; resurrection; autumn; intoxication; evanescent pleasure; commemoration of the dead on Armistice Day; associated with Taurus, occasionally the Passion of Christ; attribute of Hypnos, Morpheus, the personifications of Sleep, Night, Cunning, Lethargy • **China** associated with December • **flower language** evanescent pleasure; *red or corn poppy*: consolation; *scarlet poppy*: fantastic extravagance: *white poppy*: sleep, my bane, my antidote

porcupine blind anger • *see also* **hedgehog**

porpoise lust; presage of a storm • *see also* **dolphin**, with which the porpoise is frequently confused, especially in classical times

portrait *see* **picture**

post *see* **pillar**

pot (usually an earthen pot) connected with rain, fertility, the Great Mother, the womb, Nature's inexhaustible womb, rejuvenation, the underworld, any body moisture (blood, sweat, semen, tears, urine, saliva); attribute of St. Justina, St. Ruffina; emblem of Aquarius •

water pots the first miracle of Christ • water pot with asperges attribute of St. Martha • see also potsherd; potter; jug; jar; urn; vase; amphora

potato tranquillity; dullness; commonness; the ordinary; poverty; the subconscious; considered an aphrodisiac; fertility; emblem of Ireland • flower language benevolence

potsherd dryness; thrown on the grave of a suicide

potter a creator deity; connected with the womb

potter's wheel the Christian's life shaped by divine influence; attribute of Jeremiah

prayer, praying • youth praying in a barnyard the Prodigal Son • praying saint before Saints Peter and Paul, receiving staff and book St. Dominic • saint praying before an angel and eating a scroll or book St. John • praying saint surrounded by angels St. Charles Borromeo • praying desert hermit with an erotic or monstrous vision St. Anthony the Great • saint praying in the desert or the wilderness St. Jerome, St. Bruno • saint praying in a hollow tree St. Bavo • praying monk with a skull St. Francis of Assisi, sometimes others • praying monk among plague victims St. Frances of Rome • praying bishop attacked by soldiers St. Thomas Becket • praying pope with a monk, surrounded by flames the pope is St. Gregory the Great • several people praying before an altar on which wands are piled associated with St. Joseph • praying saint before an image or vision of the Virgin and Child — aged saint, X-shaped cross: St. Andrew; lily lying nearby: St. Philip Neri; Virgin presenting a scapular: St. Simon Stock; Virgin placing veil on the saint's head: St. Mary Magdalene of Pazzi; Virgin handing the Christ child to: St. Mary Magdalene of Pazzi, St. Francis of Assisi, sometimes others; Virgin and St. Joseph handing cloak to: St. Teresa • praying saint before an image or vision of the crucified Christ — Christ reaching down: St. Bernard of Clairvaux, St. Francis of Assisi; Christ inclining his head to: St. Margaret of Cortona, St. John Gualberto; Christ presenting instruments of the Passion to: St. Mary Magdalene of Pazzi; Christ presenting the Crucifixion nails, or showing wounds: St. Teresa; Christ bearing a cross: St. Gregory the Great, St. Ignatius of Loyola

praying mantis see mantis

precipice suggestive of the Fall of Man; euphemism for vulva

pregnancy goddess accusing a pregnant nymph: Diana and Callisto, respectively

press (tool) passion; harvest; autumn; the wrath of God

prickly pear in flower language: satire

Pride of China in flower language: dissension

priest spiritual mentor; promoter of spiritual growth; the Church

Priest (tarot) see High Priest

Priestess (tarot) see High Priestess

primrose youth; gaiety; dalliance; herald of spring; death; inconstancy; innocence • flower language early youth; evening primrose: inconstancy; red primrose: unpatronized merit

prince rejuvenated form of the king; the hero; often has powers of intuition; sometimes has the powers of the demiurge • prince rescuing a sleeping princess conjunction; the sun awakening the spring; the awakening of a girl's sexuality • see also princess

princess the anima • princess sleeping or in a secluded palace a passive potential • see also prince

prison crime; confinement; punishment; the early state of the soul in which the spirit is in bondage to the lower instincts and desires • **saint in prison, aroused by an angel** St. Peter • **saint in prison, released by an earthquake** St. Paul • **saint with a dog in a prison cell** St. Roch • **old man dying in prison with dead children** Ugolina della Gherardesca • **old man in prison, surrounded by youths** Socrates

privet *see* **hedge**

procession a cycle; the passage of time; monsters carried or imitated in a parade indicates that they are dominated • **procession in church** Christ's entry into Jerusalem; Good Friday

Prometheus freedom; the artist; prophecy; the will to resist oppression; sublimation; the intellect, in the merely technical and non-spiritual sense, in open rebellion against the soul; magnanimous endurance of unwarranted suffering; prefiguration of Christ

prophet the dawning of a higher consciousness; the beginning of a new era

prostitute the spirit seeking satisfaction instead of wisdom; an idol worshipper; lower nature; instability which is caused by object interest; the allurement of sensation and desire, which capture the soul; Pride personified

Proteus changeableness; evasiveness

prune prostitute, especially where stewed prunes are referred to; suggestive of constipation, both physical and mental

pruning hook peace; attribute of Pomona

Psyche the soul; the mind

pulpit the Word of God; religious instruction; attribute of St. Vincent Ferrer

pulse passion; life; time

pumpkin autumn; feminine symbol of containment; related to the moon and witches; charm against evil spirits; emblem of Hallowe'en; the two

worlds, earthly and celestial • **flower language** bulkiness

Punch and Judy the anti-hero overcoming learning, domesticity, death, and the Devil; contagious humor and common sense overcoming all obstacles

puppet man as the plaything of fate, deities • *see also* **doll**

puppy *see* **dog**

purgative drives out evil spirits or ghosts

purple royalty; noble birth; dignity; mourning; wisdom; power; spirituality; a religious color; penitence; sublimation; fasting; abstinence; love; justice; wisdom; knowledge; imperial power; sorrow; Advent; Lent; attribute of God the Father; associated with Sagittarius • **China** worn by an educated person • **heraldry** dignity; justice; rule; temperance in plenty; sometimes used in place of violet, which see • **purple-blue** tranquillity • **purple-red** severity; anger

purse penury; charity; avarice; philanthropy; finance; the scrotum; attribute of bankers, almoners, merchants, pilgrims, Hermes, Priapus, Fortunatus, Judas, St. Matthew, St. Lawrence, St. Thomas of Villaneuva, St. Cyril of Jerusalem, St. Matilda, the personifications of Avarice, Melancholy, Vanity • **three purses** attribute of St. Matthew, St. Nicholas of Myra • **open purse** charity to the poor; Christian benevolence • **purse with thirty coins** attribute of Judas • **still life** the possessions that death takes away • **heraldry** a liberal blessing; a treasurer • *see also* **wallet; bag; money bag**

pussy willow in England; emblem of Palm Sunday

putrefaction *see* **rotting**

putto harbinger of profane love; angelic spirit; attribute of Erato, Venus

Pygmalion inhibitions overcome

pyramid firmness; strength; endurance; stability; the sun; eternal light; the abode of the dead; the whole work of Creation; composure; aspiration; death; immortality; princely glory; time; the Mystic Center; the androgyne; emblem of Egypt; attribute of Glory personified • **pyramid and star** the flight into Egypt; Israel in Egypt

Pyramus and Thisbe perfect love

pyre death on a funeral pyre: associated with Dido, Hercules, Petroclus

pyrus Japonica fairies' fire

Pytho falsehood

python a demon; a soothsayer • **man shooting python with arrows** Apollo • *see also* serpent

pyx the Last Supper; the Blessed Sacrament; attribute of St. Longinus, the archangel Raphael when accompanying Tobias • **pyx bearing the Host** attribute of St. Clare of Assisi

Q

Q phallus and vulva; world axis and universe; associated with fertility, happiness, digestive organs, Aries, Mercury, mysticism, martial qualities, personal magnetism, the number eight primarily, but also the numbers one and seven, the Star in tarot deck

quadrant (astronomical device) attribute of Astronomy personified

quadriga partakes in the symbolism of the number four, which see; attribute of Athena

quail courage; poverty; resurrection; lasciviousness; fertility; pugnacity; God's providence; a female child up to 10 years of age; attribute of Malignity personified • **China** pugnacity; courage; poverty

quaking grass in flower language: agitation

quamoclit in flower language: agitation

quartz integrity • **rose quartz** remembrance in prayer; related to Taurus; said to enhance inner and outer beauty • **smoky quartz** related to Libra

quatrefoil the four Gospels, the four Greek Doctors of the Church, the four Latin Doctors of the Church, etc.; partakes of the symbolism of the number four, which see

Queen (tarot) the soul

queen's rocket in flower language: fashionable; you are queen of coquettes

quetzel emblem of Guatemala • **Latin America** freedom • **Aztec, Maya** the God of Air

quicksand enchantment; the obstruction of destiny; danger; the unconscious threatening to engulf the conscious

quicksilver *see* **mercury**

quill *see* **pen**

quince fertility; marriage; disappointment; scornful beauty; Christ; associated with Venus; attribute of Marriage personified; in hotter countries, may be used for the fruit of the Tree of Good and Evil, and may partake of other symbolism of the apple, which see • **flower language** temptation

quiver (for arrows) vagina, but also may stand for the phallus as it contains the shooting arrows (semen); attribute of deities, as it holds lightning, sun rays, arrows of desire, etc. • **"Cupid's quiver"** euphemism for the vagina

quivering sexual excitement; timidity; apprehension

R

R often stands for rex (king) or regina (queen); associated with Aquarius, Venus, the heart, tremendous force for either good or evil, the occult, rapidity, regeneration, the number nine, the Moon in the tarot deck

rabbit gregariousness; timidity; skepticism; suspicion; wisdom; fecundity; inhibited (but often immature) sexuality; euphemism for female genitals; speed; witty trickery; browsing; desultory reading and learning; watchfulness; cowardice; mildness; distraction; humbleness; a peasant; a victim; resourcefulness; connected with Easter; hope, life (especially the young); attribute of Venus, Lust personified • **heraldry** a peaceful and retired life • **Orient** on a disk of gold or white: the moon • **rabbit skin cap** a fool • **rabbit at the feet of the Virgin Mary** the victory of chastity • **rabbit's foot** phallus; good fortune (exposed genitals were supposed to bring good luck) • see also **hare**

Rachel the contemplative life

radiance related to fire and daylight in both the positive and negative aspects; suggests the supernatural or divine • see also **glory; nimbus; aureole**

radish thinness; redemption; dieting; spring; supposed to be an aphrodisiac; related to Mars; thought to prevent poisoning, drunkenness

rag(s) poverty; despair; self-deprecation; wound to the soul (the particular garment that is in rags gives a more precise meaning to this) • **rag hung on a tree** substitute for human sacrifice • **rag thrown in the water** substitute for drowning; an offense cast off

ragged robin in flower language: wit

rail (communion rail) the separation between heaven and earth, or between the Church Militant and the Church Triumphant

rain fertility; purification; the grace of God; life; spiritual influences from heaven; an increase in spiritual energy; initiation; mercy; the impartiality of Christ • **rain of gold** sun rays • **wind and rain** physical love • **torrential rain** punishment; divine vengeance • see also **deluge**

rainbow blessing; good fortune; the bridge between heaven and earth; hope; God's mercy; God's covenant with Noah, man; union; divine pardon and reconciliation; emblem of Iris • **tri-colored rainbow** the Trinity • **rainbow with ark** the Deluge; God's covenant with Noah

rake (implement) avarice

ram (sheep) resurrection; sacrifice; the sacrifice of Isaac; strength; Christ; emblem of the Creator, Persia; associated with Aries, March, Mars • **heraldry** patience; temperance; reconciliation; the right to keep sheep; a leader; a duke • **ram as a sacrifice** peace • **ram with its pugnacity emphasized** power; war • **ram with four horns** attribute of Daniel • **ram's horn** seven ram's horns: the fall of Jericho; see also **shofar** • see also **sheep**

ranunculus in flower language: you are radiant with charms; I am dazzled by your charms; *Asiatic ranunculus*: your charms are resplendent; *garden ranunculus*: you are rich in attractions; *wild ranunculus*: ingratitude

raspberry envy; the human heart; joy; kindly feelings; gentle-heartedness • **flower language** remorse

rat decay; passing time; infirmity and death; has phallic implications; enmity; evil; disease; major troubles; plague; an infernal animal; meanness; slander; destruction; the Devil;

an informant; sneakiness; a ghoul; attribute of St. Fina • **one black rat with one white rat** attribute of Night personified

ratsbane lechery leading to disease and death

rattle rainmaker; birth; protection against evil spirits, death

rattlesnake virulence; malignity; independence; danger

raven the Devil; solitude; melancholy; stubbornness; the lower mind; desire for solitude; materialism; wisdom; evil; bad tidings; sin; an ill omen; a messenger of the gods; dawn; trust in divine providence; unrest; death; the indifferent or unpenitent sinner; the passing of time; attribute of Noah, St. Boniface, St. Vincent of Saragossa, Rapacity personified (especially with a ring in its back); emblem of Danes, Woden, Apollo • **heraldry** a man who has made his own fortune; victory; courage • **China** an ill omen • **two ravens** attribute of St. Meinrad • **raven with a loaf of bread** attribute of Elijah, St. Anthony the Great, St. Benedict, St. Onuphrius, St. Paul the Hermit • **Elijah's raven** God's providence • *see also* **crow**, which is closely related and frequently confused with the raven

ray *see* **sting ray**

reaper a death deity

reaping harvest; reward or consequence; slaughter; castration

rear the unconscious; related to the left side, which see

recessional in the Church: Christians going forth to work in the world

rectangle the most rational, secure, and regular of geometric forms • **rectangular nimbus** indicated the holiness of a person still living

red love; virility; courage; anger; war; divine zeal; creative force; imperial power; love of God; patriotism; sacrifice; revolution; charity; sentiment; sin; primitive wildness; disease; martyrdom; blood; loyalty; attribute of Mars, dawn deities, martyrs, St. Anne, St. John, the Holy Spirit; associated with Hell, the Devil, the body of man, Pentecost, All Saints Day, Thanksgiving, dedications, martyr's days • **heraldry** desire to serve one's country as a knight; victorious power; triumph; rule; courage; magnanimity • **China** joy; happiness; the yang principle the sun; the soul; good fortune; the "life" color; anything red had "healing" qualities; *red clouds*: calamity and warfare; *red faced person* (on the stage): a sacred person • **dark red** associated with Scorpio • **brilliant red** associated with Aries, Mars • **orange-red** associated with Taurus • **red-violet** associated with Pisces • **red and black** life and death; associated with Satan • **red rose** love; divine love • **red flag** danger; auction; provocation; revolution; socialism; communism; anarchy • **red cap** invisibility

Red Sea deliverance through God's protection; salvation; purification; baptism; rebirth

reed weakness; indiscretion; resilience; divine protection; vulva; woman; humiliation of greatness; humility; justice; attribute of the Passion of Christ, Pan, river gods • **flower language** music; compliasance; *feathery or split reed*: indiscretion; *flowering reed*: confidence in heaven • **nymph hiding in the reeds** Syrinx • **reed with hyssop and/or sponge, ladder, scarlet robe** the Passion of Christ • **small cross of reeds** attribute of John the Baptist • **reed surmounted by a Latin or Tau cross** attribute of St. Philip • **two looped reeds** attribute of Ishtar

reef the obstruction of destiny; danger lurking in the unconscious

reflection consciousness

rein(s) intelligence; will; power; law;

the relationship between soul and body • **cutting reins** dying; freedom to go wild

reindeer primitive life; steeds of Santa Claus; emblem of the north polar region

relief when lacking in force; futility; falsity; equivocation • **powerful relief** the powerful surge of an idea or emotion in all its nascent strength

remora an omen of disaster; the self contained in the unconscious; Christ • **heraldry** obstacle • **remora pierced by an arrow** attribute of Prudence personified

renaming *see* **name**

reptile primordial life; cold bloodedness; lack of human warmth; old age; materialism; sexuality; heresy; an infernal animal

rescue *see* **relief**

reseda tenderness; modesty

resin embalming; resurrection; depilatory

rest *see* **peace**

return fulfilment; to return home, to one's birthplace, or to one's homeland, is the equivalent of dying in the positive sense of reintegration of the spirit with God

Reynard the Fox carnal appetite; cunning; the Church

rhinoceros bravery; victory; culture; short sighted passion; lack of sensitivity; materialism • **heraldry** one who does not seek combat, but will defend to the death when attacked • **China** rhinoceros horn: happiness

rhododendron fire; danger of intoxication • **flower language** danger; beware

rhomb the female sex organ

rhubarb bitterness; brouhaha • **flower language** advice

ribbon award; distinction; sun-ray; pleasure • **blue ribbon** first prize; marriage • **red ribbon** second prize; Order of the Bath • **knotted ribbon** fraternity • **ribbon knotted to form a circle** immortality; an undertaking fulfilled; attribute of the hero

rice fecundity; wisdom; fertility; a spermatic image; productiveness; happiness

riches wisdom, especially when they are gifts from gods or fairies

riding (usually an animal) adventure; triumph; supremacy; pride; coition

right side associated with the felicitous, evolution, openness, the normal, the legitimate, life, birth, the higher virtues, the future, the forces of reason, action, extroversion, the sun

ring continuity; wholeness; marriage; an eternally repeated cycle; delegation of authority; a contract; union; the female genitals; power; bond; slavery; fertility; female love; authenticity; justice; legitimacy; invisibility; mourning; eternity; partakes of the symbolism of the circle, which see • **heraldry** a fifth son; rank; fidelity • **China** authority; eternity; *a perfect ring*: the emperor's pleasure; *an imperfect ring*: the emperor's displeasure • **wedding ring** marriage; attribute of Saint Catherine of Siena, St. Catherine of Alexandria • **two linked rings, side by side** permanent marriage union • **two linked rings, one above the other** earth and sky; the physical and the spiritual • **three linked rings** the Trinity • **five linked rings** emblem of the Olympics

river fertility; the irreversible passage of time; the sense of loss; oblivion; life; peace; refreshment; the creative power of time and nature; rebirth; entrance to the underworld; obedience to time, life, the law • **four rivers** the four Gospels

road life; potentialities; progress; adventure; experience; difficulty; associated with the pilgrim, the prostitute • **one way road** death

robber *see* **thief**

robe concealment; may reveal the wearer's personality, or the personality shown to the world (especially a full robe) • **white robe** innocence; virtue • **gold robe** the fire of the sun • **black robe** mourning; magic; sinisterness; night; judgment • **scarlet or purple robe** the mock robe of royalty the soldiers gave to Christ • **seamless robe** attribute of the Passion of Christ • **flowing or full robe** righteousness; peace; wisdom; knowledge; beneficence • **rich robe** worldly pomp and vanity • **yellow robe** those condemned by the Spanish Inquisition; attribute of Jews • **velvet and ermine robe** rank; royalty

robin spring; tameness; love; friendliness; associated with May

rochet loving administration

rock solidity; permanence; cohesion; the source of human life; truth; the spirit as foundation; the Spirit; the Creator; the Church; Christ (especially when surmounted by a cross); St. Peter; Christian steadfastness; hiding place; durability; immortality; constancy; justice; solitude; conservatism • **water flowing from a rock** associated with Moses • **four rivers gushing from a rock** the four Gospels • **to be thrown from a rock** punishment of a traitor • **man chained to a rock, attacked by eagles** Prometheus • **man chained to a rock, attacked by a monster** Andromeda, Hesione • **to hide under a rock** trait of a low animal • *see also* **stone**

rocket (plant) in flower language: rivalry; *queen's rocket*: fashionable; you are the queen of coquettes

rod punishment; official power; correction; wickedness; liberty; phallus; light; the universal axis; support; attribute of the Passion of Christ, the sibyl Tiburtina • **flowering rod** attribute of Aaron, the Virgin Mary, St. Joseph • **rod with snake** attribute of Aaron • **Rod of Jesse** attribute of Christ, the Virgin Mary

roebuck nimbleness; speed; gentleness; Christ; love; wisdom; foresight • *see also* **deer**

roll *see* **scroll**

Rome associated with heroic death, suicide, holiness, past glory, greatness

rood *see* **cross**

rood beam the necessity of the cross of Calvary in passing from the Church Militant to the Church Triumphant

rood screen the gates of heaven

roof protection; safety; hospitality; stage for preaching; peeping spot; place of idolatry, mourning, lamentation, hiding

rook (bird) dawn; April; spring; gregariousness; a priest • **Egypt** marriage; when dead: sunset • **rooks flying in a great flock** presage of rain

room individuality; loneliness; privacy of mind and body • **closed room without windows** virginity; non-communication • **closed room with windows** the possibility of understanding and communication

rooster vigilance; the sun; activity; resurrection; the male principle Christianity; incest; egotism; defiance; self-confidence; the Crucifixion; associated with Mercury; emblem of France; attribute of St. Peter (especially when crowing), his denial and repentance, also of the personifications of Lust, Adultery • **China** the yang principle; *red rooster*: protection against fire; *white rooster*: purity; protection against evil; the only capable guide of transient spirits • **Orient** on a red or gold disk: the sun • **young rooster** foolishness • **red rooster** Catholicism • **white rooster** good fortune; dawn; a man of holy ways • **black rooster** bad luck; death; night • *see also* **chicken; chick; hen; capon**

roots foundation, but they do not necessarily imply stability

rope bondage; enslavement; entanglement, which see; mythic ascension; despair; fetter; betrayal; link; sun ray; the prerogative of power, especially a short piece; hanging; attribute of the Passion of Christ, St. Andrew • **rope around the neck** a penitent; attribute of St. Charles Borromeo, St. Mark, Judas • **putting a rope on one's head** repentance • **gold rope** divine power • **hanging man** Judas; Despair personified • **rope and vase** attribute of Nemesis • **rope binding a chariot** the Gordian knot, associated with Alexander the Great

rosary perpetual continuity; devotion; meditation; inane repetition; circle of perfection; futility of aspiration; prayer; emblem of Catholicism; attribute of St. Dominic, St. John Berchmans, occasionally St. Catherine of Siena

rose (color) associated with Libra

rose (flower) completion; perfection; the heart; God; the beloved; paradise; messianic hope; Christ; beauty; the Virgin Mary; female sex organs; integration of the personality; associated with Taurus; attribute of Venus, the Three Graces, the Erythraean sibyl, St. Rita • **heraldry** youth; beauty; charm; joy; innocence; silence; gentleness • **blue rose** the impossible; faithful unto death; martial honor • **gold rose** absolute achievement; fame; papal benediction • **purple rose** sorrow • **red rose** divine love; martyrdom (especially in painting); emblem of the House of York; motherhood • **white rose** inspired wisdom; joy; purity (especially in painting); emblem of the House of Lancaster • **yellow rose** infidelity; jealousy; emblem of Texas • **red and white roses together** emblem of the Virgin Mary • **eight-petalled rose** regeneration • **rose on a corpse** the death of Christ • **thornless rose** associated

with the Virgin Mary • **rose with thorns** thesis and antithesis; conjunction of opposites • **entwined around a crucifix** attribute of St. Therese of Lisieux • **roses in an apron or lap** attribute of St. Elizabeth of Hungary • **basket of roses and apples** attribute of St. Dorothea • **angels with rose garlands** exultation of St. Dorothea • **garland of roses** an allusion to the rosary of the Virgin Mary; reward of virtue • **garland of red and white roses** attribute of St. Cecilia • **wreath of roses** indicative of heavenly joy • **rose garden** the new Jerusalem; regeneration • **roses springing from blood drops** associated with St. Francis of Assisi • **flower language** love; beauty; *Australian rose*: thou art all that is lovely; *bridal rose*: happy; *burgundy rose*: unconscious beauty; *cabbage rose*: ambassador of love; *campion rose*: only deserve my love; *Carolina rose*: love is dangerous; *China rose*: beauty always new; *Christmas rose*: the Nativity of Christ, tranquillize my anxiety; *daily rose*: I aspire to your smile; *damask rose*: freshness, brilliant complexion, beauty ever new, a maid's blushing; *deep red rose*: bashful shame, martyrdom; *dog rose*: pleasure and pain, simplicity; *full red rose*: beauty; *hundred-leaved rose*: pride, dignity of the mind, emblem of the Three Graces; *Japan rose*: beauty is your only attraction; *Lancaster rose*: union; *maiden blush rose*: if you love me you will reveal it, if you love me you will find it out; *May rose*: precociousness; *moss rose*: love, voluptuousness; *moss rose bud*: confession of love; *full moss rose*: superior merit; *mundi rose*: variety, you are merry; *musk rose*: capricious beauty; *musk rose cluster*: charming; *pompon rose*: gentility; pettiness; *red rose*: love;

red leaved rose: beauty and prosperity; *red rosebud*: you are young and beautiful, you are pure and lovely; *rock rose*: safety; *unique rose*: call me not beautiful; *white rose*: silence, girlhood, heart of ignorant love; *dried white rose*: death is preferable to loss, unfaithfulness; *full white rose*: I am worthy of you; *withered white rose*: transient impression; *red and white roses together*: unity, warmth of hearth; *multiflora rose*: grace; *guelder rose*: winter, age, good news, bound; *full grown rose placed over two buds*: secrecy; *single rose*: simplicity; *thornless rose*: early attachment; *York and Lancaster roses together*: war; *rose in a tuft of grass*: there is everything

Rose of Sharon Christ's love for the Church

rose window eternity • *see also* **lotus**

rosemary remembrance; madness; Nativity of Christ • **flower language** your presence revives me; memory; fidelity between lovers; remembrance; remembrance of the dead

rosette *see* **lotus**

rotting spiritual decay

rowan oracle; death; immortality; protection against witches, but also used by them

rubber tree associated with Cancer

rubbing (motion) friction; impediment; difficulty; annoyance; transfer of magical power

ruby divine zeal; human love; July; charity; love; passion; beauty; dignity; divine power; royalty; light; elegance; happiness; rashness; associated with Leo, sometimes also with Capricorn, Taurus, Cancer • **ruby changing color** presage of mischief • **ruby regaining color** the danger is over

rudbeckia in flower language: justice

rudder safety; government; moral rectitude; control; power; skill; knowledge; intuition; navigation; guide; authority; prudence; wisdom; divine will; attribute of Nemesis, the personifications of Chance, Fortune, Abundance • **rudder on a globe** sovereignty • **rudder with a caduceus and cornucopia** the government of Caesar

rue (plant) grace; goodness; pity; mercy; repentance; sorrow; disdain; purification; bitterness; antidote for madness, poison • **flower language** disdain; *goat's rue*: reason

ruins life defunct; sentiments, ideas, or customs which are dead and irrelevant to present life, but which nonetheless persist • **columns in ruins** attribute of St. Titus

rule (for measuring) standard of morality; reason; choice; attribute of St. Thomas, the personifications of Geometry, Arithmetic, Melancholy

rune magic; ancient knowledge

rush (plant) fertility; wantonness; transitoriness; docility; humility; quietness • **flowering rush and white crown** emblem of the Upper Kingdom of Egypt • **flower language** docility

russet (cloth) earth; filth; heat; violence; oppression; dawn; love of darkness and lies • **russet mantle** loss of good reputation; attribute of Dawn personified

Russia darkness; dreariness

rust disuse; age; distruction; infirmity; suffering

rye connected with love

S

S associated with a new cycle, the wheel of fortune, the number one, the creative impulse for intangible things, incentive, the serpent, health, wisdom, the Holy Spirit, the sun in the tarot deck, the lungs, Pisces, Cancer

sack attribute of Isaiah

sackcloth especially when with ashes: mourning, penitence, affliction

sacrifice giving up something of lower value for something of value on a higher plane

saffron charity; associated with Buddhism; attribute of the Virgin Mary (especially when with spikenard) • **flower language** beware of excess; do not abuse; *crocus saffron*: mirth; *meadow saffron*: my happiest days are past

sage (herb) remembrance; longevity; immortality; egotism; emblem of Health personified • **flower language** esteem; domestic virtues; *garden sage*: esteem

sagebrush good fortune; emblem of the West in the U.S.

Sagittarius the complete man in both animal and spiritual nature

sail(s) breath; the Holy Spirit; venture; adventure; action; creative breath; the spur to action; attribute of Venus, Fortune personified; the wind; related to **boat, ship, sailboat,** q.q.v. • **full sail** pregnancy; swelling powers; emblem of Air personified • **striking sail** defeat; surrender; humbleness • **purple sails** attribute of Cleopatra's barge

sailboat the Church; attribute of St. Simon, St. Jude (especially when mast is cross shaped) • **sailboat on the Nile** attribute of St. Athanasius • *see also* **boat; ship; sail**

sailor conductor of the soul; coming to grips with the unconscious; partakes of the symbolism of the sea, sail, sailboat, boat, ship, q.q.v.

sainfoin in flower language: agitation

St. John's wort in flower language: animosity; superstition; you are a prophet

salamander fire; the ardent lover;

chastity; virginity; baptism; enduring and triumphant faith; the Christian who resists temptation by grace; the Devil personified, but also Christ as the king of fire; a soldier surviving a battle; attribute of Fire personified • **heraldry** constancy • **Greece** emblem of winter

salmon wisdom

Salome wantonness; pleasure

salt strength; superiority; perpetuity; hospitality; wisdom; wit; sterility; piquancy; worth; preservation; incorruptibility; truth; immortality; friendship

salt water sterility; truth; the ocean; tears • **Jewish** the tears shed by the race

sanctuary lamp in Catholic and Anglican churches: the presence of the Host at the altar

sand barrenness; fruitless labor; endurance; time (from its use in the hourglass); instability; connected with sleep

sandals liberty; freedom; humility; the lowest material life; attribute of monks, pilgrims, royalty, the wealthy (especially in ancient art) • **winged sandals** loftiness of spirit; attribute of Mercury, Perseus • **golden sandals** attribute of royalty • **sword and sandal under a rock** associated with Theseus • **one sandal** attribute of a warrior • **carrying sandals** humility • **going without sandals** poverty; mourning • *see also* **shoes; foot**

sandalwood exoticism; sacredness

sap celestial milk or the mother goddess; life fluid (blood, semen, etc.)

sapphire heavenly truth; sincerity; conscience; hope; heavenly meditation; heavenly reward; purity; emblem of the Virgin Mary; associated with Saturn, Libra, Virgo, September; attribute of Apollo • **heraldry** piety and sincerity • **sapphire ring** attribute of a cardinal

sarcophagus the feminine principle

of containment; death; woman; earth as the beginning and end of material life

sardony in flower language: irony

sash (clothing) distinction; office; attribute of St. Monica; carries all the symbolism of the belt, which see

Satan anger; witchcraft; delusion

satinflower in flower language: sincerity

Saturday *see* **days**

Saturn (god) destructive and devouring time; fertility; agriculture; consciousness; man as an existential being; activity; communication; endurance; reserve; subjective evil

Saturn (planet) associated with caution, conservatism, restriction, discipline, the number seven, Aquarius, the knees and calves, the god Saturn

saturnalia the invocation of primordial chaos; a desperate quest for a way out of time; the desire to concentrate all the possibilities of existence in a small period of time

satyr abandon; folly; lust; a child of the Devil; revelry; lasciviousness; evil; fertility; associated with Bacchus; attribute of Lust personified

saucer feminine symbol of containment; dish for bloodletting

Saul perfect friendship

savage the darker side of the personality; the natural man; instincts; desires • *see also* **wild man**

saw (tool) attribute of Isaiah, Melancholy personified, St. Joseph, St. Jude, St. Matthias, St. Euphemia, St. Simon (especially a large saw, or a saw with one or two oars), St. James the Less (especially with the handle upright) • **heraldry** industry

scabbard feminine symbol of containment; vulva

scabious mourning • **flower language** unfortunate love; *sweet scabious*: widowhood

scaffold hanging; building; theater

scales (balances) *see* **balances**

scales (fish) protection; defense; related to water and the underworld; moral or cosmic inferiority • **scales on mermaids, dragons, the Devil** the past continuing in the present; the inferior continuing in the superior

scallop shell *see* **shell**

scapegoat vicarious atonement

scapular the yoke of Christ; attribute of St. Simon Stock

scar remnant of mutilation (which see), usually with a sinister connotation

scarab the sun; self-creation; fertility; immortality; eternity; the rising sun; reincarnation; resurrection; the creation and revival of life; related to the ladybug, which see • **male scarab** attribute of Kheperi • *see also* **beetle**

scarecrow originally a fertility deity; powerlessness; old age; the soul; disguise to avoid facing reality

scarf love; romance; false front; often related to middle age • **black scarf** death

scarlet energy; life; fire; fervor; worldliness; protection; jurisprudence; general virtue and merit; mutual love; sin; steady drinking; a loud color • **scarlet coat** attribute of huntsmen, British soldiers • **scarlet hat** attribute of a cardinal • **scarlet letter A** an adulterer • **scarlet robe** the mocking of Christ • **"scarlet" woman** prostitute; woman of loose morals

scepter fertility; power; phallus; fecundation; royalty; authority; military command; world axis; any higher office; the creative power of the Word; the power of chastity; the connection between heaven and earth; attribute of the archangel Gabriel, Osiris, Mithra, Jupiter, Zeus, Oybele, the personifications of Philosophy, Justice, Fortitude, Good Government, Europe • **scepter in**

still life the power that death takes away • **scepter underfoot** attribute of Melpomene, St. Louis of Toulouse (often also with crown) • **split scepter** peace; reconciliation of opposites • **scepter of lead** night • **scepter and chain** Joseph's advancement • **scepter and trumpet** attribute of Joshua • **scepter with censer** attribute of Melchizedek; messianic hope • **scepter tipped with eagle** attribute of Roman consuls, triumphant generals • **scepter tipped with a fleur-de-lis** attribute of the Virgin Mary, French kings • **scepter tipped with a dove** peace and reconciliation; attribute of English kings • **scepter tipped with orb and cross** attribute of English kings • **scepter tipped with a cuckoo** attribute of Juno • **scepter tipped with an eye** attribute of Modesty personified, signifying Temperance • **scepter tipped with a cross** temporal power; Christ as king • **scepter tipped with cross and lily** attribute of Principalities • **scepter with scroll** attribute of Solomon

schinus in flower language: religious enthusiasm

scimitar emblem of Arabian countries, the Middle East; attribute of St. Bartholomew • **scimitar with book** (usually closed) attribute of St. Matthias • **U.S.** emblem of the Shriners

scissors creation; birth; destruction; death; conjunction of opposites; physical extermination; spiritual decision; fate; attribute of the Fates, barbers, tailors, sheep shearers, Delilah • **heraldry** usually an occupational sign (barbers, tailors, sheep shearers, etc.) • *see also* **shears**

Scorpio related to sexual function, material life

scorpion the Devil; sin; remorse; torture; evil; suffering; mischief and discord; contempt; treachery; flattery; a Jew; Judas; Scorpio; unbend-

ing pride; defensive stewardship; fire; lust; suicide; associated with October; attribute of Isis (usually seven scorpions), Selk(et), the personifications of Envy, Dialectics, Hatred, Heresy, Africa, Earth, Logic

Scotland associated with thrift, obstinancy, perseverance, roughness; puritanism

scourge (whip) discipline; divine chastisement; form of penance, torture; a sharp tongue; punishment for Roman debtors, Elizabethan prostitutes; promotion of fertility; related to hunting; remorse; persecution; attribute of Bellona, St. Boniface, St. Gervase, St. Protase, St. Peter, St. Ambrose (usually with three knots, sometimes two scourges with a beehive), the sibyl Agrippa, the Passion of Christ (usually two, often crossed) • **two scourges and a pillar** persecution

scourging *see* **flagellation**

scratch weed in flower language: hardness

screech owl *see* **owl**

screw security; tightness; sexual activity

scrip pilgrimage

scroll wisdom; life; time; the Pentateuch; the Law; prophecy; Holy Scripture; punishment of God; decrees of fate; divine revelation; writing skills; contract; legal document; sometimes merely ornamentation; attribute of Clio, Calliope, Thalia, writers, prophets, saints, Isaiah, Jeremiah, authors of the Old Testament, the archangel Uriel, the Apostles (especially the Evangelists), St. James the Great, the personifications of the Seven Liberal Arts (especially Logic, but also Music, Astronomy, Arithmetic, Geometry, Rhetoric, and Grammar) • **unrolling scroll** the unrolling of life, the upper roll is the future, the lower roll is the past • **scroll with Gregorian music** attribute of St. Gregory the Great, St. Ambrose • scroll with harp music • scroll with pencil or quill literature • twelve scrolls the twelve Epistles of St. Paul • scroll and red vestment attribute of Elijah • four scrolls the four Gospels • scroll with scepter attribute of Solomon • bishop's miter on scroll attribute of St. Asaph • winged scroll associated with Zechariah • scroll with two keys attribute of St. Peter • scroll with a sheaf of wheat Old Testament Pentecost • scroll with the word "Theotokos" attribute of St. Cyril • scroll with tall cross attribute of St. Philip • scroll with the words "Ecce Agnus Dei" attribute of John the Baptist • scroll with the words "Vox clementis in deserto" attribute of John the Baptist • scroll with the words "Ora pro nobis Deum" attribute of St. Gregory the Great • scroll being eaten St. John at the Apocalypse • scroll on Jewish graves divine presence • scroll in the hands of a Patriarch the darkness faith was enveloped in before Christ

Scylla the immediate expectation of the fruits of action as an impedance to moral progress

scythe time; death; autumn; harvest; death of the old year; related to the moon (because of the crescent blade); weapon of peasants; passivity; castration; phallus; the inexorable march of time; self-mutilation; renewed hopes for rebirth; attribute of Saturn, Cronus, Father Time, the Grim Reaper, occasionally Ceres, the personifications of Summer, Death

sea see ocean

sea gull see gull

sea horse see hippocampus

sea lion boldness

sea serpent on old maps: unexplored waters • see also ocean; serpent

sea urchin sun emblem; life force; the primordial seed; resurrection; immortality

seal (animal) the circus; exhibitionism; protection; steed of sea deities; a human being under a spell

seal (stamp) ownership; individuality; security; secrecy; authenticity; identity; power; authorization; individuation; preservation; virginity; love • wax seal virginity; repression; narrowmindedness • Abraham's seal circumcision • seven seal the seven principle events in Christ's life (incarnation, baptism, the passion, the descent into Hell, resurrection, ascension, descent of the Holy Spirit) • see also Solomon's seal

seat stability • seated man or woman supreme deity or the earthly representative thereof • see also throne

seaweed the eternal; bondslaves; maternal fertility; God; eternal life

secret the power of the supernatural

sedan chair in China, a green sedan chair is the attribute of a lower government official

sedge refuge of the lover • absence of sedge desolation

seed latent possibilities; hope; the Mystic Center; fertility; growth; potentiality; children; divine instruction • three seeds of the Tree of Life associated with Seth • germinating seed the mother • see also mustard seed

see-saw balance; vacillation; choice; coition; attribute of wind deities

semen the purest part of an individual or of one's being; fertility; the life force

sensitive plant see mimosa

senvy in flower language: indifference

septfoil the Seven Gifts of the Holy Spirit, the seven sacraments of Pre-Reformation times, etc. • see also seven

sepulchre death; corruption • whitened sepulchre that of a hypocrite • red hot sepulchre that of a heretic •

model of a sepulchre attribute of St. Helena

seraph guardianship; might; swiftness; heavenly messenger; wisdom; zeal; the spirit of love and imagination • heraldry dignity; honor; high position

serpent evil; sin; energy; force; night; subterranean life; fertility; wisdom; power to heal; generative energy; regeneration; the Devil; secrecy; hiding; danger; death; materialism; slavery; temptation; fascination; jealousy; wisdom of the deep; guardian of the springs of life, immortality, the superior riches of the spirit; great mysteries; forces of destruction; seduction of strength by matter; the inferior within the superior; the evil inherent in all worldly things; the evil side of nature; the feminine principle; a phallic symbol; the unconscious expressing itself suddenly and unexpectedly with terrible or frightening results; emblem of the tribe of Dan; attribute of Saturn, Janus, Father Time, Asclepius, Minerva, Ceres, St. Patrick, the personifications of Time, Earth, Logic, Innocence, Africa • heraldry strategy; military fame; courage; vigilance; instinct; the subconscious • China evil; cunning • horned snake water; intensified duality; opposite forces in conflict • feathered snake duality (good/evil, heaven/earth, etc.) • brass snake associated with the Crucifixion • snake with head erect human wisdom • rising snake retrospection • snake in a circle, or biting its own tail eternity; time; union of the sexes (has to have its tail in its mouth); the zodiac • snake encircling a globe the spread of sin; the omnipresence of sin • snake encircling a tree the Fall of Man • woman holding a mirror and a serpent Prudence personified • serpent at the foot of the Cross Christ's overcoming of the evil that leads man into sin • plumed serpent beneficence; reconciliation of opposites; the angel of dawn • serpent with sheep's head spring; initiation; spiritualization • serpent with rod or staff the miracles of Aaron, Moses • serpent over a fire associated with St. Paul at Melita • twin serpents death; all binary opposites (good/evil, male/female, life/death, etc.) • three coiled snakes attribute of St. Hilda • serpent sloughing its skin rebirth; healing • kissing a serpent's head fellatio • serpent on a Tau cross Christ • the Virgin Mary with a serpent underfoot victory of the Seed of Woman • bruised serpent attribute of the Virgin Mary indicating her victory over sin • serpent battling with a fish Satan tempting Christ • serpent emerging from a cup or chalice the attempted poisoning of St. John • serpent on a sword attribute of St. John • serpent in a loaf of bread or in other food attribute of St. Benedict • woman with serpents for hair Medusa • woman with serpent to breast Cleopatra • woman treading on serpent the Persian sibyl • serpent entwined around a woman's arm or leg Eurydice • serpent with a woman's head Deceit personified • serpent entwining a corpse, with other victims nearby Cadmus • two youths and a man wrestling with a serpent Laocoon and his sons • infant wrestling with two serpents Hercules • man shooting python with arrows Apollo • image of a serpent with a human head on a shield attribute of the Iron Age personified • serpent around man's wrist at campfire St. Paul • serpent with infant in a basket Erichthonius • see also viper; asp; wyvern; sea serpent; python

service free in flower language: prudence

seven completeness; perfect order; planetary order; exceptional value; transformation and unification of all hierarchical orders; conflict; pain; the moon; the sun; charity; grace; the Holy Spirit; holiness; consecration; stability; safety; rest; creation; cosmos; space; wisdom; an indefinite number (that is, it means "many"); associated with the closing of a cycle, Uranus, culture, coldness, intellect, music, wealth, health, philosophy, deceit, stubbornness, unexpected and willful action, fate, courage, heavy responsibilities, the color gray, the archangel Gabriel; has the value of letters G, P, Y; may stand for the seven liberal arts, the seven virtues, the seven vices, the seven gifts of the Holy Spirit, the seven joys and seven sorrows of the Virgin Mary, the seven sacraments of the Church, the seven planets known in the ancient world, the seven last words on the Cross, the seven penitential psalms, the seven trumpets of Jericho, the seven days in the week, the seven stars in the Pleiades, etc., etc. • kabala victory

seventeen associated with the angel Uriel

seventy a fortunate number; multiplies the qualities of seven, which see; associated with finality, death, resurrection • kabala catastrophe

seventy-two a ritual number involving solar increase and lunar wisdom; associated with angels, mercy, but also evil and confusion

sewer the unconscious; the instincts; the base and the vile

sewing life; the temporal; the transitory; the cyclic; typical occupation of the housewife

sextant navigation; attribute of Astronomy personified

sexual intercourse union of the male and female principles

shadow the evil or base side of the physical body; existence between the soul and the body; the alter ego; the soul; the primitive side of an individual; a departed soul; gloom; obscurity; the past; protection; a ghost

shaft see column

shaking sainfoin in flower language: agitation

shamrock the Trinity; loyalty; emblem of Ireland; attribute of St. Patrick, St. Gerald • flower language light-heartedness

Shangri-la retreat from the world; eternal youth

shark danger; evil; rapacity

sheaf unification; agriculture; integration; strength; discipline; God's bounty; plenty; Joseph's dream; Thanksgiving • sheaf with scroll Old Testament Feast of the Pentecost • fourteen sheaves Joseph, his wife, and their twelve sons • sheaf with a sickle death; harvest; autumn • see also wheat; entanglement

shears attribute of Atropos, St. Agatha of Sicily, Fury personified

sheen time

sheep the congregation; the faithful; the higher qualities and virtues of the soul; innocence; simplicity; love; gentleness; charity; sacrifice; guilelessness; gregariousness; helplessness; obstinacy; stupidity; straying; clouds; attribute of Eve, Usury personified • China the retiring life • sheep with its feet bound the sacrificial lamb • sheep on a man's shoulders the Good Shepherd • twelve sheep the Apostles • sheepskin connected with parchment, which see; diploma • coat or cloak of a sheep's skin fertility • see also ram; lamb; fleece; wool

sheet bed; coition; death; ghost; sail; garb of ghosts • winding sheet death • sheet with cross the Passion of Christ

Shekinah God's presence

shell related to the moon, woman; fertility; the female principle of containment; vulva; related to Venus, the Virgin Mary, virgin birth; alludes to the presence of water; attribute of pilgrims, St. Roch, St. Augustine of Hippo, St. James the Great, St. Michael, Folly personified • **heraldry** pilgrimmage, especially to Santiago in Spain; any successful distant journey • **chariot of shell** the vehicle of Neptune, Galatea, Fortune personified • **shell shaped stones** attribute of St. Stephen • **shell dripping with water** baptism • **kneeling youth offering a shell as a cup to a maiden** Granida and Dafilo • **scallop shell shown with a snail** attribute of St. Lydia • *see also* **conch shell**

shepherd the conductor of souls to the land of the dead; Christ; the priest; a protector; bishops of the Christian church; guardian of ancient wisdom; the moon; the rustic lover • **twelve shepherds** the Apostles

shield defense; protection; faith; salvation; virtue; defense of the spirit; divine defense; attribute of Diana, the personifications of Rhetoric, Chastity, the Church • **blank shield** attribute of Judas • **highly polished shield** attribute of Perseus • **shield inscribed "Maria," "A.M.," or "AMGPDT"** attribute of the archangel Gabriel • **white shield with a red cross** attribute of St. George of Cappadocia • **shield with an image of Medusa's head** attribute of Minerva • **shield with an image of a lion or a ball** attribute of Fortitude personified • **shield with an image of a serpent with a human head** attribute of the Iron Age personified

Shiloah (pond in Jerusalem) God's protection

ship consciousness; transcendance; safety; hope; confidence; the womb; a feminine symbol of containment; the Church; attribute of St. Peter, St. Ursula, St. Vincent, St. Nicholas of Myra, St. Francis Xavier, St. Julian, Christ calming the Sea of Gali-lee, Hope personified, occasionally St. John • **heraldry** veteran of sea expeditions; merchant riches; happiness; power; succor in extremity • **ship with a staff** attribute of St. Wilfred • **model of a ship in the hand of a woman** Claudia, Fortune personified • **model of a ship in the hand of a bishop** St. Erasmus • **ship in a harbor** associated with Zebulum • **twelve men rowing a ship** the Apostles moving the Church • **man preaching from the stern of a ship** St. Peter leading the Church • **ship on the Nile** attribute of St. Athanasius • **ship with windmill and fish** attribute of St. Mary of Cleophus • **young man bearing woman off to ships** abduction of Helen of Troy • **tattoo of a full rigged ship** in the 19th Century, an attribute of a sailor who had sailed around Cape Horn • **ship on a stormy sea** the Church surviving persecution, heresy, schism; alludes to Christ's calming of the Sea of Galilee • **ship ploughing waves** joy; happiness • **ship sailing** living to transcend existence • **hold of a ship** the unconscious; experience on the lower plane • *see also* **ark; boat**

ship of fools sailing as an end in itself and not in the sense of seeking a safe arrival in heaven

shipwreck tragic fortune

shittim Ark of the Covenant; the Burning Bush of Moses

shiver a sudden shiver for no apparent reason is considered a bad omen

shoe(s) liberty; usefulness; utility; vagina; fertility; love; humility; pleasure; power; royalty (especially golden shoes) • *see also* **sandal; foot**

shofar the call of God; obedience to divine will; supreme loyalty to God; attribute of Abraham

shooting star a heavenly omen; related to angels, which see

shoulder(s) strength; responsibility

• **giant with child on shoulders** St. Christopher carrying the Christ child • **giant with youth on shoulders** Orion • **man with old man on shoulders** Aeneas

shovel fertility; the androgyne; labor; attribute of Adam after the Fall

shower of gold: sun rays • *see also* **rain**

shrimp smallness; shyness

shroud death; attribute of St. Joseph of Arimathea • **shroud with cross** the Passion of Christ • **shroud pierced with knife and bleeding** St. John's shroud (usually held by St. Gregory the Great)

shuttle (weaver's) man's life; transitoriness; lightness

sibyl the intuiting of higher truths; prophetic powers

sickle time; death; agriculture; fertility; reaping; end of the world; instrument of castration; attribute of Saturn, Cronus, Perseus, Priapus, Ceres (occasionally), the personifications of Summer, Hope • **held by Christ enthroned with angels about the Apocalypse** • **hammer and sickle** emblem of the U.S.S.R., communism

sickness *see* **disease**

sieve purification; perfection; wisdom; self knowledge through action; small talk; vanity; hope; chastity; attribute of Tuccia, Chastity personified • **broken sieve** attribute of St. Benedict

sigma, sigmoid divine power; communication or connection with heaven

silk beauty; extravagance; luxury; upper classes; the bonds of social behavior; sensuality; purity; virtue; riches • **woman in silk** a loose woman, as opposed to a virtuous woman in linen

silk worm in China: emblem of industry

silver purity; faith; chastity; eloquence; innocence; clear conscience; virginity; fidelity; associated with Cancer, the moon • **heraldry** chastity; innocence; wisdom; sincerity; justice; peace; joy; victory • **China** brightness; purity; protects children from evil influences • **silver as payment** bribery; betrayal • **thirty pieces of silver** the betrayal of Christ by Judas • **silver weapons** bribery • **silver doors** associated with the palace of the sun

singing fostering and bring forth life • *see also* **music**

siren (mechanical) danger; a human cry; hysteria; psychic disturbance

siren (mythology) temptation; a treacherous woman; the base forces in woman; sensual pleasure; death bearer; death wish; corrupt imagination; desire leading to self destruction; sorcery; empty or deceptive attraction; involutive fragmentation of the unconscious

Sirius death; plague; summer fever; war; wantonness; an evil omen

sistrum fertility; wedding; prostitution; war; attribute of Isis • *see also* **tambourine**

Sisyphus senseless human endeavor; the rise and fall of the sun

sitting sovereignty; judgment; council; peace; leisure • **act of sitting down** acquiescence • **sitting on the ground** desolation; mourning; penance; leisure • **sitting at a window** mourning; yearning • **sitting in darkness** slavery

six a perfect number; the six days of Creation, the six hours of Christ on the cross, the six sins against the Holy Ghost, the six gifts of the Holy Spirit, etc., etc.; associated with divine power, majesty, justice, creation, perfection, material comforts, education, marriage, institutions, harmony, responsibility, beauty, art, balance, happiness, family life, love, peace, life, good fortune, wisdom, mercy, spirituality, virginity, stabilizing influences, trial and effort, the soul, equilibrium, ambivalence, the duality of all things, Venus, the angel Raphael, the colors yellow and light blue, the letters F, O, and X • **kabala** experiment

six hundred perfection

six hundred and sixty-six the Beast of the Apocalypse; also applied to Adolf Hitler, Martin Luther and other protestants

sixpence cleanliness; a lucky coin

sixteen associated with happiness, luxury, love, sensuality, fertility, increase, the angel Samael; the ideal age for a lover

sixty a multiplication of the qualities of six, which see; associated with time, happiness, harmony, destiny • **kabala** destiny

sixty-nine a lucky number; associated with Cancer (the numbers are usually on their sides, one above the other) • **U.S.** simultaneous oral-genital sex

skeleton death; vanity; usually has infernal implications; Death personified • **skeleton at a feast** reminder of mortality

skidding loss of control of the Id by the Ego and Superego

skin • **human skin** death by flaying; attribute of St. Bartholomew • **animal skin** associated with death and rebirth, John the Baptist • **coat or cloak of**—*cat, mouse, ass skin*: humility; *ox skin, sheep skin*: fertility; *lion skin*: attribute of Hercules, Fortune personified, sun heroes • *see also* **fleece**

skirt a woman • **spreading a skirt over someone** copulation; protection; taking possession

skull mortality; the worldly survival of the dead; death; the transitory nature of life on earth; the useless nature of earthly things; sin; the Fall of Man; attribute of Adam, Hosea, Hamlet, St. Francis of Assisi, St. Romuald, St. Mary Magdalene, St. Paul, St. Jerome, and other hermit

and penitent saints, the personifications of Old Age, Melancholy • **skull in a portrait** a mark of piety; when shown with a laurel crown: fame that will endure • **skull with a cross** meditation upon eternal life that comes after death • **skull and crossbones** pirates; poison; the brevity of life; danger to life • **skull and crossbones at the foot of the Cross** refers to the legend that the Cross rested upon the bones of Adam • **skull at the foot of the Cross** Adam's skull representing sin

skullcap dignity; reverence; distinction

skunk offensiveness; obscenity; truculence; complete defeat

sky the active male principle; the father; holiness; purity; the supreme deity or his dwelling

skylark *see* **lark**

slavery subjection to lower nature

sleep ignorance; retreat; withdrawal; wisdom; giver of prophetic dreams; connected with coition; opportunity for the soul to leave the body; susceptibility to evil

sleeping beauty passive potential; ancestral memories lying dormant in the unconscious; the anima; sexuality lying dormant in a woman until the right man appears; fertility awakened by the sun

slime substance of Chaos; stagnancy; decay; inertia preceding rebirth; evil; sin

sling especially with five stones: attribute of David in his battle with Goliath

slipper *see* **shoe; sandal; foot**

slithering things *see* **creeping things**

sloe difficulty; austerity; the berry of the blackthorn, which see

slug (animal) the male seed; the origin of life; the tendency of darkness to move toward light; attribute of Sloth personified

sluice as a verb: a euphemism for coition • **sluice gate** vagina

smell bridge to heaven • **evil smell** sin • **pungent smell** protection against evil spirits

smelling apprehension; discrimination; investigation

smoke evanescence; all that is fleeting; the shortness of life; vanity; the anger and wrath of God; mental darkness; evil; love; protection; punishment; war; industrialization; illusion obscuring truth; the futility of earthly glory; the supernatural or supra-natural

snail fruitfulness; resurrection; slowness; humility; the sinner; laziness; emergence of sexual power; sensitivity; the self (the shell representing the conscious, the soft inner part the unconscious or one's personality); tenderness; attribute of Sloth personified • **heraldry** deliberation; perseverance; acquired possessions to be preserved and enlarged • **snails when eaten** sexual power • **snail with scallop shell** attribute of St. Lydia • **snail's track** the Milky Way; connection between heaven and earth

snake *see* serpent

snake's foot in flower language: horror

snake's lounge in flower language: slander

snapdragon in flower language: presumption, indiscretion

snare sin; temptation; a strange woman

sneezing the soul trying to leave the body; generally an ominous sign, but in Greece and Rome, a good sign • **days associated with sneezing** • **Monday**, you sneeze for danger • **Tuesday**, you kiss a stranger • **Wednesday**, you sneeze for a letter • **Thursday**, you sneeze for something better • **Friday**, you sneeze for sorrow • **Saturday**, see your sweetheart tomorrow • **Sunday**, for safety seek, the Devil will have you the whole of the week

sniffing *see* smelling

snipe a fool; a simpleton

snood virginity

snow death; blindness; nothingness; purity; chastity; impotence; frigidity, especially in women; virginity; cocain • *see also* **ice**

snowball in flower language: bound; age; winter of age; good news

snowdrop friendship in adversity; purity; herald of spring; connected with Candlemas; emblem of the Virgin Mary • **flower language** consolation; hope

sock (stocking) comedy

Sodom carnal passion

soil *see* earth

solar wheel life; fertility; the sun, which see

soldier bravery; defense; vigilance; service; devotion to a cause; striving mental qualities; St. Sergius; St. Bacchus • **soldier, blind and begging** Belisarius • **soldier throwing his sword onto a scale pan** Brennus • **soldier placing his hand into a brazier** Mucius Scaevola • **soldier on a couch with a woman, his weapons aside** love conquering war; Mars with Venus • **woman hammering a tent peg into a soldier's head** death of Sisera • **soldier holding a mirror for his mistress** Rinaldo and Armida • **soldier kneeling before a fleece** Gideon • **soldier accompanied by Mercury** Hercules • **soldier on horseback, leaping into a pit** Marcus Curtius • **soldier with dragon** St. George, Perseus, St. Theodore, St. Angelica • **soldier stabbing a woman before a judge** death of Virginia • **soldier in bedchamber, holding a naked woman at swordpoint** the rape of Lucretia • **soldier before a tomb, woman at swordpoint** the sacrifice of Polyxena • **soldier in camp, maiden being threatened by arrow** martyrdom of St. Ursula • **several soldiers attacking women and children** the

Iron Age • **several soldiers killing babies** slaying of the Holy Innocents • **soldier with wings** the archangel Michael • **soldier standing with sword, and shield or lance** St. Demetrius • **soldier holding cloak and sword** St. Martin of Tours • **soldier with palm, banner with eagle and red cross on breastplate** St. Maurice • **soldier receiving monk's habit from abbot** St. William of Aquitaine • **soldier fighting enemy on bridge** Horatius Cocles (Horatio) • **soldier fighting with naked man on bridge** Rodomont (in armor) and Orlando (naked) • **soldier slaying a sage** death of Archimedes • **soldier on a white horse, killing Saracens** St. James the Greater • **soldier with anvil** St. Adrian • **soldier with palm and banner of the Resurrection** St. Ansanus • **soldier with falcon on wrist** St. Bavo • **soldier with stag** St. Eustace • **soldier with millstone, or bucket, or pitcher** St. Florian • **soldier with crocodile** St. Theodore • **soldier with keys** St. Hippolytus • **soldier with lance, on horseback** St. Longinus • **soldiers scaling city walls, observed by nuns** associated with St. Clare • **female soldier** Minerva; Fortitude personified • **female soldier, dying, comforted by male soldier** Clorinda and Tancred • **female soldier with shepherds and basket makers** Erminia

Solomon human wisdom combined with human weakness • **Solomon's ring** wisdom and power • **Solomon's knot** divine inscrutability

Solomon's seal the Bible; key to the kingdom of heaven; health amulet; inspiration; perfection

Solon legislator; wisdom

solvent, universal the undifferentiated

son heir; rebirth; earthly spirit; beauty; sun-prince

Sophia wisdom of the universe; creative spirit of God

sorb prudence • *see also* apple

sorcerer the Terrible Father; the evil demiurge; the wise old man; the dark unconscious of man

sores the suffering of lower nature

sorrel parental affection; purification; resignation to sorrow • **Jewish** the bitterness of their bondage • **flower language** affection, especially parental; *wild sorrel*: ill-timed wit; *wood sorrel*: joy, maternal tenderness

soul reason; aspiration; man's creative or immortal part

south summer; light; youth; midday; the full moon; warmth; sun; the infernal regions; spiritual light; the direction of escape; the south wall of a church was often dedicated to defenders of the faith; to face south was to speak with the authority of the gods; associated with the New Testament, particularly the Epistles

southernwood (plant) mockery; pleasantry • **flower language** jest; bantering

sow (swine) fecundity; the fecundity of evil; brutalization; grossness; attribute of Cybele, Demeter, etc. • *see also* swine

sowbread in flower language: diffidence

sower October or November personified • **woman sower** as above, or the Silver Age personified • **sower of dragon's teeth** Cadmus

sowing dissemination; creation

spade (shovel) fertility; death; hatred; toil; winter; the male principle; the Fall of Man; attribute of Adam after the Fall, St. Maurus, Spring personified • **heraldry** emblem of Mercury

Spain associated with bragging • **to the Greeks, Celts** associated with the underworld • **to Romans** associated with thievery

spaniel fawning; subservience; faithfulness; emasculation; attribute of St. Margaret of Cortona spark God; the heavenly father; the initiator; life; the spiritual principle giving birth to each individual; souls scattering from the Mystic Center into the world of phenomena

sparrow love; lasciviousness; lechery; fecundity; humility; pugnacity; boldness; chattering; melancholy; solitude; purification; the Devil; vandalism; the traveler; insignificance; attribute of the personifications of Lust, Solitude, Wantonness

sparrowhawk sharp vision; brave warrior; jealousy; associated with the sun, Osiris, Apollo • see also eagle; hawk

Sparta obedience through custom; simplicity; frugality; courage; brevity of speech

spear sun ray; lightning; world axis; knighthood; fertility; war; phallus; martyrdom; attribute of the Crucifixion, Mars, Minerva, Juno, soldiers, St. Liberalis, the Bronze Age personified, and in ancient times, royalty • heraldry honor; martial readiness • spear with pillar attribute of Constancy personified • spear with V-shaped frame attribute of St. Andrew • spear with inverted cross and/or fuller's bat attribute of St. Jude • man pierced with spears St. Thomas (especially when on a cross) • spear with builder's square, arrows or book attribute of St. Thomas • spear with patriarchal cross or tau cross and long staff attribute of St. Philip • see also javelin; lance

spearmint burning love; severity • in flower language warmth of sentiment

spectacles (glasses) old age; bookishness; learning; binary functions (love/knowledge, revelation/learning, illusion/clear sight, etc.); any twin deities; attribute of Temperance personified

speculum see mirror

speed energy

speedwell in flower language: female fidelity; Germander speedwell: facility; spiked speedwell: semblance

sphere the world; intellectual life; thought; abstraction; perfection; unity; God; creative motion; a celestial or terrestrial form; the wheel of life; deity form • see also ball; orb; globe

Sphinx intellect; power; enigma; spirit triumphant over matter; secrecy; pestilence; the Terrible Mother; silence; mystery; pleasures of the body; union of binary functions (spirit/matter, intellect/physical power, harmony/peace, creator/created, etc.); the libido; Israel in Egypt; the Flight into Egypt; watchdog over the ultimate meaning of life, which remains beyond man's reach forever; sometimes associated with lust; emblem of Egypt • ancient Greece arcane wisdom • ancient Egypt power; vigilance • see also androsphinx

spice love; fertility; sexual activity; sanctity; purification; rejuvenation; spiritual qualities which purify the mind

spider patience; subtlety; industriousness; ambition; cunning; presumption; temptation; envy; aggressiveness; malice; a miser; the Devil; the supreme deity; the Creator; avarice; craftiness; despair and hope; heaven; continuous sacrifice; physically and/or morally repulsive sex; attribute of fertility goddesses • heraldry wisdom; prudence; labor • spider in a chalice or cup attribute of St. Norbert • woman turning into a spider Arachne • tarantula or black widow spider repulsiveness; danger • see also web

spiderwort in flower language: esteem, but not love; transient happiness • Virginian spiderwort momentary happiness

spikenard perfume; allurement; purification; holiness; death • spikenard with saffron or camphor emblem of the Virgin Mary

spindle life; the temporal; transitoriness of life; mutual sacrifice; phallus; axis of the universe; coition; union of heaven and earth; attribute of Eve after the Fall, Clotho, Lachesis, female deities of the moon, earth, vegetation

spindle tree associated with sculptors • **flower language** your image is engraved in my heart; your charms are engraved in my heart

spine firmness; stamina; courage; life; force; aspiration

spinning (thread) creation; fate; bringing forth and fostering life; attribute of the Fates

spinning wheel the revolving heavens; emblem of femininity; vulva

spiral mystery; complexity; escape from the material to the spiritual; resurrection; immortality; breath; spirit; authority; mystery of life and death; evolution of the universe; growth; the spirit • **double spiral** binary functions (life/death, evolution/evolution, etc.); DNA (dioxyribonucleic acid) • **clockwise spiral** creation; evolution; growth; attribute of Pallas Athena • **counterclockwise spiral** destruction; involution; death; decrease; whirlpool; attribute of Poseidon

spire heavenly aspiration; bridge to heaven; universal axis; creative force; aspiration; purity • **on churches...** • **the largest spire** God the Father • **the smaller spires** God's celestial offspring • **with a finger pointed to heaven** one God; reminder of heaven • **weathervane** a challenge to face difficulties and changing conditions

spirit (the spirit) the ideal; perfection; unity

spitting disdain; idleness; indifference; a sign of truth; binding oneself to a bargain or bet • **spitting into the ocean** inconsequence

spleen seat of emotions (sexual passion, mirth, impetuosity, capriciousness, melancholy, but especially anger)

sponge parasite; obliteration; attribute of the Crucifixion

spoon the maternal; female symbol of containment

spot the female

spread-eagle exaggeration; boastfulness; flogging; death; torture • **when lying down** female surrender

spring (season) regeneration; revival; youth; innocence; especially female; rebirth; sweetness; mildness; courtship; time; associated with early morning, the live, Aries, Taurus, Gemini, the color green, occasionally white

springwort fertility

spruce *see* **pine**

spur(s) stimulus to action; knighthood; emblem of a cowboy; qualification • **heraldry** fighting spirit; knightly dignity

spy limitation; the inclination to trust the flesh rather than the spirit

square (implement) right conduct; truth; honesty; carpentry in particular, the building trades in general; attribute of St. Matthias, St. James the Less, the personifications of Melancholy, Geometry • **square with cross** attribute of St. Philip • **square with spear or arrows** attribute of St. Thomas • **square with boat hook** attribute of St. Jude • **square with lily** attribute of St. Joseph • **T-square** attribute of Geometry

square (shape) firmness; stability; material things; the merely rational; the instinct; the earth; limitation; order; organization; man not yet at one with himself; tense domination; earthly existence; the unwavering firmness of the Church; mortality • **heraldry** truth; equity; constancy; stability • **square nimbus** an indication of the holiness of a person still living

squill attribute of Envy and other vices personified

squinch owl *see* **owl**

squinting attribute of Envy personified

squirrel forethought; nimbleness; playfulness; hoarding; providence; thrift; heavenly meditation; the striving of the Holy Spirit; the messenger on the Tree of Life, or Yggdrasil • **heraldry** service as an important messenger; courage; impartiality; a great hunter; sylvan retirement • **squirrel tail** emblem of a scout in the American Revolution

stable the Nativity of Christ; a guarded place; light and revelation arising from ignorance; realm of darkness from which light emerges

staff support; blindness; old age; a royal weapon; an instrument of punishment; guidance; fertility; resurrection; the sun; phallus; the axis of the universe; faith; attribute of pilgrims, travellers, shepherds, bishops, the Nativity of Christ, Christ, Abel, Amos, Moses, David, Asclepius, Dionysus, Mercury, the lover (especially with purse), St. James the Great • **China** staff of ash: mourning for a father • **broken staff** famine • **staff striking rock and producing water** Moses, Rhea • **flowering staff** innocence; forgiveness; attribute of Tannhauser, St. Joseph • **staff made of a palm tree** attribute of St. Christopher • **staff surmounted by a Latin or Tau cross** attribute of St. Philip • **staff surmounted by a crescent** conjunction of opposites • **staff and white banner with red cross** attribute of John the Baptist, St. Ursula, St. Jerome • **staff with ship** attribute of St. Wilfrid • **staff with gourd** attribute of the archangel Raphael • **staff with serpent • attribute of Moses and Aaron before Pharoah** • **staff with wallet or hat, or letters "S.J." or crossed with a sword** attribute of St.

James the Great • **staff with sword and wallet** attribute of the archangel Raphael • **staff with cup** attribute of the archangel Chamael • **staff crossed with sword** associated with the Passion of Christ • **long staff and spear** attribute of St. Philip • *see also* **crook**

stag piety; religious aspiration; devotion; the faithful Christian longing for God; longevity; regeneration; growth; related to heaven and to light; a messenger of the gods; the life of solitude and of purity; agility; grace; fertility; rejuvenation; immortality; beauty; mildness; chastity; the word of God; attribute of Father Time, Diana, St. Jerome, St. Aidan, St. Julian the Hospitator, the personifications of Hearing, Prudence • **heraldry** lover of justice and harmony; skill in music; mildness; kindness; political providence; lover of faith and trust; possessor of hunting rights • **stag with a crucifix between its antlers** attribute of St. Eustace, St. Hubert • **hunted stag** persecution of early Christians • **stag trampling on a snake or dragon** Christ's power over Satan • **stags pulling chariot** attribute of Diana, Father Time • **two stags drinking** baptism • *see also* **deer; hart**

stage (theater) the world

stain death; the passage of time; the transitory; the abnormal or defective; dishonor

stairs spiritual ascension; aspiration; transcendence; Christian pilgrimage; world axis (especially when surmounted by a cross, fleur-de-lis, star, or angel); communication between different worlds • **ascending stairs** journey to the Mystic Center; pilgrimage; longing for the higher world • **descending stairs** entry into the infernal world

stake • stake being driven into the heart nailing the soul in a particular place; the prescribed method for killing a vampire • **being bound to a stake** martyrdom, particularly of St. Agnes, St. Sebastian, St. Dorothea; death of a fertility king • **soldier being killed by a woman pounding a tent stake into his head** the soldier is Sisera

standing respect

star(s) the spirit; the forces of the spirit struggling against the forces of evil; destiny; supremacy in a particular area; disintegration; immortality; the soul; guidance (especially spiritual); hope; purity; constancy; vigilance • **four pointed star** emblem of Shamash; the Cross • **five pointed star** Epiphany; the manifested nature of God; the Virgin Mary; Horus • **heraldry** the third son; divine grace; learning; virtue • **five pointed star, inverted** the infernal; witchcraft • **six pointed star** the human soul; good and evil; the upper and lower worlds; God the Creator; the androgynous nature of the deity; union of the male and female principles; the natural and supernatural; good luck amulet; the androgyne; the six days of Creation; the six points indicate the omnipresence of God; the twelve corners signify the twelve tribes of Israel; emblem of Israel, the Jewish faith, David • **seven pointed star** the Holy Spirit; the seven gifts of the Holy Spirit; cyclic progression; human skill; attribute of Cybele • *see also* **Star of the Sea** • **eight pointed star** baptism; regeneration; the rising sun; the Wheel of Fortune; attribute of Venus • **nine pointed star** the Holy Spirit; the nine gifts of the Holy Spirit • **ten pointed star** the ten Apostles who neither denied nor betrayed Christ • **star on the breast** attribute of St. Nicholas of Tolentino • **star on the forehead or on a halo** attribute of St. Dominic • **day star** Christ • **morning star**

Christ • **stars in a constellation** order • **stars and a knife on a blue shield** attribute of Abraham • **stars on the forehead of a god** a planet personified • **starry crown** (sometimes also with lilies) attribute of the Virgin Mary, usually at the Immaculate Conception • **seven stars** the seven gifts of the Holy Spirit • **seven stars falling** the Apocalypse • **nine stars** the nine gifts of the Holy Spirit • **twelve stars** the Apostles • **twelve stars surrounding the sun and the moon** Jacob, his wife, and their twelve sons • **crown of twelve stars** attribute of Urania

Star of Bethlehem (plant) in flower language: guidance; purity

Star of David *see* entry under **star** (six pointed) •

Star of the Sea (usually seven pointed) emblem of many mother or sea goddesses (Isis, Aphrodite, Venus, etc.); emblem of the Virgin Mary

starfish inextinguishable power of true love; the grace of God not quenched in a sea of sin

starling connected with mid-winter; life in death; a messenger • **U.S.** a pest

starwort in flower language: afterthought • **American starwort** welcome to a stranger; cheerfulness in old age • **Christmas starwort** the Nativity of Christ

statue attribute of Idolatry personified • **life sized female statue with sculptor** the sculptor is Pygmalion • **life sized male statue with a god** the god is Prometheus • **statue of the Virgin Mary carried by a Dominican over water** the Dominican is St. Hyacinth

steed the animal in man; the force of the instincts; the control of baser forces; the body • *see also* specific steeds (horse, goat, ass, etc.)

steel strength; war; industry; armor; weapons; the all-conquering spirit; cruelty; chastity; trustworthiness

steelyard *see* balances
steeple *see* spire
stem world axis
stepmother jealousy; cruelty; the Terrible Mother
steps *see* stairs
stick punishment; world axis; leadership; death; starvation; wisdom; attribute of St. Hilary • burnt stick death and wisdom • stick dance war rite; fertility rite • *see also* staff
stigmata a person of high religious character; attribute of St. Catherine of Siena, St. Francis of Assisi
stilts deceit
sting death; sexual appetite; the ploy of a confidence man
sting ray cunning
stock (plant) in flower language: ten week stock; promptitude; lasting beauty
stockings in the Middle Ages, green stockings were worn at weddings by an older unmarried sister of the bride • *see also* sock
stocks (for restraint) loss of liberty; confinement; marriage; constancy; a form of entanglement, which see
stole (religious garment) willing servitude; innocence; the yoke of man's sin borne by Christ; the hope of immortality; a sign of ordination; priestly dignity and power; obedience; patience; submission to God's will; the reign of Christ • when worn crossed celebration of the mass • when worn on the left shoulder and across the breast attribute of a deacon
stomach seat of courage, anger, temper, resentment, nausea, disgust; endurance; learning and truth • *see also* belly
stone cohesion; harmonious reconciliation with the self; the spirit; the spirit as a foundation; the first solid form of creation; firmness; hardness; unity; strength; witness; silence; remembrance; blindness; martyrdom; punishment; testicles;

attribute of St. Stephen, Jacob, Jeremiah, St. Barnabas; emblem of the Creator, Christ • broken stone dismemberment; psychic disintegration; death; infirmity; annihilation • stones with spear or girdle or arrows attribute of St. Thomas • man at prayer, beating his breast with a stone St. Jerome • stone full of eyes associated with Zechariah • stone with open Bible and whip attribute of St. Jerome • stone held in hand of kneeling hermit the hermit is St. Jerome • stone held in the hand of a soldier with a falcon the soldier is St. Bavo • stone held in the hand of a beggar woman Poverty personified • man carrying large stone St. Bavo • monk offering a stone to Christ the Devil tempting Christ in the wilderness • stones on a book attribute of St. Emerantiana • crane with a stone in a raised foot Vigilance personified • bloodstained stones attribute of St. Stephen • two stones attribute of St. Matthew (especially with battleaxe) • three stones attribute of St. James the Less • three stones with lance attribute of St. Matthias • three stones with dalmatic attribute of St. Stephen • five stones and sling attribute of David • black stone sin; defeat; restraint; *Greece:* cast as a vote for guilt • white stone victory; theater admission; virtue; resurrection; immortality; happiness; *Greece:* cast as a vote for acquittal • stone rubbing stones were thought by some to be the homes of ancestors; rubbing a stone into a round shape was to perfect it into a home for the Self
stone mason *see* mason
stonecrop in flower language: tranquillity
stool (for sitting) attribute of St. Mary of Bethany • *see also* footstool
stork filial piety; parental affection; longevity; birth; domestic peace and

happiness; obedience; fertility; vigilance; pretension; self-conceit; chastity; harbinger of spring; emblem of the traveler; attribute of Mercury (the god), the Annunciation, the personifications of Help, Commerce • **China** longevity • **Britain** in ancient times: adultery

storm creation; creative intercourse between the elements; passions of the soul; psychic disruption • *see also* **wind; hurricane; thunder**, etc.

stramonium in flower language: disguise

stranger the possibility of unforeseen change; the future made present; mutation; the replacement of reigning power

straw a thing without value; a sinner • **broken straw** quarrel; dissension; renunciation of an agreement or of allegiance • **making bricks without straw** punishment • **flower language**—*broken straw*: the rupture of a contract; *whole straw*: union

strawberry good works; fruits of the spirit; righteousness; good hidden under evil; emblem of love goddesses, the Virgin Mary, John the Baptist • **strawberries and violets** the truly spiritual are always humble • **strawberries with other fruit** the good works of the righteous; the fruits of the spirit • **strawberry leaves** aristocracy • **flower language** perfect excellence

strawberry tree in flower language: esteem and love

stream peace; righteousness

Strength (tarot) power through conscious awareness of eternity; the triumph of intelligence over brutality; insensitivity; fury; spiritual power; triumph of love over hate; the spirit ruling over matter

string cohesion of all things in existence; world axis; bondage • *see also* **entanglement; rope; cord**

stubble (in a field) transitoriness • *see also* **chaff**

sturgeon preservation; security; longevity; wisdom; courage; sacred to Venus • **China** literary eminence; scholarly excellence, particularly in examinations • *see also* **fish**

sty (animal pen) corruption

Styx death

submarine the irrational; the unconscious; a vehicle of the unconscious; the means of exploring the unconscious

succory *see* **chicory**

succubus the Devil in female form; the Anima

sugar sweetness; flattery; deceit; a plea for happiness; a palliative

sulphur the desire for positive action; reason and intuition; vital heat; the passions; infernal fumes • **sulphur and eggs** purification

sumac resoluteness • **flower language** Venice sumac: splendor; intellectual excellence

summer maturity; abundance; youth; love; extended peace or happiness; beauty anticipating decline; perfection; charity; innocence; heat; ripening

sun potential good; the will; the hero; the eye of God; creative light; the spiritual; the source of light; blessing; youth; sovereignty; fertility; the active power of nature; the promise of salvation; the guiding light; the male; the creator; the mind; splendor; magnificence; authority; heaven; paradise; Christ (seldom used in modern times); associated with the heart, authority, domination, masculinity, Leo, the number one; attribute of Apollo, Truth personified; emblem of Louis XIV of France • **heraldry** authority; glory; magnificent example • **sun with the letters IHC in the middle** Christ • **sun on the breast** attribute of St. Thomas Aquinas • **sun and moon together** attribute of the Virgin Mary • **sun and moon together at the Crucifixion** the sorrow of all creation • **sun and full moon with twelve stars** Jacob, his wife, and their twelve sons • **sunrise** Christ; resurrection; the beginning of a cycle • **sunset** death; the end of a cycle • **eclipse of the sun** the Day of the Lord is at hand; omen of the death of kings, the end of the world, the start of war or plague

Sun (tarot) renewal of life; Mother Nature; balance between conscious and unconscious, physical and spiritual; liberation from physical limitations

Sunday *see* **days**

sundial natural time, in the general rather than the personal sense; daytime as opposed to the hourglass which indicates night

sunflower gratitude; affectionate remembrance; religious remembrance; turning the soul to Christ; worship; false riches; infatuation; the sun; emblem of Kansas; attribute of Mithra, Daphne; loyalty; devotion • **flower language** – *dwarf sunflower*: adoration; *tall sunflower*: haughtiness

sunrise *see* **sun**

sunset *see* **sun**

surgical instruments attribute of St. Cosmas, St. Damian

surplice innocence; purity; man renewed in justice and in truth

suspension unfulfilled longing

swallow (bird) wandering spirit; spring; domesticity; resurrection; hunger; prayer; the incarnation of Christ; contentment in poverty; hope; diligence; obedience; sociability; equality; wantonness; instability; babbling; chattering; the inexorable march of time; filial piety; attribute of Venus, Isis, Equity personified • **Jewish** paternal inheritance • **China** emblem of good luck; a woman's voice; *swallow nesting on a house*: success, prosperity; *swallow nest*: insecurity, danger • **heraldry** courage; depen-

dence; messenger of good news; good fortune

swan grace; purity; poetry; music; solitude; beauty; the hypocrite; the androgyne; the Mystic Center; the union of opposites; hermaphroditism; chaste female nudity; time; transcience; mortality; dignity; nobility; haughtiness; jealousy; the soul; eternity; wisdom; resurrection; return to the womb; incestuous maternal relationships; Christian retirement; connected with prophecy; emblem of the Virgin Mary, Aphrodite, virgins in general (usually a white swan in the foregoing cases), attribute of Venus, Clio, Apollo, occasionally Erato • **heraldry** a learned person; a lover of harmony; *with a crown on its neck*: dignity, high rank, liberal views • **swan neck** phallus; masculine • **swan body** feminine • **red swan** sunset • **five swans** the five Scandinavian countries • **swan song** the desire which brings about self destruction; melancholy; self-sacrifice; martyrdom; death; tragic art • **swan embracing a young girl** the girl is Leda, the Swan is Zeus • **youth changed into a swan** Cygnus

swastika revival; prosperity; good fortune; felicity; the sun; agriculture; the succession of generations; speed; rotation; the Mystic Center • **China** good luck; the seal of Buddha's heart • **swastika over a door** protection against fire • **swastika in a circle or triangle** cosmic harmony; if the tops are curved, death • **clockwise swastika** increase; growth; spring; sun; good luck; white magic • **counterclockwise swastika** decay; darkness; death; the autumnal sun; ill fortune; black magic; emblem of Nazi Germany

sweat toil; sin; venereal disease; anxiety • **sweat on the face** falsity; illusion • **a sweating image** omen of danger

sweet brier related to fairies; talent; funeral bouquet • flower language — *American sweet brier*: simplicity; *European sweet brier*: I wound to heal, poetry; *yellow sweet brier*: decrease of love

sweet flag in flower language: fitness

sweet pea in flower language: departure

sweet sultan in flower language: felicity; supreme happiness; *when the flower is alone*: widowhood

Sweet William in flower language: gallantry; finesse; a smile

sweetbrier *see* sweet brier

swine impurity; uncleanness; abomination; an unbeliever; gluttony; greed; lasciviousness; lethargy; grossness; lack of feeling; obstinacy; viciousness; desire that seeks sustenance is matter rather than in spirit; transmutation of the higher into the lower; the moral plunge into corruption; Satan; a pagan; sensuality; sloth; self-indulgence; filth; selfishness; voracity; ingratitude; corruption; lust; a boor; attribute of Dionysus, Demeter, Circe, St. Anthony Abbot, the personifications of Lust, Sloth, Gluttony • swine in a palace associated with Circe • youth praying among swine the Prodigal Son • Jewish an unclean animal • pig skin bag attribute of a tinker • *see also* boar; sow

swineherd a low job

swinging life's changing fortunes; purification by air; coition

sword liberty; strength; knighthood; strife; the Crusades; the Word; authority; the administration of justice; destruction of the physical; conjunction of the physical and spiritual; purification; antithesis of the monster, q.v.; the 10th Plague of Egypt; a cross; spiritual evolution or ornament; leadership; a "spiritual" weapon; death; war; attribute of soldiers, Christian martyrs, Elijah, Melpomene, Simeon, the sibyls Euro-

peana and Erythraea, St. Justin Martyr, St. Boniface, St. Edmund, St. Jude, St. John Gualberto, St. Catherine of Alexandria, St. Agnes, occasionally St. Julian the Hospitator, the personifications of Justice, Fortitude, Wrath, Choler, Rhetoric, Constancy (with pillar), City of Venice (with two lions), Temperance (with sword in a sheath and/or the hilt bound) • heraldry defense; justice; execution; a free man • straight sword masculine; solar; the European style • curved sword feminine; lunar; sometimes the Eastern style • crossed swords battle; military strategy or power; emblem of St. Paul (one refers to his martyrdom, the other to his good fight for the faith) • blunted sword mercy • obtusely pointed sword religion • pointed sword justice • flaming sword the authority of God; ardent zeal; attribute of the archangel Jophiel driving Adam and Eve from the Garden of Eden, the archangel Michael • sword held by the point attribute of St. Matthias • sword held with the hilt upward consecration; allegiance; the cross • two-handed sword civil power; the State • sword hanging over walled city (Jerusalem) associated with Zephaniah • sword hanging overhead associated with Damocles; constant threat; immediate danger; vulnerability to fate; the suddenness of fate • sword and water pitcher associated with Levi • sword and scabbard crossed attribute of St. Paul • sword with an anvil attribute of St. Adrian • sword and palm martyrdom • sword and sandals under a rock associated with Theseus • sword and book offered to a sleeping soldier Scipio • sword offered to a plowman by a Roman soldier the plowman in Cincinnatus • sword and pilgrim's staff crossed, or sword with a scallop shell attribute of St. James the Great • **flaming sword and a shield** attribute of the archangel Michael; Christian conquest • **sword on a book** attribute of St. Matthias • **sword behind a book** attribute of St. Paul (the book is usually inscribed "Spiritus Gladius") • **woman with scales and sword** Justice personified • **sword and children** charity • **sword and serpent twined around it** attribute of St. Paul • **sword and trumpet** associated with Joshua • **broken sword with lance** associated with Micah • **sword and torch crossed** the Passion of Christ • **sword with balances** (scales) justice • **sword and staff** the Passion of Christ • **sword and cloak** attribute of St. Martin • **sword and broken lance** attribute of St. George of Cappadocia • **two saints, one with a sword, one with a whip** St. Protase carries the sword, St. Gervase carries the whip • **broken sword** peace; defenselessness • **two edged sword lying between a sleeping man and woman** chastity • **sword through the throat or breast** attribute of St. Justina of Padua • **sword through the head or hand** attribute of St. Peter Martyr (usually shown as a monk) • **woman killing herself with a sword** Despair personified • **sword piercing a skull** attribute of St. Thomas à Becket (usually shown as a bishop) • **sword piercing a book** attribute of St. Boniface (usually shown as a bishop) • **sword piercing a woman's bosom with a lion present** St. Euphemia • **sword piercing a woman's neck** St. Lucia

swordfish assoc. with unicorn, q.v.

sycamore abundance; variety; curiosity; wisdom; love • **Christian** the wood of the cross; cupidity; the unbelieving Jew • **Great Britain** fertility • **flower language** curiosity; reserve

symmetry achievement; triumph; supreme equipoise

synagogue Jewry; Judaism; the Old Testament personified

syringa in flower language: memory • **Carolina syringa** disappointment

syrinx lust; attribute of shepherds, Pan, Polyphemus, Daphnis and Chloe • *see also* **pipe** (musical)

T

T the first letter of the Greek word for God (Theos), and hence, God himself; the Cross; associated with cooperation, the feminine principle, following, indecision, devotion, generative power, change, the number two (especially magnified ten times), perfection

t-square attribute of Geometry personified • *see also* **square** (carpenter's)

tabernacle the body; the Eucharist • **tabernacle in a tent** Old Testament worship • **three tabernacles** (usually on a mountain top) the Transfiguration • **tabernacle on an altar** the reserved host; the Real Presence

table fellowship; banquet; conviviality; conference; memory; earth; an altar; the Last Supper; Communion • **round table** the universe; the sun; equality; attribute of King Arthur and his knights • **table with showbread** (shewbread) Old Testament worship • **two tables of stone** associated with Moses, the Ten Commandments • **writing table, pen, and books** attribute of St. Ambrose

tablet justice; law; divine word; divine order • **tablet with stylus** attribute of Clio, Calliope, the personifications of History, Arithmetic • **old man beside youth who has tablet and stylus** the old man is Homer •

two **tablets of stone** associated with Moses, the Ten Commandments; when oak leaves are in the background, they indicate sturdiness and regeneration • **broken tablet** injustice

tabor festivity; instrument of beggars • *see also* **drum**

tabret religious ecstasy; ecstasy of victory; instrument of goddess feasts • *see also* **drum**

tail animal power; expression of an animal's mood; false prophet; attribute of a devil • **animal without a tail** may be a witch in animal form

tailor the Creator; sexual curiosity; impotence; imperfect humanity, or an incomplete person; coward; a bad shot with a weapon

tallit when worn by the entire congregation in a synagogue: a sign that all men are equal before God

tamarisk fertility; resurrection; attribute of Crime personified • **flower language** crime

tambourine joy; Bacchanalian worship; rejoicing in the Lord; attribute of Miriam, the Maenads, Jepthah's daughter, Hercules when dressed as a woman, Vice personified, occasionally Erato • *see also* **sistrum**

tansy in flower language: I declare against you

taper (wick) attribute of St. Gertrude, St. Blaise

tapster false geniality; a very ignorant person; a falsifier of accounts

tar connected with sailors and ships; blackness; stickiness

tares sinners • **wheat and tares** the Church on earth

tarot deck comprises an image of initiation; portrays the complementary struggles in man's life (practical reason vs. pure reason, self vs. others, reflection vs. intuition, physical vs. spiritual) • **gold suit** material forces • **suit of goblets** sacrifice • **sword suit** discernment and the meeting out of justice • **club suit** power of command • **cards I to XI** the solar way: the active, the conscious, the reflective, the autonomous • **cards XII to XXII** the lunar way: the passive, the unconscious, the intuitive, the dependent • *see also* the names of specific cards, such as **High Priest**, **World**, **Fool**, etc.

tartan *see* **plaid**

tassel sun ray; friendliness

tattoo a rite of entry; declaration of allegiance to what is signified by the mark; a "turning point" in a man's life; has magical properties; a cosmic activity; protection; sacrifice; mystic allegiance; counter-magic; adornment • **tattoo of a full-rigged ship on a 19th century sailor** a veteran of sailing around Cape Horn

Taurus associated with fecundation, creation, primordial sacrifice, invigoration, long-suffering, slowness to anger, but furious once provoked, strength, stolidity, reliability, lack of intelligence, laziness, secretiveness

tea exoticism; the Orient; connected with amorous intrigue and scandal; sociable life; the brew of life; connected with the British

teacher *see* **poet**

tear (rip) for Jews: a torn garment is a sign of mourning and grief

tear (weeping) sorrow; grief; weakness; suffering endured in pursuit of truth; ecstasy of joy; fertility; attribute of St. Monica

teasel in flower language: • **fuller's teasel** misanthropy

teat *see* **breast**

teeth an expression of activity, especially sexual activity; guardian of the inner person; means of enforcement • **loss of teeth** fear; castration; failure; inhibition • **dragon's teeth** associated with Cadmus, warfare, seeds of dissension

Temperance (tarot) generally has a favorable significance; universal life; ceaseless cycling through formation, regeneration, purification; the flow of life; the cyclic; the seasons; that which is always different yet always the same; the union of the male and female principles; interaction of spirit and matter; adaptation and coordination; successful combination; perpetual evolutive movement from the past to a golden future

temple the Mystic Center; the soul; throne of the deity; the intersection of heaven and earth • **circular temple** the sun • **triangular temple** the Trinity • **temple on a mountain** associated with Micah; the spiritual Zion; the Church • **temple under construction** associated with Solomon, Haggai • **model of a temple** attribute of Solomon, Habakkuk • *see also* church

ten associated with kingship, infinite power, the wonders of the world, beginning, originality, perfection, completeness, finality, the androgyne, marriage, spiritual achievement, the totality of the universe, order, the angel Lumiel; multiplication of the powers of one, which see; the ten sibyls, the Ten Commandments, the Ten Plagues of Egypt, the ten faithful disciples, the ten wicked brothers of Joseph, the ten virgins (five wise, five foolish), the ten servants of Joshua, etc., etc. • **kabala** wealth

tendrils in flower language: ties

tennis ball *see* ball

tent protection; the world; temple; tabernacle; the heavens; transitoriness; often has spiritual significance; often protects and hides something, such as the mystery of the universe; partakes of the symbolism of clothes, which see; associated with shepherds, nomads, Israel in the wilderness • **heraldry** readiness for war or battle; hospitality • **tent of boughs** assoc. with Feast of the Tabernacles

tern *see* gull

terror lack of intellectual will

tetractys the beginning and the end; birth, growth, and death

tetragrammatron the Father

tetramorph the four Evangelists

thaw the return of fertility; corruption; dissolving of the flesh

theater the world of phenomena; this world and the next; social life • *see also* stage; playwright

theta a blue theta on the shoulder: attribute of St. Anthony Abbot

thief the lesser nature which robs the self of primordial wealth; time; death; personification of natural calamities (flood, frost, drought, etc.)

thigh(s) strength; dynamic support of the body; sexual vigor; euphemism for genitals; holy, sacrifical spot • **plague spot on thigh** attribute of St. Roch • **smiting one's thigh** mourning

thimble insignificance; femininity; vagina

thirst the blind appetite for life

thirteen associated with the angel Raphael, bad luck, betrayal, faithlessness, misfortune, death, birth, beginning anew

thirty associated with sacrifice; a multiplication of the powers of three, which see • **kabala** sacrifice • **thirty pieces of silver** associated with Judas

thirty-three associated with mystery, perfection, culmination; the number of years in Christ's life; often the number of buttons on a cleric's cassock

thirty-six Jewish: the renewal of life

Thisbe *see* Pyramus

thistle sin; sorrow; the Fall of Man; austerity; rejection; vengeance; misanthropy; earthly sorrow and sin; the Passion of Christ; emblem of Scotland • **flower language** — *common thistle*: austerity; *Scotch thistle*: retaliation

Thomas (Saint) doubt; skepticism

thorn error; evil; the flesh; suffering;

grief; obstacle; sin, sometimes only minor; tribulation; the Crucifixion; austerity; remorse; materialism killing spiritual aspiration; sharp intelligence; affliction; annoyance; deprivation; temptation of the flesh; associated with Aries, Mars, war; the road to salvation, fame, truth, chastity; attribute of martyrs • **branch with thorns** martyrdom • **crown of thorns** attribute of the crucified Christ, Delphica the sibyl, St. Catherine of Siena, St. Ignatius Loyola, St. Louis of France, Martyrs • **roses and thorns** thesis and antithesis; conjunction of opposites (pleasure/pain, etc.) • **flower language** — *a branch*: severity, rigor; *evergreen thorn*: solace in adversity • *see also* **brier; bramble**

thorn apple in flower language: deceitful charms

thorn tree Glastonbury thorn: associated with the Nativity of Christ, St. Joseph of Arimathea

thousand *see* **one thousand**

thread world axis; ascension; the connection between planes (spiritual-biological-social, etc.); sublimation; escape; connection in general; life; destiny; semen • **three women spinning thread** the three Fates • **thread wrapped three times around the thumb** associated with Seth

three related to the right side, which see, moral and spiritual dynamism, intellectual and spiritual order, sufficiency, heaven, the Trinity, childbirth, the resolution of conflict, perfection, the beginning, middle and end, love, joyfulness, hope, destiny, children, achievement, carelessness, intrigue, marriage, good fortune, happiness, material success, fame, activity, catalyst, concern for others, Jupiter, the angel Anael, the color red; generally, a favorable number; a "God" number; the three sons of Noah, the three days of Christ in the tomb, the three days

of Saul's blindness, the three temptations of Christ, the three elements of faith, the three theological virtues, etc. • **kabala** energy; action

three hundred a large or infinite number; associated with the breath of God • **kabala** compensation

threshing harvest; fertility; destruction; involution • **threshing floor** world navel; the universe; the Mystic Center; fertility

threshold transition between two worlds; transcendance; the reconciliation and separation of two worlds (sacred-profane, life-death, etc.) • **threshold monsters at entrance to holy place** (lions, dragons, etc.) warning against profanation

thrift (plant) in flower language: neglected beauty

throat vagina

throatwort in flower language: neglected beauty

throne support; exaltation; equilibrium; security; stability; unity; majesty; seat of a deity; the Mystic Center; authority; justice • **empty throne** God; the Second Coming • **empty throne with dove and crucifix** the Trinity • **burning throne** attribute of the Devil • **ebony throne** attribute of Night personified, Pluto • *see also* **cathedra**

thrush melodiousness; bird of spring; love; shyness; wisdom; heavenly aspiration

Thule (classical land) the Mystic Center

thumb when up: phallus; mercy; favor • **when down** disfavor; death • **thumb with three turns of thread around it** attribute of Seth • **cutting off thumbs and great toes** incapacitation of a warrior

thumbscrews torture

thunder divine power or warning; threat or precursor of war; war itself; cosmic disturbance or upheaval; voice of the supreme deity; fertility • *see* **thunderbolt; lightning**

thunderbolt supreme creative fire; dawn; illumination; sovereignty; action of the higher world upon the lower; divine wrath; the male orgasm; weapon of the supreme deity; divine power; the Word piercing the darkness; power or speed (especially with wings); attribute of the supreme deity, Jupiter, Fire personified • *see also* **lightning; thunder**

thurible *see* **censer**

Thursday *see* **days**

thyme activity; courage; bravery; the opposite of hyssop, which see; attribute of Diligence personified • **flower language** activity

thyrsus life; fertility; regeneration; gaiety; ecstasy; attribute of satyrs, Bacchus • **Rome** euphemism for phallus

tiara temporal power • **triple tiara** the three estates of the Kingdom of God; the Trinity; attribute of popes, Aaron, St. Gregory the Great, St. Sylvester • *see also* **crown; coronation**

tickling expectancy; ignominious death; playfulness

tide balance of nature; bringer of the divine; the ebb and flow of fortune • **turning of the tide** changing of fortune • **ebb tide** finish; completion; low fortune • **flood tide** success; high fortune

tie *see* **necktie**

tiger wrath; cruelty; bloodthirstiness; ferocity; courage; beauty; grace; deceit; cunning; brutality; jealousy; violent desires; repressed sex; treachery; martyrdom; energy; drive; emblem of Christ; attribute of Asia personified, Bacchus • **tamed tiger** strength and valor in the fight against evil; the defense of order against chaos

tiger flower in flower language: for once may pride befriend me

Tigris River fertility; refreshment; wisdom

timbers associated with Haggai

timbrel rejoicing; religious ecstasy; usually an instrument of women

tin dross; cheapness; associated with Saggitarius, Pisces, Jupiter

tinker a man living outside the conventions of society; an impressive drinker; a sexual freebooter; associated with eroticism

Tiresias the androgyne; lunar knowledge

titan a wild and untamable force of primeval nature

titmouse imprudence

toad the Devil; evil spirit; fertility; wisdom; inspiration; vice; connected with witches; the inverse and infernal aspect of the frog, which see; attribute of the personifications of Injustice, Death (especially with skull and crossbones); ugliness • **bloated toad** attribute of Pride personified • **toad hanging from the breasts of a woman or eating female genitalia** attribute of Lust personified • **toad as a steed** attribute of Avarice personified • **heraldry** three toads, erect, saltant: an ancient crest of France

toadstool connected with ecstatic visions, death

tobacco ephemeral pleasure; forgetfulness • *see also* **smoking; pipe**

toe direction; a man's way of life; phallus; a ray of light • **amputation of great toes and thumbs** incapacitation of a warrior • **extra toe** good fortune • **second toe longer than the first toe** a sign of a cruel husband • *see also* **foot**

Tom (Peeping) Lechery personified; lechery (Lady Godiva symbolized fertility)

tomahawk attribute of American Indians; related to war • **to bury a tomahawk** to make peace

tomato love

tomb transformation; the unconscious; the feminine; the maternal; the womb; the body and its fleshly desires; involution with the hope of

regeneration; finality; attribute of Lazarus, St. Joseph of Arimathea • **empty tomb** the Resurrection of Christ • *see also* **sarcophagus**
tombstone mortality
tongs attribute of St. Eloi, St. Agatha • **tongs holding a glowing coal** attribute of Isaiah • *see also* **pincers**
tongue gossip; malicious talk; lasciviousness; eloquence; persuasion; inconstancy; perfidy (especially a double, or forked tongue); scandal; lies; blasphemy; taste (as a sense); substitute for phallus • **blister on the tongue** sign of a lie
tonsure Christ's crown of thorns; humility; asceticism; spiritual thoughts; dedication to divine service; rejection of the temporal; reminder of the perfect life (Christ's); attribute of a monk (although in the early Church, it was also worn by secular clergy)
tooth primitive weapon; cruelty; power; transcience; wisdom; divination; ingratitude; potency • **loss of teeth** fear of castration, potency, failure • **tooth in pincers** attribute of St. Apollonia
toothwort in flower language: secret love
topaz felicity; fruitfulness; November; friendship; fidelity; integrity; divine love and goodness; ardent love and gentleness; wisdom; associated with Sagittarius; attribute of cherubim
torch the truth; progress; the sun; the active, positive power of nature; enlightenment; fervor, especially religious; victory; high ideals; purification; spiritualization through illumination and guidance; vigilance; marriage; regeneration; life of tradition passed from one generation to another; the solar or masculine; phallus; anarchy; revolution and ultimate liberty; Christ; Christian witness; the Gospel; attribute of the Libyan sibyl, Ceres, Venus, Cupid,

Aurora, Hecate, Hymen, Prometheus, the personifications of Sight, Peace, Temperance, Fury, Lust, Slander • **heraldry** science; fame • **flaming torch** hope of resurrection • **upright torch** life • **inverted torch on a tombstone** end of verted torch on a tombstone end of a family line • **torch held by a dog** attribute of St. Dominic • **torch held by a woman tied to a stake** St. Dorothea of Cappadocia • **torch in Nativity scenes** Christ as the light of the world • **monk driving off a young woman with a torch** St. Thomas Aquinas • **woman on a seashore with a torch** Hero (of Hero and Leander) • **woman with a torch dragging a youth before a judge** the woman is Calumny personified • **torch crossed with a sword** refers to the Passion of Christ • **two torches burning** Christ as the light of the world
tornado invincible power; destructiveness; a hole through which one may pass out of space and time
torrent attribute of St. Christopher
tortoise longevity; fecundity; divination; the feminine principle; the androgyne (the head is phallic, the body feminine); caution; foresight; Chaos with the hope of renewal of life; chastity; sloth; silence; the earth; attribute of Industry personified • **China** strength; endurance; longevity; associated with winter • **heraldry** steadfastness; invulnerability; glorious development of family • *see also* **turtle**, with which it is often confused
touch-me-not in flower language: impatient desire
tourmaline generosity; thoughtfulness; courage; associated with Pisces, Libra
towel a spotless towel: attribute of the Virgin Mary • **towel with pitcher** refers to Pilate washing his hands during the Passion of Christ •

throwing a towel in a boxing ring
admission of defeat

tower ascent; the link between
heaven and earth; man; strength;
power; purity; aspiration, especially
toward God; isolation; phallus;
height; the supreme deity; salvation;
world axis; hope; virginity; the Virgin Mary; watchfulness; refuge; philosophical retirement; hidden truth;
beauty; treasure; conscience • heraldry solidity; strength • round
tower connected with solar worship
round tower surmounted by crescent
the androgyne • tower with three
(usually) windows attribute of St.
Barbara • leaning tower emblem
of Pisa, Italy; sometimes used as an
emblem of Italy Itself • two towers,
one leaning attribute of St. Petronius • see also Babel, Tower of
Tower (tarot) see House of God

toy temptation; childhood

tragelaph(us) generation and preservation; body, soul, and spiritual life

train (transportation) progress; life;
human communication • see also
locomotive

tramp (hobo) the primitive, instinctual, natural self

transvestitism identification with a
deity, parent, or ideal of the opposite sex; sign of homosexuality; overcoming a castration anxiety

trapezium in comparison with a trapezoid, it shows a greater degree of
abnormality and irregularity • see
also trapezoid

trapezoid sacrifice; abnormality; irregularity; an inferior form • see
also trapezium

traveller seeker after truth; someone
engaged in personal development,
especially spiritual or religious

traveller's joy in flower language:
safety

treasure something of spiritual value
• treasure in a cave the Mystic
Center; the self being reborn; the
value to be found in the unconscious

• hidden treasure the fruits of supreme illumination • search for
treasure the search for spiritual evolution

tree immortality; the life of the cosmos; the link between the three
worlds (heaven, earth, the underworld); longevity; fertility; mythic
ascension; the slow process of individuation; wisdom; universe; eternal life; divine wisdom; the Cross;
the Church; life; the home of spirits
or the gods; the feminine; earth's
fecundity • heraldry justice; prosperity; constancy in faith; possession
of wooded land • felling a tree castration • tall tree aspiration •
withered tree death • pearl or gem
bearing tree sacred significance •
flowering tree life; attribute of St.
Zenobius • man praying in, or in
front of tree St. Bavo • tree with
many branches the divisions of Protestantism • three tree seeds attribute of Seth • see also specific kinds
of trees (oak, pine, palm, etc.)

tree of life in flower language: old
age

trefoil (design) the Trinity

trefoil (plant) foresight; inspiration
• flower language revenge

tremella nestoe associated with alchemy; once thought to be an ema-
nation from a star • flower language resistance; opposition

triangle (geometric form) the Trinity
(especially when formed with fishes);
the number three, which see • triangle with apex up the male principle; fire; sun; the active; the god-
head; aspiration of all things toward
unity; the urge to escape from this
world to the Origin • triangle with
apex down the female principle;
water; moon; the passive; underworld powers • triangle within a
circle man and woman; Trinity and
unity • triangle within three circles
the Trinity • two triangles, one
apex up, one apex down, one upon

the other union of the male and female principles; *see also* **star, six pointed**

triangle (musical instrument) an occasional attribute of Erato

trident the sea; sin; the unconscious; the Tree of Life; destruction; the male as creator; in ancient times, the Trinity or a disguised cross, later it was used as an inversion of the Trinity; attribute of Satan, Neptune, sometimes his wife Amphitrite • **heraldry** maritime dominion; upper class merchant

trillium in flower language: modest beauty

tripod achievement in song or dance

triquetra the Trinity

triscele, triskele the sun; the revival of life and prosperity; motion; energy; victory

Tristram self sacrifice in an unendurable situation

Trojan lower emotions; diligence; endurance; war

troll (mythic being) malice; evil; sin

trombone voluptuousness • **when being played** sexual intercourse

trousers superiority

trout jealousy; sexual activity; adaptibility; stubbornness in overcoming obstacles

truffle in flower language: surprise

trumpet the call to action; the call of the spirit; power; glory; war; the yearning for power, glory, fame; praise; death; rallying cry; resurrection; the call to worship; associated with Judgment Day, the Resurrection of Christ; attribute of the archangel Gabriel and other angels, Clio, Calliope, Euterpe (occasionally), St. Jerome, St. Vincent Ferrer, the personifications of Fame, Terror • **trumpet with sword, pitcher, or scepter** attribute of Joshua • **seven trumpets** the fall of Jericho; the seven archangels • **Trumpet of Zion** associated with Hosea • *see also* **shofar; cornet; horn**

trumpet flower in flower language: fame • **ash leaved trumpet flower** separation

tub three children in a tub with a bishop: the bishop is St. Nicholas of Myra

tuberose in flower language: dangerous pleasures; voluptuousness • **when received from the hands of a lady** mutual affection

Tuesday *see* **days**

tulip fame; charity; constancy; declaration of love; chalice of the Eucharist; eloquence; extravagance; renown; magnificence; spirituality; spring; separation; inconstancy; emblem of the Netherlands; associated with Pisces • **flower language** fame; *red tulip*: declaration of love; *variegated tulip*: beautiful eyes; *yellow tulip*: hopeless love; *Near East tulip*: inconstancy, violent love

tuna wisdom; sovereignty

tunic the soul; the inner self • **soldiers gambling for a tunic** associated with the Crucifixion • **bloodstained tunic presented to an old man** Joseph's garment presented to Jacob

tunicle service; joy and contentment of heart; worn by a subdeacon at a high mass

tunnel hazardous passage; birth trauma; vagina • **entering a tunnel** sexual intercourse • **exiting a tunnel** birth

tunny wisdom; sagacity

turban attribute of Middle Eastern peoples (especially Mohammedans), Old Testament figures, Saracens, the sibyls, the Orient generally

turkey arrogance; pride; foolishness; lunacy; senseless anger; ostentation; vanity

turnip associated with peasants • **flower language** charity

turquoise (gemstone) sincere affection; September; earth and water; associated with Capricorn, Aquarius, Saggitarius

turtle lubricity; material existence; natural evolution as opposed to spiritual; longevity; obscurity; slowness; stagnation; highly concentrated materialism; involution; the marriage of heaven and earth; silence; safety; the body is maternal, the head phallic; the androgyne • *see also* **tortoise**, with which the turtle is occasionally confused

turtle dove fidelity; affection; love; purity; constancy; joy; plaintiveness; timidity; seclusion; gentleness; a victim; Christ; obedience to God's law • **two doves** Christ's presentation in the Temple • *see also* **dove**

tusk phallus; an offensive weapon; spiritual power overcoming ignorance and evil; power; strength; an aphrodisiac • **tusk on a grave** immortality

tussilage in flower language: sweet scented tussilage—justice shall be done to you

twelve universal order; the Apostles of Christ; salvation; perfection; completeness; holiness; harmony; power; the Church; justice; temperance; beauty; grace; mildness; associated with the angels Uriel and Gabriel jointly, space and time; the tribes of Israel, sibyls, legions of angels, Epistles of St. Paul, sons of Jacob, etc.

twenty continuity; dynasty; an intensifier; an indefinite number; shares in the symbolism of ten, which see; multiplication of the powers of two, which see; associated with the angel Lumiel • **kabala** physical strength

twenty-eight an unlucky number

twenty-four the four and twenty elders; generally, a lucky number

twenty-one absolute truth; the coming of age; associated with the angel Cassiel; a lucky number

twenty-two generally an unfavorable number

twilight dichotomy; the dividing line which both joins and separates pairs of opposites; lack of definition; ambivalence; threshold of day and night; perception of a new state of being • *see also* **dawn; dusk**

twins two opposites that have a complementary function (life/death, sunrise/sunset, etc.); Gemini; the duality of all things; St. Cosmas and St. Damian • **twin lions back to back** sunrise and sunset

twisting deviation; abnormality; irregularity

two the duality of all things; positive and negative; day and night; counter-balanced forces; related to the left side, which see; echo; reflection; counterpoise; equilibrium; nature; shadow; disintegration; an ominous sign; polarity; diversity; conjunction of opposites; resistance; may also refer to the dual nature of Christ, the sun and moon, the parents of mankind, the thieves on the crosses, the angels at the tomb of Christ, etc., etc.; associated with opinion, the material, the feminine, intuition, emotion, cooperation, tact, diplomacy, timidity, deceit, secrecy, domesticity, helpfulness, instability, the moon, cycles, reproduction, pacification, balance, inner peace, the angel Gabriel, the color green • **kabala** knowledge

two hundred in the kabala: reincarnation

U

U the "world pot"; womb; cauldron of plenty; receipt of a gift; associated with Pisces, the number three, the Cup in the tarot deck, charm, inspiration, profligacy, good but tenuous fortune, misery, grief

Ulysses cleverness; versatility; perseverance; adventure

Ultima Thule *see* **Thule**

umbrella protection; honor; position; mourning; dome of the sky; sun emblem; divine or royal power or protection; popular attribute of an Englishman • *see also* **parasol**

undine the perilous nature of water

unguent divine love and truth

unicorn feminine chastity; purity; the noblest of animals; uprightness; the word of God; Christ; high birth; peace; prosperity; solitude; the monastic life; it was so wary it could only be captured by a virgin, hence it is associated with virginity; unified, absolute monarchy; sometimes considered an enemy of man; steed of Faith personified; attribute of the Virgin Mary, the Annunciation, the Incarnation of Christ, St. Justina of Antioch, St. Justina of Padua, Chastity personified • **heraldry** royalty; knightly power; courage; pugnacity; the word or spirit; trademark of chemists or druggists, signifying the purity of their goods • **China** longevity; grandeur; felicity; the wise administration of government; the illustrious offspring of a family; a good omen; an emblem of perfect good

universal solvent the undifferentiated

uraeus fire; motion; sovereignty; power over life and death; protection; attribute of Ra • *see also* **asp**

Uranus (god) the unconscious; man's ancestral memory; latent thought

Uranus (planet) associated with originality, personal magnetism, the number eight, the ankles, Aquarius

urn death; mourning; fate; the feminine principle; health; purification; cauldron of plenty; attribute of Alpheus and other river gods (especially when lying on its side), the Virgin Mary • **funeral urn** attribute of Artemesia • **severed head placed in an urn by two women** Tomyris with the head of Cyrus •

urn held by woman with boat Agrippina the Elder • **river god by urn** Water personified • **urn with a lid on it** the state of supreme enlightenment which triumphs over birth and death • **urn of gold or silver with a white lily** attribute of the Virgin Mary • **four urns with water flowing from them** the four evangelists and the four Gospels • *see also* **vase; jar; jug; pot; amphora**

utensils their symbolism is derived from their practical function as applied to a spiritual plane; secondary implications are derived from shape, color, or material

V

V joining; support; until modern times, identical with the letter U, which see; associated with the number four, metaphysical gifts, earthly success with spiritual gifts, trial, hard work, losses, Taurus, Venus; corresponds to the Lovers in the tarot deck

vale protected life; gloom; declension

valerian benevolence; formerly a perfume, but now found offensive • **flower language** accommodating disposition; *blue flowered or Greek valerian*: rupture, warfare; *red valerian*: readiness, thought to restore strength, sight, spirits

valley neutrality; death; the soul's secret retreat; peace

vampire sin; death; the Devil; a harlot; the aftermath of orgasm

vase feminine symbol of containment; womb; attribute of the Virgin Mary, Virgo, Aquarius, Pandora, Psyche, Nemesis, the personification of Smell • **full vase** fertility •

empty vase the body separated from the soul • woman holding two vases Temperance personified • lily or lilies in a vase attribute of the Virgin Mary • birds drinking from a vase eternal bliss • pottery vase man • vase of ointment (usually with a lid) St. Mary Magdalene, St. Irene • lily or other flower in a vase in the presence of the Virgin Mary the Annunciation • vase with flame coming from the mouth Venus, the personifications of Charity, Sacred Love • see also jar; jug; urn; pot; amphora

vegetation an abundance of vegetation shows fertility and fecundity; vegetation growing in cycles represents death and resurrection

vehicle the type of vehicle reveals the character, the mind, or the ideas of the driver • see also specific types of vehicles or steeds (horse; motorcycle; chariot, etc.)

veil invisibility; concealment of certain aspects of truth or of the deity; truth; protection from a deity; fertility hidden underground; mystery; chastity; modesty; virginity; mourning (usually a black veil); atonement; renunciation of the world; attribute of nuns, St. Agatha, the personifications of Chastity, Prudence, Lust, Hypocrisy • veil with Christ's likeness on it attribute of St. Veronica • black veil death; mourning • white veil chastity; virginity • painted veil mystery; life and death • veil with likenesses of animals on it fecundity

vein vital male energy; maternal links

Venus (goddess) love in the physical or sexual sense; occasionally love in a spiritual sense

Venus (planet) associated with sexual emotions, love of beauty, the arts and crafts, love in all forms, happiness, the number six, Taurus, Libra, the throat, back, kidneys

Venus' car in flower language: fly with me

Venus flytrap in flower language: deceit

Venus' looking glass in flower language: flattery; vanity

verbena marriage; faithfulness; fertility; sanctity; peace; good fortune; used in amulets to bring protection and good luck; venerated by the Druids • flower language enchantment; reconciliation; prophecy

Vergil worldly wisdom

veronica in flower language: fidelity (especially female)

vervain see verbena

vesica associated with Christ

vessel a place for the intermingling of forces; the feminine principles • see also urn; ewer; pitcher; etc.; and ship; boat; etc.

vestments red vestment and scroll: attribute of Elijah • see also clothes, and particular vestments (cassock; surplice, etc.)

vetch in flower language: shyness

vial feminine symbol of containment; attribute of St. Philip Neri • dove with a vial in its beak attribute of St. Remigius • two vials on a book attribute of St. Januarius

victory subdual of lower nature; that which is conquered often represents the very inferiority of the conqueror himself

Victory (personified) implies spiritual worth

vine autumn; resurrection; safety; happiness; affection; an unfailing source of natural creation; foundation, root, or basis; Christ; the relationship between God and his people; the Christian faith; associated with Libra; attribute of Noah, the personifications of Autumn, Gluttony • heraldry hospitality; liberality; happiness; truth; belief • flower language drunkenness; intoxication • vine with branches Christ and his followers; Christ and the Church (especially when the emblems of the Apostles—keys, ship, shell, saw, etc.—are shown in the branches) • **vine wood staff** authority • **vine garland** attribute of Bacchus, Silenus • **vine with wheat** the Eucharist • **vine with twelve bunches of grapes** Christ and the Apostles • **elm and vine** the ideal husband and wife (respectively) relationship

vinegar bitterness; sadness; poor man's wine; final consolation; attribute of the Crucifixion • **vinegar and gall** attribute of the Crucifixion

vineyard a place of joy; the female body; the Church; a place where the children of God flourish • **work in a vineyard** the work of good Christians for the Lord

viol attribute of Thalia, Terpischore, Erato, Orpheus, Apollo, Arion, Music personified; instrument of a "godless" feast • **old man playing a viol covered with laurel** Homer

violet (color) humility; secrecy; suffering; sympathy; fasting; nostalgia; memories; repentance; love of truth; purification; sickness; sadness; authority; constancy; mourning; penitence; fasting; love of truth; preparation; a transitional stage (as between sleeping/walking, worldliness/spirituality); a feminine color; associated with Advent, Lent, the Passion, Cancer, Aquarius • **violet-blue** associated with Capricorn • **red-violet** associated with Pisces • **slate violet** associated with the planets Mercury, Jupiter

violet (flower) modesty; sweetness; loyalty; humility; spring revival; mourning; death; love; faithfulness; constancy; humble life; watchfulness; true virtue; chastity; transcience; emblem of Bonapartists • **white violets sprouting from death bed** attribute of St. Fina • **violet crown** attribute of Eurydice, the Pleiades, occasionally Athena • **flower language**—*blue violet*: faithfulness, love; *dame violet*: watchful-

ness, you are the queen of coquettes • **purple violet** you occupy my thoughts • **sweet violet** modesty • **wild violet** love in idleness • **yellow violet** rural happiness

violin passion; the androgyne

viper unnatural treachery; evil genius; ingratitude; the Devil; sin; the undifferentiated • *see also* **serpent**

Virgil *see* **Vergil**

virgin innocence; fear; wisdom; self-love; purity; purified emotions; Virgo

Virgin Mary virtuous womanhood; the Mother Church which Christ left in the world • **Virgin Mary appearing to a bishop in a vision** the bishop is St. Andrew Corsini • **the Virgin Mary's image being painted** attribute of St. Luke

Virginia creeper *see* **clematis**

virgin's bower (plant) in flower language: filial love

Virgo hermaphroditism; the duality of all things; the supreme expression of dynamic consciousness; associated with the birth of a demigod

viscera lower qualities

voice unmaterial existence; conscience

volcano fertility; evil destruction; the fire of creation; primary forces of nature; divine destruction or punishment; tremendous passions • **erupting volcano** the male orgasm; the sudden attack of the unconscious on the conscious

volkemania in flower language: may you be happy

vowel the male principle

Vulcan intellect rebelling against the soul; the demiurge; the creative mind which has been captured by the lower qualities; a weak, materialistic and corrupt soul; associated with cuckholds

vulture a mother image; death; punishment; remorse; purifications; compassion; portent of evil tidings, death, major troubles; protection;

fertility; sun; wind; righteousness; summer; heat; sedition; rapacity; gluttony; hypocrisy; the Devil; ruthlessness; revenge; evil; a woman 60 to 70 years old; attribute of a desolate place, Nature personified • **vulture tearing at the liver of a naked man** the man is Tityus

W

W associated with wavering emotions, change, acquisition, adventurousness, words, travel, any twin formations (such as Gemini), surprises, things held in abeyance, the number five, the liver, the World in the tarot deck

wafer the sun; the Host of the Eucharist; sacrifice to the moon goddess

wagtail amorousness; attribute of Comeliness personified

wake robin in flower language: ardor

wall defense; safety; prohibition; woman; wisdom; salvation; prosperity; impotence; delay; resistance; a limiting situation; the separation between worlds; protection (especially when the wall is viewed from the inside)

wallet female symbol of containment; memory; pilgrimage; attribute of pilgrims, Perseus • **beggar with wallet as shoulder bag** St. Felix of Cantalice • **saint with wallet and staff, sword, or letters S.J.** St. James the Greater • **archangel with wallet, staff and gourd or fish** Raphael

wallflower (plant) in flower language: shyness; fidelity in misfortune; *garden wallflower*: lasting beauty

wallowing depravity; a sacrificial act to encourage inversion or change

walnut hidden wisdom; longevity; fertility; selfishness • **flower language** intellect; strategy • **split walnut** Christ (the outer casing represents his flesh; the hard shell, the wood of the cross; the kernel, his divine nature) • *see also* **nut**

wand intensity; direction; phallus; authority; conjuring; measuring; attribute of Grammar personified • **flowering wand** attribute of Aaron, St. Joseph • **magic wand** attribute of magicians, sorcerers, Circe • **wand and staff** official authority; attribute of Jeremiah

wanderer *see* **fugitive**

Wandering Jew alludes to the imperishable side of man which cannot die

war the struggle of good against evil

warmth love; comfort; protection; maternal comfort • *see also* **heat**

warrior ancestor; forces of consciousness warring within a personality; various forces, hostile or friendly; latent force in the personality ready to come to the aid of the conscious • **warrior(s) seen in the sky** portent of war

wart associated with the Devil, sexual potency, boorishness, crudity

washing purification from guilt or from ritual uncleanness; washing in a stream can be a death omen

wasp evil; viciousness; irritation; petty danger; generally an unfavorable symbol, but it can mean love

watch *see* **clock**

watchtower consciousness; alertness • *see also* **tower**

water the source of life; mystery; fertility; the personal or collective unconscious; mother; innocence; sexuality; baptism; regeneration; refreshment; the Deluge; attribute of Reuben • **immersion, or ritual immersion** (baptism) purification; rebirth; regeneration • **looking into water** contemplation • **drinking or drawing water from a well** the soul or mind acquiring truth • **water mixed with wine at the Eucharist** Christ's humanity (water) and divinity (wine) • **holy water** purification; expulsion of evil

water buffalo serenity; contentment; agriculture

water cress old age; renewal of life; rejuvenation; redemption • *see also* **cress**

water fly busy fertility; something small and unimportant; an effeminate homosexual

water jug *see* **pot**; **jug**

water lily eloquence; fertility; charity; companionship; companionability; beneficence; associated with Pisces, the moon • **flower language** purity of heart

water mill time; the material world of phenomena; fertility • *see also* **mill**; **water wheel**; **water**; **wheel**

water pot *see* **pot**

water wheel fate; time; industry • *see also* **water**; **wheel**; **water mill**

watermelon in the U.S.: associated with Negroes in a pejorative sense • **flower language** bulkiness

waves (ocean) regeneration; righteousness; the feminine principle; the female orgasm; maternity and death; the flux and reflux of life; dreams; the unconscious; purity; renewed spiritual vigor; associated with dancing; not to be confused with an ocean swell (which see, under **ocean**)

wax secrecy; elevation; associated with Icarus • **sealing wax** *see* **seal** • **melting wax** fear; hot love

wax plant in flower language: susceptibility

weapon conflict; the will directed toward a certain end; thesis and antithesis as the counterpart to monsters or enemies; the powers of spiritualization and sublimation; attribute of the personifications of Europe, the Iron Age • **woman reclining on weapons** Victory personified • **woman destroying weapons** Peace personified • **weapon in a blacksmith's forge** attribute of Vulcan • **thun-**derbolt, net weapons of sky gods • **scepter, staff, mace, whip** weapons of kings • **sword, spear, dagger** associated with knights • **knife, poniard** weapons of villains • **bow and arrow** weapon of common soldiers or men • *see also* specific weapons (**spear**; **sword**; **lance**; **knife**; etc.)

wear signs of wear indicate weariness of spirit, poor health, or an extinct or outmoded idea

weasel vigilance; courage; slenderness; bloodthirstiness; arrogant quarrelsomeness; avarice; killer of vermin; squirminess; emblem of Christ

weather cock, weather vane inconstancy; frivolity; foolhardiness; versatility; showiness • **weather cock on a church** St. Peter (especially when crowing); his denial and subsequent repentence; hence, also a reminder to be humble; when red, an occasional emblem of Catholicism • *see also* **rooster**

weaving creation; life; snare; ladder to heaven; peace and concord • **weaving as a feminine activity** the world of matter; creation; life; vegetation; order and balance in nature; love; poetry • **weaving as a masculine activity** an incomplete man • *see also* **loom**

web destiny; entanglement, which see; the Mystic Center and the unfolding of Creation; illusion; the Labyrinth; rays of the sun; the world of phenomena; false trust or hope; the laws of man; sin; sorrow; despair; entrapment • **spider web** human frailty; the negative side of the universe; decay; desolation; fine work; transcience; the laws of man, which catch small transgressors, but let the big ones break through • *see also* **web**, above • **spider's web with woman at loom** the woman is Arachne • *see also* **spider**; **net**

Wednesday *see* **days**

weed disorder; grossness; sin; carelessness; the lower qualities driving out the higher

well baptism; life; rebirth; refreshment, especially spiritual; fortune; time; access to earth gods; the Gospel; attribute of the Great Goddess • **sealed well** the Virgin Mary • **well with trees** divine marriage; vulva and phallus • **well with fruitful bough above** attribute of Joseph • **peering into a well** contemplation • **drawing water from a well** acquiring truth • **putting money or other offerings into a well** an offering to the gods, especially earth gods

werewolf the irrationality latent in man and the possibility of its reawakening

west death; autumn; middle ages; evening; the waning moon; the setting sun; abode of evil; completion; darkness; abode of demons; to turn west is to prepare to die

whale the world; Christ and his resurrection; the Devil; cunning; deceit; hell; lust; avarice; the Mystic Center; the grave; brawn without intellect; attribute of Jonah • **the open jaws of a whale** the gates of Hell • **fish swimming into a whale's mouth** unsuspecting souls trapped by the Devil • **modern use** conservation of the earth's resources; the grandeur or nobility of Nature

wheat prosperity; wisdom; the bounty of the earth; the bread of the Eucharist; a spermatic image; attribute of Ceres • **wheat with grapes** the Eucharist; agriculture; attribute of Saturn, earth goddesses • **wheat with tares** the believers and nonbelievers (respectively) in the Church that will be separated out at Judgment Day • **stalk of wheat** associated with Ruth • **flower language** prosperity • *see also* **sheaf**

wheel the sun; the passage of time; fortune; the zodiac; mutability; torture; transcendance; progress; completion; power; associated with the lotus, which see; attribute of the expulsion of Adam and Eve from the Garden of Eden, the personifications of Fortune, Inconstancy • **flaming wheels with wings or eyes** the throne of God • **wheel with eyes on rim** Ezekiel's vision • **wheel with candles in rim** attribute of St. Donatian • **winged wheel** the Holy Ghost, Cherubim or Thrones • **wheel with knives or spikes in it** (may be broken) attribute of St. Catherine of Alexandria • **wheels within wheels** male and female; complex influences at work

Wheel of Fortune (tarot) manifestation; fecundity; the equilibrium of contrary forces of expansion and contraction; the principle of polarity; the mystery of all things; the intermingling of the disparate; law of cause and effect; unchanging reality despite changing events; unexpected turn of luck; irreversible fate; divine will; evolution; progress; success; fecundity; balance

wheelbarrow labor; poverty; suffering; drunkenness (because of its movement)

whetstone lying; wit

whin in flower language: anger

whip domination; mastery; superiority; punishment; slavery; sovereignty by force; fecundity; impetus; fertility; victory; hunting; phallus; penitence; remorse; conscience; attribute of royalty, the Terrible Mother, Hecate, Poseidon, the Passion, Christ's cleansing of the Temple, St. Vincent of Saragossa, the Agrippine sibyl, Grammar personified, occasionally St. Mary Magdalene • **whip with three knots** attribute of St. Ambrose • **whip with open Bible and stone** attribute of St. Jerome • **whip with pile of bricks** Israel in bondage • **two saints, one with a whip, one with sword** St. Gervase (whip), St. Protase (sword) • *see also* **lash**; **scourge**; **flagellation**

whipping post attribute of the Passion

whirlpool passions; emotions • *see also* **spiral**

whirlwind universal evolution; invincible power; violence; destruction; transcendance; space; the angry voice of a sky deity • *see also* **spiral; whirlwind**

whisky *see* **intoxicants**

whisper secrecy; witchcraft

whistling idleness; frittering away time; boredom; signal; a magical act; cleanness; pretense of innocence; a typical male activity, sometimes considered a taboo for women

white peace; purity; faith; timelessness; ecstasy; the moon; lividness; spiritual intuition; simplicity; cowardice; blandness; reason; amnesty; nobility; consumate wisdom; humility; integrity; the purest of all colors; light; joy; detachment from worldliness; glory; perfection; attribute of Christ, the Creator, the Virgin Mary, St. John, saints who did not suffer martyrdom • **Orient** mourning • **China on the stage—** *white face*: a cunning, treacherous, but dignified man; *white nose*: a comedian • **white rose** inspired wisdom; chaste love; purity • **white flag** surrender; truce; peaceful intent

Whitsunday *see* **Pentecost**

whore *see* **prostitute**

whortleberry in flower language: treason

wild man (or wild woman) primeval force; the primitive, instinctive, baser part of the personality; the unconscious in its perilous and regressive aspect • **heraldry** as supporters: base forces of nature subjugated and transcended • *see also* **savage**

wildflower the short, perhaps unhappy, life • *see also* the names of specific flowers

will o' the wisp *see* **fox fire**

willow sadness; mourning; desperation; abandonment; the Gospel; sterility; celibacy; forsaken love; eloquence; poetry; joy, but in later times, mourning; misery; quick growth; endurance; femininity; slenderness; associated with Pisces; emblem of the East, the rising sun; attribute of Prometheus • **China** spring; power over demons; purification; emblem of meekness • **willow branch** mercy • **willow switch** whipping; punishment • **flower language** forsaken; *creeping willow*: love forsaken; *French willow*: bravery and humanity; *water willow*: freedom; *weeping willow*: mourning • *see also* **osier**

willow-herb in flower language: • **spiked willow-herb** pretension

wimple • in Germany and elsewhere worn by married women • **white wimple and black robe** mourning

wind destruction; evil powers; air in its active and violent aspects; desire; regeneration; freedom; inconstancy; fickleness; caprice; inducer of ecstasy, poetic inspiration; life force; the spirit; time; nothingness; speed; madness • **rushing wind** occasionally the Holy Spirit • **north wind** destruction; creativity; winter; frost; cold; religious persecution • **south wind** heat; warmth; summer • **east wind** morning; bringer of rain; wantonness; comforter; an ill omen; • *see also* **Khamsin** • **west wind** mildness; gentleness; fertility; the autumn; evening; death • *see also* **breeze; Khamsin; whirlwind**

winding sheet *see* **shroud**

windlass compulsion

windmill fertility; harvest; combines the symbolism of air or wind, and the wheel, q.q.v.; emblem of the Netherlands, and in the U.S., the West and Midwest; attribute of St. James the Less and Temperance personified • **windmill with ship and fish** attribute of St. Mary of Cleophus • **knight charging a windmill** Don

Quixote • **children playing with toy windmills** allegory of Air

window consciousness; possibility; communication; possibility of understanding; the idea of penetration; the eyes; vigilance • **rose window** eternity • *see also* lotus • **red lattice window** an alehouse

wine blood; sacrifice; youth and eternal life; the spiritual nature of love and wisdom; the Eucharist; a spiritual drink; intoxication; inspiration; wisdom; resurrection; lust; truth; violence; purification; gladness; rejoicing; revelry; attribute of Bacchus • **pouring out wine** blood letting in ritual sacrifice • **mixed wine** euphemism for semen • **napkin and cruse of wine** attribute of the Good Samaritan • **Jewish** on Seder nights a glass of wine is set out for Elijah, messenger of the Messianic Age • **wine mixed with water at the Eucharist** the wine signifies Christ's divine nature, the water his human nature

wine press the wrath of God; slaughter; destruction; thirst; Christ; patient or solitary labor or suffering • **Strength personified standing on a wine press** the conquest of the spirit over the heart

wineskin sin; evil mindedness; heavy conscience; attribute of Silenus, satyrs

wings spirituality; spiritualization; imagination; thought; intelligence; justice; the possibility of spiritual evolution; aspiration; divine mission; victory; healing; misfortune; chance; elevation; virtue; authority; power; glory; protection; time; speed; fancy; meditation; the soul; resurrection; divinity; personification of a fleeting occurrence; healing; ubiquity (especially four wings); generally only put on benign beings; attribute of Nemesis, Hermes, Artemis, Athena, Eros, Aphrodite, angels, heavenly beings, St. Matthew

(occasionally), Father Time, the personifications of Fame (usually with trumpet), History (usually with tablet), Peace (usually with doves), Fortune (usually blindfolded with globe), Opportunity, Fate, Night (usually with two infants), Melancholy (usually sitting) • **heraldry** protection; when on a shield: the joy of flourishing prosperity • **wings of skin** perversion of the higher qualities of wings; attribute of the Devil, infernal creatures • **four wings** ubiquity • **wings on an orb** spiritual elevation • **winged animals** the sublimation of that animal's specific virtues (such as a winged bull — courage; nobility) • **wings of many colors** attribute of the archangel Gabriel • **winged hand** attribute of Poverty personified • **winged sandals and/or hat** attribute of Mercury, Perseus • **man making wings** Daedalus • **man and youth flying with wings** Daedalus and Icarus • **the wings of Icarus** functional insufficiency • **winged deacon** St. Josaphat

winnow, winnowing sublimation; selection; separation of the good from the bad; attribute of Bacchus, occasionally Hermes

winter old age; death; dormancy; hate; darkness; misery; coldness; involutive death with the promise of rebirth

wisteria welcome; the gentleness and devotion of womanhood

witch hazel in flower language: a spell

wolf rapacity; rapine; hunger; hypocrisy; lust; cruelty; fraud; deceit; the Devil; war; warrior; cunning; ferocity; corruption; heresy; darkness; masher; a thief; untamed nature; inversion; murder; avarice; greed; false doctrine; a false prophet; the principle of evil; the lesser instincts taking control of more human instincts, but with the possibility of improvement; swiftness; poverty; melancholy; night; winter; protection; cowardice; valor; fertility; a man 50 to 60 years of age; attribute of Odin, Apollo, Mars, St. Maurus, the archangel Michael, the personifications of Avarice, Gluttony • **heraldry** caution in attack; prudence; martial cunning • **China** cupidity; greed • **wolf devouring children** fear of incest • **wolf with lion** associated with the tribe of Benjamin • **tame wolf** attribute of St. Francis of Assisi • **female wolf** attribute of Romulus and Remus; emblem of the papacy *see* Rome • **wolf with lamb** peace • **wolf with eagle** emblem of the elect part of Valhalla

wolfsbane deadliness; illicit love; remorse; vendetta • **flower language** misanthropy

woman the passive principle in nature; receptiveness; the changing and intuitive; submissiveness; the mother; the unconscious; the involutive; associated with the left side; the anima; the Terrible Mother; often used as the personification of an idea or principle: Summer, Europe, Justice, etc. — they are differentiated by their attributes: sword, globe, serpent, etc., which see • **woman as captive** higher nature held latent by desires • **man's head on a woman's body** solid and profound judgment • **seven women** the seven virtues (faith, hope, charity, temperance, prudence, fortitude, justice — these may be identified by their attributes: globe, serpent, scales, etc., which see) • *see also* **maiden; virgin; prostitute; wild woman;** and specific women: **Helen; Eve;** the **Virgin Mary,** etc.

womb beginning; morning; night; the tomb; protection from reality

wood wisdom; mother; life and death; celestial goodness in its lowest corporeal plane • **touching or knocking on wood** a charm against

evil • **burnt wood** wisdom; death • *see also* specific kinds of trees and their woods (**ebony; palm;** etc.)

wood pigeon *see* **pigeon**

wood sorrel in flower language: joy; maternal tenderness; praise of God

woodbine in flower language: fraternal love; bond of love; domestic happiness; I will not answer hastily

woodcock goodwill; affection; fool; dupe; simpleton

woodpecker presage of a storm; perseverant action; the Devil; heresy; fertility; lust; immortality; distinction; associated with Romulus and Remus

woodruff in flower language: modest worth

woods *see* **forest**

wool a homely, simple life; noiselessness; vagueness; fertility; warmth; shroud • *see also* **sheep; fleece**

woolsack wealth; emblem of the Lord Chancellor in Great Britain

work the endeavor of the soul to attain perfection

works days related to works • **Sunday** light • **Monday** divination • **Tuesday** wrath • **Wednesday** science • **Thursday** politics, religion • **Friday** love • **Saturday** mourning

World (tarot) transitory life; the body; the senses; the totality of the manifest world as a reflection of permanent creative activity; major fortune; the attainment of unveiled truth; the final blending of personal consciousness with universal completion; perfection as the end of creation out of Chaos; final crown of the initiate; truth and spiritual evolution attained on earth; cosmic consciousness; merging of the subconscious and the super-conscious with the conscious

worm connected with death; baseness; the Devil; lowliness; contempt; weaknes; insignificant man; death; the insidious destroyer; conscience;

wiles; laziness; secrecy; sin; Hell; a
killing libidinal figure • **silk worm**
in China: emblem of industry
wormwood affection; purification;
false judgment; punishment; bitter
labor; intoxication; weaning •
wormwood and gall bitterness •
flower language absence
wound punishment; the conscience;
sacrifice to placate powerful forces;
damage to the soul; martyrdom •
wound in the neck poet's stigma •
three wounds attribute of St. Cecilia
• **five wounds** the wounds of Christ
in the Passion
wreath eternity; celebration; mourning; victory; valor; resurrection;
memory • **wreath on the head**
honor • **ivy wreath** conviviality •
oak wreath strength; hospitality;
victory on the seas; attribute of Jupiter • **laurel wreath** distinction in
literature or music; attribute of
Apollo, Clio • **olive wreath** peace
• **bay wreath** death; mourning •
willow wreath bereavement; death;
mourning • **cypress wreath**
mourning; attribute of Pluto •
pine wreath attribute of Pan • **yew
wreath** immortality • **myrtle
wreath** attribute of a bride
wren modesty; maternity; heroism;
lust; death; consolation; small size;
insignificance
writing table with pen and books: attribute of St. Ambrose
wryneck feminine lust
wyvern guardianship; Satan

X

X negation; elimination; a variable
quantity; an unknown; illiteracy;
spiritual love; signature; a kiss; emblem of Christ; St. Andrew's cross;

associated with the number six, abnegation, responsibility, humaneness • **U.S.** an inferior product;
pornographic material
XP (Chi Rho) usually shown with the
staff of the P bisecting the X, from
the Greek word for Christ
xanthium in flower language: rudeness; pertinacity
xeranthemum in flower language:
cheerfulness under adversity

Y

Y the androgyne; an unknown quantity; associated with the number
seven, the search for the esoteric or
the mystic
yang see **yin and yang**
yarmulke submission to God
yarrow war; treatment for wounds;
used in casting spells
yeast fermentation; love; high spirits
• see also **leaven**
yellow the sun; fruitfulness; beneficence; joy; truth; kingship; intuition; magnanimity; intellect; cowardice; inconstancy; adultery; jealousy; death and decay; sensational-
ism; melancholy; enmity; lowest
rank; earth; the mind of man; infernal light; degradation; treason;
deceit; associated with God the Son,
Venus, Gemini, Leo, Judaism, the
executioner in the Spanish Inquisition; partakes of the symbolism of
gold, which see • **yellow shield** Judas • **dirty yellow** unpleasantness;
decay; associated with Judas •
bright yellow marriage; fruitfulness; divine wisdom, goodness, glory
• **bright yellow mantle** attribute of
St. Peter, St. Joseph • **yellow garments** in the Middle Ages: attribute

of heretics • **yellow star** in Nazi Germany, Jews were forced to wear a yellow Star of David • **yellow cross** sign of the plague • **yellow flag** disease • **China** the national color; sacred to the emperor and his son; the yin principle; earth; *yellow clouds*: prosperity • **orange-yellow** divine wisdom or goodness; glory • **yellow-green** associated with Virgo

yew death; sadness; mourning; immortality; sorrow; constancy; faith; forgetfulness; sacred to the Druids • **flower language** sadness; despair; sorrow

Yggdrasil wisdom; the All Father • *see also* **ash tree**

yin and yang spirit and matter; life and form; good and evil; any pair of related opposites • **yin** (the dark color) the material; the feminine • **yang** (the light color) the spiritual; the masculine

yoke union; discipline; sacrifice; agriculture; balance; tyranny; toil; patience; sacrifice; burden bearing; the Law; patient service; Christ bearing the sins of the world; trials; meekness; obedience; attribute of Cain, the personifications of Obedience, Patience, Toil • **broken yoke** associated with Nahum

youth *see* **man; boy**

Z

Z the thing that completes perfection; an unknown quantity; super-

fluity; associated with the number eight, lightning, potential for good and/or evil, the stomach

zenith the point at which one passes out of time into timelessness

zephyr *see* **breeze; wind**

zephyr flower in flower language: expectation

zero the latent and potential; eternity; non-being; the female principle; the womb; vulva; nothingness; failure; an intensifier after a number; associated with the planet Pluto, the infinite, eternity, ether, the angel Lumiel

zigzag disquiet; confusion; the material world; lightning; electricity; waves of the sea; regeneration; spiritual purification and rebirth; emblem of Zeus and other thunder deities • **two zigzag lines** emblem of Aquarius

zinnia in flower language: thoughts of absent friends

zircon associated with Capricorn, Virgo

zither the cosmos; the synthesis of heaven and earth; the strings correspond to the various levels of the universe

zodiac the year; the dignity of labor; the first six signs (Aries, Taurus, Gemini, Cancer, Leo, Virgo) relate to involution or matter; the last six signs relate to evolution or materialization • **days related to the zodiac** • **Sunday** the sun • **Monday** Cancer • **Tuesday** Scorpio • **Wednesday** Gemini • **Thursday** Saggitarius • **Friday** Taurus • **Saturday** Capricorn • *see also* the separate signs under their individual headings